Compton Abdale

in the Cotswolds

Researched and written by
Katja Kosmala

Pen and ink drawings by
Andy Aston

 Longhouse Publishing

Compton Abdale in the Cotswolds

First published in Great Britain in 1993

Longhouse Publishing
72 North Street Winchcombe Glos. U K GL54 5PS
7 Linwood Avenue Tewksbury MA 01876-3835 USA

Designed and produced by Rupert M. Kosmala

Set in Palatino

Printed in the U.K. by Witley Press Ltd. 24 Greevegate Hunstanton Norfolk PE36 6AD

ISBN 0 9520125 0 2

Library of Congress Cataloging-in-Publication Data applied for.

British Library Cataloging-in-Publication Data.
A catalogue record for this book is available from the British Library.

Front cover photograph by kind permission of Mr. & Mrs. Ron Owens

Contents

List of Illustrations

Pen and ink drawings

Brasses

Maps

Wild Plants

Foreword

Every village has a story to tell and it is the good fortune of all those who love Compton Abdale that its story teller is Katja Kosmala.

Countless "foreigners" delight in discovering the Cotswolds. Many of these, myself included, seize upon the opportunity to settle in this delectable area and having put down their roots deep into its hospitable soil, are content to adjust their lives to the easy restful tempo of this serene landscape.

A few, however, feel compelled to respond to their peerless surroundings in a tangible way, giving of themselves in return for the enrichment their lives have received from their chosen corner of the Cotswolds.

Katja Kosmala is one of this number. During her twenty-six years' residence in Compton Abdale, she immersed herself in its geology, history, architecture and wild life. She devoted hours of her time to researching its elusive past, to interviewing its inhabitants, and - most important of all - to exploring its every facet with a seeing eye, an inquiring mind, and an empathy borne of exceptional intellectual powers.

Should these words appear in any way extravagant, put them to the test. Open the book, settle down to read, and begin an armchair discovery of Compton Abdale through the dedicated scholarship of one who knows and loves it well.

You will not be disappointed.

Gordon Ottewell   Winchcombe, November 1992

A note from the Author

As Gordon Ottewell pointed out in his Foreword, I am not a native of Compton Abdale, but a newcomer; a curious newcomer who questioned what to anybody born and bred in the village was unquestioningly taken for granted. "St. Oswald, King and Martyr." King of what? Why Martyr? What happened? How old is the Crocodile? Nobody was quite sure, it had always been there. It soon became clear that if I wanted to know, I would have to find out for myself.

It took me ten years, on and off, to satisfy this curiosity and to write down what I had discovered.

But why write about Compton Abdale? It has no obvious claim to fame, no Roman Villa like Chedworth, no famous hostelry like Withington - two neighbours who take the tourists' attention. It is, in fact, so unknown that one frequently has to spell its name in Cheltenham, only ten miles away. It is just one of thousands of ordinary villages - yet worth knowing? I think so, and so did William the Conqueror. He was aware how important his humble subjects were, for what is a King without subjects? Kings are important, certainly, but they are few and have many willing chroniclers. Ordinary people in small villages are just as important and no justification is needed for wanting to know them, even if they "have no History."

This history of Compton Abdale was completed in 1971, but not published and, though never quite forgotten, it slumbered on a bookshelf for 20 years. In response to a suggestion that the chapter about the church be converted into a leaflet for sale in St. Oswald's, Compton Abdale, my son, Rupert, proposed that we publish the whole book, even if we do it ourselves.

After having re-assured myself that the history was not hopelessly out of date and overtaken by the archaeological and historical research of the intervening years, I agreed to his plan. So, with the help of his wife, Daisy, and their home computer, he turned the yellowing, curling pages into something fit to see the light of day.

I am glad of this opportunity to offer my sincere thanks to the many friends and contributors who from the start unstintingly cooperated. Some, who shared their memories with the stranger and patiently answered never-ending questions, others who gave of their specialised knowledge just as freely. Mr. and Mrs. P. Sparks contributed the lists of birds and mammals, Mrs. B. Midwinter (then Rideout) undertook the mammoth task of searching for and listing the wild flowers and plants in the parish. To them not only mine, but also the conservationists' thanks are due. We hope the lists are still valid.

Even a quick glance will show how much the book owes to the drawings of Compton scenes so generously contributed by Andy Aston, who lives in the village. His wife, Maggie, equally generous, is responsible for the maps.

It is with appreciation that I thank my ex-neighbours in Compton, Ron and Barbara Owens, for their cheerfully and freely given help with some of the many tasks encountered in the preparation of this book.

Having lived in the village longer and felt more at home there than anywhere else, I left Compton (in 1986) with great regret, fearing I should go out into a friendless wilderness - I did not know Winchcombe then, or my luck. My luck because it must be rare to twice be blessed with such friendship and neighbourly concern, even including assistance with the preparation of this book.

I am indebted to Mrs. Freda Humble for the many hours she spent on many tasks. I also thank Mr. Gordon Ottewell for his Foreword, his encouragement and constant interest.

I would like to thank Mr. D. Smith, the Gloucestershire County Archivist for his interest and his staff for help and research. Also for permission to use documentary material in the Record Office, the Diocesan Register and the Public Library which are acknowledged in detail in the Notes, as are the Transactions of the Bristol and Gloucestershire Archaeological Society. Is any book ever written without the ever ready, smiling, knowledgeable help from the staff of the Public Library? My thanks for their patience.

The plant illustrations are based on *Flowers of the Field* by the Rev. C.A.Johns, edited by Prof. G.S.Boulger, published by the Society for Promoting Christian Knowledge, London 1902.

Lastly, I wish to express my gratitude to my family for rallying round and giving their support and active assistance: to the Rev. Ruth Kosmala for her generous contributions to help defray the cost of publishing; to my granddaughter, Allison Taylor (Norwich), for her technical and artistic advice as well as general liaison; to my son, Alex (USA), for his much appreciated assistance in technical matters; to my son, Rupert (also in the USA), and his wife, Daisy, for months of hard work, for patience with my "ideas" and for many letters across the Atlantic. In short, without Rupert there would be no book for which to write this note.

K.K.

"…. Manors belonging to St. Oswald's….. were placed under the protection of Thomas, Archbishop of York, and remained in the hands of his successors till the dissolution. Parishes thus held have no history. Their inhabitants lived and died in peace."

Bristol and Gloucestershire Archaelogical Society
Transactions 1913, Volume 36 Page 39

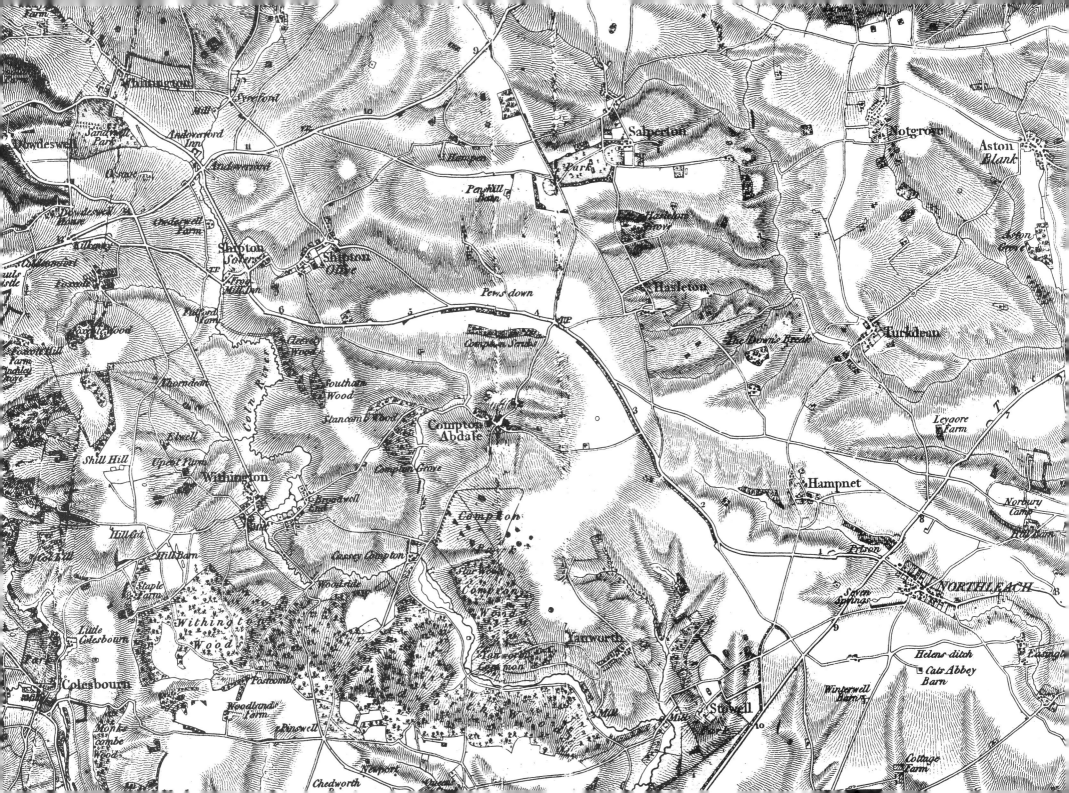

The reprint of the first edition of the one inch Ordnance Survey of England and Wales by David and Charles, Publishers, Newton Abbot, Cornwall, is based on the edition of 1867.

This map was by no means new in 1867, its origins go back to the 18th century, the age of intensive map-making.

It underwent several revisions and improvements during the 68 years between the first triangulation in 1799 and the electrotype printing of the 1860's, which David and Charles re-published in the 1970s.

The story of the cartographic development in England, the expansion of the railways, the role Mathew Arnold played in the improvement of the maps, all this and more can be found at the bottom of Sheet 60 (the Cheltenham district).

This information and the map itself offer an absorbing study of our part of Gloucestershire 130 years ago.

This portion of the Ordnance Survey is reproduced with permission from David and Charles, Publishers

A Village in the Cotswolds

Compton Abdale is a small village in Gloucestershire, ten miles east of Cheltenham in that part of the county which, as William Camden says, "riseth up with hilles, to wit

1 Cotteswold". It rises up indeed, not in gentle slopes, but as a bold escarpment, towering above the Severn Vale. These "hilles" are not an isolated range like the Malverns, but part of the Jurassic limestone formation which traverses the country from the south-west to north-east, from the south coast near Lyme Regis to the North Sea coast at Robin Hood's Bay in Yorkshire. The Cotswolds proper stretch for about fifty miles from Bath towards the north and are ten to twenty miles across, a hilly, undulating high plateau, at 600 to 1,000 feet above sea level. While this limestone shelf rises sheer and in places clifflike from the Severn Vale in the west, it dips gently and merges into the Oxford Plain in the east and the descent from the hills to the plain is so gradual, the change so subtle, that there is no point at which one could say here the Cotswolds end and the Plain begins, just as the road back from Oxford across the Cotswolds takes you up to its highest point of 850 feet almost imperceptibly and will descend to Cheltenham as gently again; in this the A40 however, is exceptional, all other roads plunge down from the escarpment in a much more spectacular fashion.

For the name of this region William Camden offers an explanation in his Brittania: "...Cotteswold, which of wold and Cotes, that is, hills and sheepfolds tooke that name. For, mountains and hills without woods, the Englishman in old time termed Woulds..." While his definition of wold is still acceptable, his derivation of the first syllable has been proved mistaken, though it is still widely used. "Cots" is now thought to refer not to sheepfolds, but to a man named Cod whose high open land lay in the hills above the upper Windrush and the

2 Dikler. The village of Cutsdean owes its name to him. From there it spread over the whole area we now know as the Cotswolds.

Not many travellers on the busy main road from Oxford and London will muse about the name of the country between the roundabout at Burford and Andoversford. They will hardly be aware that they cross the Cotswolds and even less aware of the Cotswolds themselves for the road reveals but little of their character and beauty. The infinite variety of hills and hidden valleys, the little streams, the ancient villages tucked into the folds of the hills and, by contrast, the bleakness of the open wold - these things you do not see when you stay on the main road.

Yet all this is so close to it that one can truly say of Compton Abdale that it lies in the heart of the Cotswolds, though only one mile from the A40. Just when Puesdown Hill, the highest point of this road, is reached, the trees thin out and allow a view of Compton vale, though "vale" is a misnomer if it means a low, flat plain, for this lower land consists of a multitude of lesser hills, round-backed like a flock of grazing sheep. Among this tumble of hills lies Compton Abdale. Until barely 20 years ago all that was visible of it from the main road was the top of the church tower, hardly discernible in its cloud of tree tops. Now the Council Houses and some farm buildings give the hidden village away. The small wood to the west is Compton Grove, and the road curling round its edge leads to the neighbouring village of Withington. Another road can be seen climbing toward

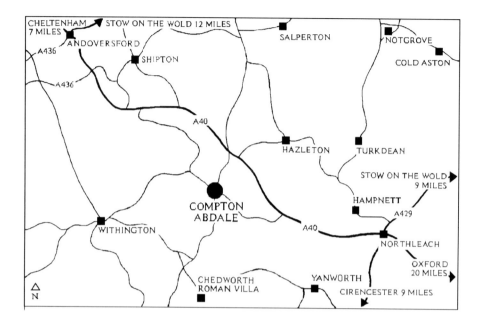

Chedworth Woods which close the view to the South. This is the ancient White Way to Cirencester, its continuation this side of Compton Abdale crosses the A40 and proceeds north towards Brockhampton and eventually Winchcombe. The village is hidden not only from the main road, but from all points of the compass, and whichever way you approach it, it reveals itself only when you descend the last hillside. No fewer than five lanes lead to Compton Abdale and they all meet in the "Square", now only a triangular widening of the road, or roads, but once the heart of the village, for here we find Compton's raison d'être: the spring which has never failed, not even in years of severest drought. Its water now gushes out of a crocodile's mouth into a large stone trough and, overspilling its mossy sides, runs along the narrow valley

towards the west until the hills bar its way and deflect it southwards to join the Coln at Compton Cassey.

The road follows the brook and both keep to the hill on the left which presses close to the valley on its south flank, and is too steep for houses, but apparently not too steep for the church which was built halfway up its slope. The houses lie on the northern side of the river valley where beyond a narrow level strip the hills are low and rise gently. The road forks soon after it leaves the village, the northern branch called Hunter's Horn curls round a steep sided spur of the hillside that closes the brook valley to the west. Two cottages, now enlarged and modernised were built long ago on the end of the spur - a strange situation for a dwelling with a strange name : Smallhope. No latter day whim, this. These cottages and their name already figure in an 18th century will.

The brook valley settlement is Compton's oldest part. In the 19th century when its population nearly doubled, the village grew out of the confines of the narrow valley and it was no longer entirely "Compton in the Hole", as it was called. A cluster of nine cottages joined the one or two which had been built long before on the lane leading north towards the main road. This group, separated by pasture from the main village, remained on its own until very recently; now a bungalow and a new house joins it to the old part. Meanwhile the houses have crept still farther up the hill until the Council Houses have reached the crest, 105 feet above the bottom of the river valley, their fronts towards the north and bravely - or foolishly - taking the worst the winter winds can do.

There are 38 houses in the parish, most of them within the village; a variety of houses, old farm houses and cottages, stonebuilt and stoneroofed, the Victorian vicarage, new houses and cottages, one bungalow and the Council Houses. Old and

"Upper Compton" in close-up. This name is used only for orientation. It is by no means official. This is the 19th century extension towards the north.

new blend well together, at least as far as the reconstituted stone of the modern buildings will allow.

Though the 2,000 acres of the parish are still farmed, Compton is not an agricultural village any more. Farming methods have changed and the village with them. The old houses and farm buildings remain, but there is not one which is used as originally intended. The farmhouses do not house the people who farm the land, the cottages have been "converted", the vicarage is a private residence, The Old School House has not seen any school children for forty years, the carpenter's shop was turned into the Village Hall and the Tithe Barn into a dwelling house. Even the Crocodile has lost its function as the main water supply to the village.

This change from a purely agricultural to a residential village is, of course, not particular to Compton Abdale, it has happened to thousands of rural settlements. But Compton is more fortunate than many, for it has become neither a dormitory nor a collection of weekend cottages; it is still a living community of people with many occupations and interests.

The valley has seen many changes since the Neolithic people watered their animals at its spring and lost their arrowheads on the hills; since the farm carts went creaking along the White Way from the Roman Villa estate to Corinium; since a Saxon queen gave Compton to her Minster of St. Oswald in Gloucester; an Archbishop of York rode up from the Vale to visit his manor of Compton Parva, or William Midwinter came over from Northleach to bargain with the farmers for their wool. So the change which has taken place in the last fifty or sixty years, and which to us seems so momentous, is only the latest of many.

"Compton Abdale"

A name is not bestowed haphazardly on a village, it expresses the special feature by which it can be distinguished from its neighbours. It may be the name of the first owner, as in Withington, or the local vegetation which gave Hazleton its name. Compton was simply named after its situation; settlement in the valley.

It is an appropriate, but not an exclusive name, for wherever there are hills there are bound to be villages in the valleys, and there are no fewer than forty-one Comptons in England. Most Cotswolds villages lie in valleys, yet only one in this neighbourhood was singled out as THE settlement in the valley for, hidden in the folds of the steep hills around it, the village was almost invisible from anywhere, particularly in the early name-giving days before the houses had crept up the northern hillside but remained huddled together in the bottom of the narrow brook valley. The original meaning of Compton was forgotten in time and the point was made again by a nickname which Bigland records in 1791 in his County History: "The surrounding Hills have so sudden a Descent to the Village, that it is usually called Compton in the Hole". This nickname is now largely forgotten; the young have not even heard of it, but old Compton people of whom, alas, few are left, still know it.

"In the Hole", however, is not Compton's only by-name ever. At different times and in differing contexts it needed different designations. When Archbishop Murdac leased his manor of Compton to the Priory of St. Oswald in Gloucester in 1154, he called it "Cuntun super montes", "Compton on the hills" - and so the place would appear to the Priory in the Severn Vale. In the 13th century it had become Compton Parva, as the smallest manor of the Barony of Churchdown. In the 15th century Compton, like many other places, acquired its official surname: Abdale.

The origin and meaning of it is obscure and even *"The Place Names of Gloucestershire"* cannot suggest a satisfactory derivation. It regards Abdale as a family affix of feudal and manorial owners, but Compton did not have a Lord of the Manor whose name could have been added to the name of the village, as was done in many places, for instance in Shipton Oliffe. The most popular explanation of it is Abbot's Valley, and, though it was ecclesiastical property throughout the Middle Ages, no abbot ever owned Compton, and -dale is a northern word for valley which is not used in Gloucestershire.

This northern sound convinced Dr. W. St.C. Baddeley, who was the Gloucestershire County Archaeologist for many years, that (Compton) Abdale, Ravensdale and Thorndale, all close together and, as he thought, the only placenames with dale in Gloucestershire, must have been Danish settlements from the time of King Guthrun's stay in Gloucestershire in A.D. 877, when he was confined there by King Alfred for a year. But this explanation is not tenable if only because Abdale was not used until nearly five hundred years after King Alfred and -dale may not be as Scandinavian as it looks. Could the old by-name "in the Hole" be a pointer? OE HALH or hale, meaning a nook or corner of land, a secluded hollow, is not uncommon in Gloucestershire, and there is one example in the *"Place Names"* of de hale being shortened into dale. If Abdale had evolved from Abd'hale by the same process, at least one syllable of it could be explained.

Ab- remains a mystery unless it can be proved to be a dialect word perhaps meaning "in" or "down". Abdale would then mean "in the Hole" and ultimately the same as Compton.

Who gave the village its name in the first place? Presumably the first settlers and the Saxons are thought to be the founders of English villages. Compton, however, is not an entirely Saxon word. It consists of two elements, one British, one Saxon. Comp- is the British coombe, -ton the Saxon tun, originally a fenced enclosure, later a settlement, a village, and coombe-tun, now Compton is simply the village in the valley. So the name of the place takes us back to its beginning. Or does it?

"Compton-in-the-Hole" as seen from the Northleach - Andoversford road, the A40.

Pre-history

At Christmas in 1085 William the Conqueror decided to make a survey of his realm of England. "He surveyed the Kingdom so thoroughly, that there was not a single hide of land throughout the whole of which he knew not the possessor and how much it was worth", says the Anglo-Saxon Chronicle. This survey of England still exists and we know it by its ancient name of Domesday Book. There are few places in England that for some reason or another are not listed in Domesday Book and so we find Compton duly recorded as it was in 1086. This, as far as I know, is the first time that Compton is mentioned by name and its existence recorded.

Domesday Book shows the place as it was in 1086, but gives no hint or help in regard to what went before. So we have to look for other ways and means to probe into Compton's past, before its debut in written records. The dedication of its church hints at some connection with the Priory of St. Oswald in Gloucester which was founded in A.D. 909. The origin of its name takes us back even further to the Saxon invasion of the village. The Saxons, however, were not the first invaders, they were among the last. Only the Danes and the Normans came after them, while before them there were the Romans and the Belgae, and before those the many nameless peoples and tribes who came across the sea; they all left their traces on the land and on our hills, however faint at times. But we shall get little help from chronicles if we want to know what happened those thousands of years ago. The chronicler appeared late on the scene, in the last but one

act so to speak; the drama of history had then been going on for a very long time indeed. It is nine hundred years since Domesday Book was compiled, but 3,500 years between Domesday Book and the building of the Long Barrows, the oldest pre-historic monuments in our neighbourhood. As far as Compton itself is concerned, we cannot expect to reconstruct every scene, the stage will be dark for intervals of hundreds and even thousands of years. This is really not peculiar to Compton, however, there are few places whose history is known in unbroken clarity from the Stone Age to the present. Among these few is Bourton-on-the-Water, where careful and patient observing and collecting, digging and recording over the years has produced evidence of continual occupation from Palaeolithic, Neolithic, Bronze and Iron Age, to Roman, Saxon, Norman and medieval times.

The first two thousand of these 3,500 years are still called Pre-history as if they were merely a prelude or ante-chamber to History. Until quite recently the distant past seemed dark and bleak indeed. But we now know that this age

9

A typical arrowhead - drawn more than twice the size of those found in the fields.

of the fundamental discoveries like farming and the introduction of metal is just as important and interesting as later documented times.

This realization and the enormous expansion of our knowledge of "Pre" history we owe to Archaeology and the patient labour of archaeologists in the field. Not all of this knowledge was gathered in one place, naturally. The pieces of this vast mosaic are scattered all over the country, even all over Europe.

Often small and insignificant things in isolation can give an astonishingly detailed picture if brought together and into relation with each other. It is true, knowledge and training are needed to recognize their significance and to fit them into the right place of the mosaic, yet many discoveries have been made through the observations and accidental finds by non-archaeologists. Interest in the past and consequently knowledge are now much greater than of old and, in our village as well as elsewhere, attention is paid to whatever comes to light. A Roman coin is not so readily tossed away because it is small, dirty and "worthless", potsherds are arefully picked up. We owe the recent discovery of a hitherto unrecorded Long Barrow in our neighbourhood to the awareness of the owner of the field that the hump which disfigured his acres might be more than a natural blemish; likewise the flint arrowheads, picked up in different fields, might easily have been overlooked save for the knowledgeable alertness of the finders. If, on the other hand, Mr. Purvey who in the early twenties dug up a bronze statuette of Venus in his garden, had realized its importance to Compton, he would not perhaps have parted with it so readily.

Both the Long Barrow and the arrowheads are recent (1962/3) and remarkable discoveries; remarkable in that the Barrow had been overlooked, despite its size and the intensive search for Long Barrows, and in that the arrowheads had been found at all, tiny specks in vast ploughed fields. If such things, large and small can be found, then perhaps there is hope that there will be more discoveries to shed light on Compton's past.

DÁCTYLIS GLOMERÁTA
(*Cock's foot Grass*)

2500BC to AD43

The Cotswolds are rich in pre-historic remains. They are, like the Wiltshire Downs, part of the uplands which were inhabited from the earliest times. The first inhabitants probably arrived on foot - about 10,000 B.C., when Britain was still joined to the Continent. These primitive hunters and gatherers left no trace. Thousands of years later some tribes who had been on the move on the Continent in search of new land made the bold decision to cross the sea which now separated Britain from the continental land mass. No doubt they had sent out reconnaissance parties before setting out with their women and children, their cattle and their bags of precious seed grain, and knew that they would find vast pastures on hilly land, open scrubby country and soil light enough for their stone implements. There would be lowlands, too, covered in swamps and forests, but they could ignore them, because there was space enough on the hills and downs. So they took possession and gradually spread northwards. Others explored the rivers and some of the tribes that settled on the Cotswolds are believed to have come up the Severn. Settled is perhaps the wrong word, for these Neolithic people were still half-nomadic. Though they had domesticated animals and were growing grain, they did not yet know how to keep the soil fertile and had to move on when it was exhausted. Nevertheless, this step from hunting to taming, and from gathering wild fruit, seeds and roots to sowing and harvesting was such a fundamental and tremendous advance, that it has been called the Neolithic Revolution. It was the first step in the mastery of the environment and towards civilisation.

These nameless tribes came to Britain 4,500 years ago, and they left traces that are still visible today. Their trackways over the hills have been used ever since, the White Way is one of them, the Ricknield Way from Bourton-on-the-Water northwards is another. Their most impressive and conspicuous memorials, however, are the graves of their chieftains, the Long Barrows. An astonishing number of them has survived to the present day; there are more than fifty on the Cotswolds alone, and they are found in other parts of England, particularly in the South and West, as well as on the Continent. Most Cotswolds Barrows are gallery graves, consisting of a forecourt and a corridor or gallery leading to one or more burial chambers, where the bones of the dead were deposited. They were built before burial and used by successive generations of chieftains' families. The burial chambers were constructed of stone slabs or rocks and surrounded by a mound of small stones, often carefully laid in the same way dry stone walls are still built today. The Barrows are oval mounds, now covered with grass, their length varying between ninety and three hundred feet, the width at the broad end between forty-five and one hundred feet, monumental and impressive even now, 4,000 years after they were built. (They were already ancient monuments when Moses led the Children of Israel out of Egypt.) The great number of Long Barrows - there are six within a three mile radius of Compton - shows that the Cotswolds must have been well populated in the New Stone Age, for each Barrow represents a clan. Had the land been covered by forest such density would not have occurred. But the Great Oolite Limestone, the prevalent rock of the Cotswolds, is not a forest bearing formation, it is good pasture and corn land.

The building of the Barrows, the quarrying of the stones and their transport to high places in which Barrows were usually erected, required organisation, great effort and time. A camp site was needed and it seems unlikely that a place on the dry, windswept wold would be chosen for it. Water was indispensable for man and beast and the shelter of the hills would have been welcome, too. Our valley with its springs must have had great attraction as a camp site at all times, but especially for a tribal gathering. The nearest Barrow, the one that was discovered recently, is only a mile or so away, so it is perhaps permissible to claim these Neolithic farmers as Compton's first, even if only temporary, inhabitants, though we have no proof that they lived in the valley. It would be difficult indeed to prove it, for any evidence of their stay had little chance to survive in this narrow valley which has been continuously inhabited for at least fourteen hundred years.

The Barrows were conspicuous landmarks before vegetation covered them. They were regarded as sacred places long after their builders had vanished, as secondary burials show, and they inspired feelings of awe and superstition ever after. Ploughmen treated them with respect and led their horses patiently round them when the land came under cultivation, and it is only in our time of mechanical farming that many are in danger of obliteration. Tales of great battles and buried treasure became attached to them and caused many a hopeful search for gold - in vain of course, but disastrous for Archaeology. Though not only the treasure hunters but the early archaeologists themselves did much damage in their enthusiasm for digging. Most of the evidence which would be so valuable today was thus destroyed and irretrievably lost. So, when in 1962 a Long Barrow was discovered which was unrecorded and unknown - to archaeologists, if not to local people who had heard it said that a great battle had once been fought in that field, the mound presumably being the grave of

the fallen - it was hoped that this Barrow might have escaped the usual fate and would yield information which through carelessness and ignorance had been lost before.

But first it has to be stated that this Long Barrow actually belongs not to Compton but to Withington, as it lies in the parish of Withington, just a few yards from the boundary with Compton Abdale. However, Sale's Lot, the field with the Barrow, belongs to a Compton farm, and parish boundaries are immaterial as far as Long Barrows are concerned, ancient though they are.

11   When the Barrow had been excavated, it was found that it had indeed escaped the attention of grave robbers ancient and modern, nevertheless the burial chamber was empty. How did it happen?

One of the unique features of this Barrow was a series of postholes in the forecourt which indicate that a wooden structure had been erected there. It had probably been thatched and it contained a hearth. The whole house, hut or whatever it was had burnt down and the forecourt floor was covered with a layer of burnt debris. The burial chamber was empty and human bones representing eighteen persons from infants to adults were scattered all over the forecourt. Only a few fragments of skull bones were found, though many teeth, and there were no bones of domestic animals. The Barrow had not been repaired after this disaster and the burial chamber remained empty, but three later graves were found in the body of the burial mound. The Barrow was built about 2,500 B.C. and destroyed towards the end of the Neolithic period.

It is, of course, impossible to reconstruct precisely what happened, or even to explain the building in the forecourt, with certainty. The absence of animal bones indicates that the hut had not been inhabited long enough to accumulate a detectable amount of household refuse. Was this structure a temporary shelter for the burial rites and the hearth a sacrificial altar? Had the tribe perhaps been ambushed while assembled for the ceremonies? Or had people taken refuge in the sanctuary of the chieftain's tomb and built a hut in the forecourt, and were attacked and overwhelmed there? We do not know, but the Barrow bears witness that the enemies did not respect the dead and were ruthless to the living. The ancestral bones were pulled from the burial chamber and scattered over the forecourt, the skulls taken away as trophies, the house was set on fire and the Barrow was left desecrated and desolate. The tribe must have been wiped out, or taken prisoner, for no one came back to replace the remains and rebuild the tomb.

Grasses and wild flowers gradually covered the stony mound and it lay undisturbed for nearly four thousand years, until it was discovered and carefully brought to light again in 1963-65. Some Roman sherds were found just below the turf on the mound, they probably came from the villa which is only a stone's throw away. The Barrow had not been disturbed.

Despite the sacrilege the Barrow remained a sacred place, as the secondary graves in the mound show. About five hundred years after the conflagration, the Beaker people who owe their name to the pottery found in their graves, buried one of their dead in the Barrow. Their bellshaped beakers and open bowls, decorated by means of finely toothed stamps with geometrical patterns, are so distinctive that they identify their graves wherever they are found.

This warrior tribe invaded Britain in c, 1800 B.C. and soon overran the country and dominated the peasant population. They brought with them a superior kind of pottery and some knowledge of metal. Knives of copper and gold

ornaments are sometimes found with their burials, but these were certainly not things of everyday use, but the dead man's greatest treasure. Flint and stone were still their working material, from arrowheads to such monumental edifices as the sanctuary of Avebury, of which the Beaker people were the builders or re-builders. They were, however, a roving race, and more interested in herding and trading than in farming. They gradually established trade routes across Britain, particularly to Ireland from where they imported metal, and so initiated the Bronze Age.

Though the Beaker people had their own burial custom, namely the individual burial in Round Barrows, a Beaker grave is occasionally found in a Long Barrow, and this happened in Sale's Lot. The top layers of the mound had been removed just behind the ruined burial chamber and the grave was inserted there. Because it was so near the surface it was damaged when the mound was about to be demolished by bulldozer in 1962, before it was realised that this was not a natural or accidental heap of stones, but man-made and of some significance. Had Mr. H.J.Cooper who then owned Grove Farm not stopped the work when he noticed the pattern of upright stones in the rubble, we should have had no knowledge of this Long Barrow at all, because not knowing of its existence, nobody would have been aware of its ultimate loss. But he suspended operations and contacted Mrs. O'Neil, the archaeologist, to have the mound inspected. When the importance of his discovery was realised, he agreed to the preservation of the mound and, later, to its excavation, despite the inconvenience this entailed for him. As far as Ancient Monuments are concerned, he might pardonably have felt that one can have too much of a good thing, as he already "owned" the Roman Villa in the Grove, scheduled, but not yet excavated in full.

To return to the Beaker grave. Though damaged, it was still identifiable as such by the sherds of the bell beaker which lay at the foot end. The incomplete skeleton was that of a man of about forty years; he owned neither a gold ornament nor a copper knife, a minute scrap of bronze adhering to a bone might have been an earring. The beaker dates the grave at c. 1700 B.C.. This solitary grave is the only witness to the presence in our neighbourhood of this great people.

Among the burnt debris in the forecourt of the Barrow, lay a complete leaf shaped arrowhead of such perfection that one can only marvel at the skill and workmanship of the Neolithic man who fashioned it from a flint with no finer tool than another flint. How many years of trying and learning, how many flints and nodules may it have taken to achieve such a symmetry and faultlessness? This beautiful thing was probably never intended to be used but was given as a votive offering to be buried with one of the chieftains. It was much bigger than the two arrowheads which were found by Mr. Rideout, (58 mm against their 40 and 25 mm length). Yet these smaller ones, used in the hunt or in wars, are hardly less perfect. They are, however, not Neolithic, they were made during the Bronze Age. Even when metal was available, it was still precious and flint was not discarded entirely, it remained in use for things that were liable to be lost easily, such as arrowheads. Mr. Rideout, whose home is in Dorset, in Pitt-Rivers country, and who knows a flint when he sees one, also found the working place of a flint chipper in yet another field. He recovered two cores and a handful of chips, among them a discarded arrowhead.

This handful of flints and some arrowheads - some more have meanwhile been picked up - are the only traces of human occupation during the years, roughly 1500, between the Beaker people and the Romans. Neither Round Barrows nor Iron Age hill forts have so far been discovered in the immediate vicinity of Compton. So far - it may still happen, for neither the Long Barrow nor the flints had been found when this excursion into the past started in 1962. Compton's history then, began with the Roman Villa in the Grove, and we had to surmise, without evidence, that it shared the generally known history of pre-Roman times. Now the period of blankness has shrunk to the Iron Age and may yet be closed altogether, for we have no reason to believe that our valley and the hills around it were deserted and uninhabited between the Bronze Age and the Roman Era.

QUÉRCUS RÓBUR
(*Common Oak*)

AD43 - 410

Only when Britain is drawn into the sphere of literate culture which spread with the Roman Empire from the Mediterranean towards the North, does written History come to the help of Archaeology. Now at last people, the tribes and their chieftains emerge from the anonymity of Pre-history. But History was written in Rome, by and for Romans, and Britain was a remote province of a vast empire and the Cotswolds only a small part of that remote province, so that information from Roman historical writers is scanty and Archaeology still remains the chief source of our knowledge.

Moreover, this Roman History of Britain was a history of conquest and campaigns, of resistance and rebellion, and peaceful people tend to get overlooked in the histories of war. If this is so, then the people who lived on the Cotswolds at the time of the Roman conquest must have been peaceful indeed, for they are hardly mentioned. They are on record as the first British tribe to surrender without fighting, probably by negotiation, but this report is marred by mis-spelling of their name and so leaves room for controversy. They are the Dobunni, who occupied the territory from Worcestershire in the North to the Wiltshire Downs and part of Somerset in the South. They probably were part of the great conglomeration of tribes which had invaded Britain in about 75 B.C. and which are collectively known as Belgae. The most powerful of the Belgic tribes were the Catavelauni who established a kingdom in the East with the capital of Camulodunum (Colchester). From there they expanded westwards and towards the South, a threat to the Dobunni whose neighbours in the West were the fierce Siluri who would soon prove very troublesome to the Romans by their hostility and resistance.

This precarious situation between two strong and aggressive tribes may have influenced the Dobunnic kings in their attitude to the Roman conquerors. The arrival of the legions may have seemed a relief and a solution to their troubles. There is a report of the early surrender of a tribe called Bodunni, otherwise unknown, which probably refers to the Dobunnni for they were not prominent enough for their name to be incised so indelibly in the annals of the Roman Empire that it could not suffer some mis-spelling. So, "if the Bodunni were in fact the Dobunni", then they surrendered after the first decisive battle, even before the Emperor Claudius and his generals made their triumphal entry into the capital of the vanquished Catavelauni. There are no reports of a campaign against the Dobunni or of a later rebellion. Occupation of the Cotswolds was swift and the Pax Romana soon established. As early as A.D. 49 only six years after the beginning of the war in Britain, the Romans established a legionary fortress at Glevum (Gloucester) to contain the rebellious Siluri and the Cotswolds were at peace and enjoyed increasing prosperity.

Sometime during the reign of Nero (A.D. 54-68) the Romans persuaded the Dobunni to leave the earthworks and huts of their "capital" at Bagendon and to move to a new city a few miles further south. In this way the leading members of the tribe were introduced to the Roman way of life and, in time, thoroughly Romanised. This new city, Corinium Dobunorum (Cirencester), became the civic and administrative centre of the tribal territory. A cavalry unit had been stationed there in the early days of the conquest, but was soon withdrawn. Corinium was a tribal capital, but, like the other tribal capitals, built by the Romans as an entirely Roman town. It had its forum and basilica, its public baths and amphitheatre, in short, the character which the Romans imprinted on the cities of their empire from Africa to Britain. In time, Corinium developed into the second largest city in Britain, the capital of Britannia Prima.

Important roads met and crossed at Corinium, the Ermine Street from the East to Glevum, Akeman Street and, later, the Fosse Way, the only Roman road not based on London. All were major roads, broad and well-paved, for the quick movement of troops or government couriers and officials. Other roads to and from Corinium were more modest, but no less important, and the White Way is one of them.

14   The White Way is not a Roman creation, it is one of the pre-historic ridgeways and was an important route over the Cotswolds long before the Roman engineers drove their highways across the length and breadth of Britain. In Roman times, however, it was re-shaped, because its function had changed. It figured no longer as a track across the hills to the North, but had become the link between Corinium and its hinterland, or, conversely, between the villa estates and their market. The White Way leaves Cirencester in the north-east of the town and, after ascending the hills above the river Churn, runs on more or less level ground for about six or seven miles. As a ridgeway it had then continued in the same direction, but the Romans here turned it to the North to drop to the valley of the Coln and to cross the river at Compton Cassey. It then climbs straight up and over the hill to the North and

passing through Compton Abdale it merges with the Salt Way near Hazelton. It is still in use and though it may have changed its course here and there, it is essentially the same route as at least 2000 years ago and it is still the quickest and shortest way between Cirencester and Compton and other villages around.

15   While the tribal aristocracy moved to Corinium, absorbed Roman civilisation and came to know new luxuries, but certainly new responsibilities as well, life for the common people outside the town continued in much the same way as before the conquest. As long as taxes were paid and peace was kept, the Romans did not interfere with custom and usage. They introduced neither new farming methods nor new implements. The Belgae had contributed more than the Romans ever did to the advancement of agriculture. They had brought with them the heavy coultered plough which made it possible to cultivate the heavier and more fertile soil of the lowlands. It is doubtful, however, if this heavy plough was used on the Cotswolds, for there are no traces of "celtic" fields to be found here, a pattern of ancient ploughland that is still clearly discernible in other parts of Britain. It therefore seems that the hill country was mainly used for pastoral farming while the lowlands provided the corn.

Although the Romans did not interfere with the rural way of life, changes were inevitable. The demand on the resources of the land was greater than ever before, for the towns had to be fed and the army to be provisioned, not only with food but with wool and leather. Roads like the White Way made the market accessible and at the same time brought town and country close together. Roman goods from the towns were traded back to the country and it was gradually Romanised through contact with the towns, for Roman culture was city culture and spread from the towns outward.

It reached its culmination in the country in the villas which fascinated the early archaeologists as much as the Long Barrows and with the same sad consequences. Roman villas, in our thinking, are almost synonymous with mosaic pavements, baths and underfloor heating, but actually only seventy-five of about six hundred and thirty identified Roman or Romanised farm and country houses come into this luxury class, and there are farm houses of all stages of wealth and comfort, according to the various strata of the population. A high percentage of the rich and luxurious country houses are found round Cirencester, mainly on the Cotswolds, clearly an indication of the prosperity of the district in Roman times.

As villas are not country seats of wealthy townsmen, but the headquarters of agricultural estates, farming must have flourished to produce these magnificent houses. They were not planned and built by the Romans, but represent the last stage of development of native farm houses and reflect the gradual increase of wealth, though not all of the them reach the splendour of Chedworth and Woodchester. Where excavation of the site was done carefully, as in Northleigh (Oxon), this process of change in growth can still be traced, but in other places, as Chedworth, much evidence was destroyed in the search for mosaic floors.

Roman sites, and in most cases identifiable villa sites, have been discovered on both sides of the White Way in an almost unbroken sequence from Cirencester to Winchcombe. There is first Chedworth villa, discovered and excavated in 16 1864, there is a Roman site in Yanworth Woods, in the neighbouring parish, and not yet examined (the two pillar bases on each side of a garden gate in Yanworth village came from Stowell Park, and so probably from Chedworth). Then we have Compton Abdale villa, not yet excavated properly; Withington villa, discovered in 1811; Whittington Court villa, which was excavated and explored; a site near Hazelton, known in 1891 but not followed up, and the villa sites at Spoonley Woods and Wadfield near Winchcombe. Others may have been destroyed before they were recorded, some may possibly still come to light, for Roman sites, unlike Long Barrows, give little indication of their existence on the surface, and were, and still are, discovered accidentally.

As late as last century, however, some walls on Roman sites were still accessible and a welcome source of stone for building field walls. These sites were well known locally, particularly to the men who built the walls, yet until the interest in Archaeology and in the remains of the past arose, people did not consider these things important. The whereabouts of such sites might be mentioned conversationally, but nobody would dream of notifying an authority of finds or discoveries. A site might be quite well known by local people but would still be unrecorded and 17 some, once known, have in fact been lost again.

Dr. W. St.C. Baddeley knew all this and he made a point of questioning people he met on his walks and in the villages. So he may have heard the rumours and speculations about Compton Grove. There is Bell Tump which has always appealed to the imagination; it was said that you could make the bells in the tump ring if you jumped on it at midnight, but apparently nobody was brave enough to try "Just stories, you know". It was also noticed

So-called Roman Snails. Thought to be indicators of Roman sites.

that there was an abundance of 'Roman' snails around Bell Tump, and this was commented on. A few people knew that the snails were not the only Roman things to be found there. How much of all this Dr. Baddeley learned must remain uncertain, for he gives no indication of how he became aware of the site, when he refers to it in an article in the *Transactions of the Bristol and Gloucestershire Archaeological*

18 *Society" in 1925:* ...It was likewise unknown, that another extensive and sheltered villa was certainly situated on the way towards the important uplands beyond Coln-Head." He adds a footnote: "The small evidence for this are; first of all the worked ground area there, and next its products - four kinds of good pottery, a gold solidus of Gratian, and a bronze statuette of Venus." This, as far as I am aware, is all that has ever been published about the Villa at Compton Abdale; Dr.Baddeley does not give its exact location.

These few sentences seem at first sight very informative, yet, when one scrutinises them closely they become more and more vague and ambiguous. What is a "worked ground area"? What is "good pottery"? Were the finds made in the same place and at roughly the same time? And by whom? By Dr.Baddeley himself or somebody else? It seems futile to ask, since Dr.Baddeley died long ago and nobody else could answer these questions.

Perhaps he handed his finds over to a museum and gave some information about them? The first place to come to mind and the most likely one is the City of Gloucester Museum. Mr. Taylor, the Curator, wrote in answer to my enquiry that there are four coins from Compton Abdale in the Museum, presented by Dr. Baddeley, but nothing else: "Neither the solidus of Gratian nor the statuette are in our collection and it is quite possible that Mr. St. Clair Baddeley retained these pieces himself. On his death the bulk of his personal collection went to the Ashmolean Museum at Oxford and it would certainly be worth your while to approach them." I did so, and the answer was: "It appears that neither the coin nor the statuette about which you write are in this museum... We have a record of only one object presented to the Ashmolean by Mr.Baddeley, and that is a section of lead piping with a Latin inscription." So it seems that he did retain the finds in his private collection which was presumably dispersed at his death, as no Museum appears to have received it as a whole. The only hint of what may have happened to the Venus is an entry in one of his numerous notebooks. A short inventory in one of the books connects a Bronze Hebe with Mr. and Mrs. Edwiger, though without giving any details as to gift, loan or anything else. As Dr. Baddeley in another entry refers to the Compton Venus as Hebe-Venus, the inventory may refer to it.

If this is where the Venus went to - where did it come from? And, for that matter , the gold solidus? The footnote says they are products of the villa, and it is generally and naturally assumed that they were found on the villa site, but this assumption is wrong. Neither the Venus nor the coin came from the Grove.

In the course of one of our conversations I asked Mrs. Kibble, who was then the oldest inhabitant and had a remarkable memory, if she had ever heard of things like coins being found. "No, not lately", she answered, "but years ago there was a Mr. Baddeley, and he came to the village now and then and he asked me, too. And I told him Harry Purvey had found a little idol. It was all dirty, of course, having been in the ground all these years, and so Harry carried it in his breeches pocket till it was clean. So Mr. Baddeley went up and asked Harry about it. Yes, Harry knew where it was, he had given it to the children to play with. He did not think it was of any value, it was so old. They still had it, so he got it and gave it to Mr. Baddeley. And you know - he gave him ten shillings for it!....Oh yes, I have seen it, it was about as long as my finger. It looked a bit like an angel, but it was rough, of course, having been buried so long. Mr.Baddeley told me to keep watch for anything that may be turned up and to keep it for him. But there was not anything more, and he did not come back either. That was many years ago, I suppose he is dead now."

It must have been in 1923/4, and Dr. Baddeley is indeed dead, and so is Mr. Purvey. He died in 1951, but Mrs. Purvey lives across the road, still in the same cottage, one of the five in a row, above the village proper, towards the A40. She can and does confirm Mrs. Kibbles' story. She, too, of course, has seen the idol and uses the same words to describe it: "angel-like, but not quite like an angel". She cannot recall details like its dress, but would recognise it if she saw it. Her husband found it when he dug the garden above the cottages. A Roman coin was found in another strip of the same gardens which lie beside the White Way, and were still fields when Mrs.Purvey's father was a young man (he died in 1958, aged 89). This figure could have originated at the villa site - or might it have been lost by some traveller on the White Way on his way to or from Corinium?

Mrs.Purvey and I went to Chedworth Villa and to Cheltenham Museum to see if we could find an "idol" which might resemble our vanished Venus, just enough to get an idea of her appearance, but we did not see one which even faintly reminded her of the angel-like figure, and so there is nothing to show for our efforts, not even a drawing or a photo of a similar statue.

So much for the Compton Venus, well known, often mentioned, even in the Little Guide to Gloucestershire, found and lost nearly half a century ago, and now an insubstantial wraith. Is Gratian's gold solidus more solid? Alas, it is at least as elusive as the Venus. Nobody seems to know anything about the coin, nobody has seen it.
Dr. Baddeley mentions it several times in his notebooks and adds the same date to each entry, and this date is 1901.

These entries are scattered over hundreds of pages of highly interesting but miscellaneous notes and jottings, and they gradually reveal the history of that solidus. One entry mentions Stowell Park in connection with it; another refers to "Maddy's farm", from where both the Venus and the solidus are said to have come, the coin is now called Lord Eldon's solidus. Yet another says that it was turned up in 1901 or 1903 by a man, called Jones, while ploughing a field on "Maddy's farm". This Compton farm, now called Manor Farm, belonged to Lord Eldon in 1901. He sold it to Mr. Maddy in 1911. Stowell Park was Lord Eldon's residence, and it seems that Mr. Jones handed in the gold coin he had turned up and that it was kept at Stowell Park. In 1925, however,

Dr. Baddeley added the last and final remark to a previous note concerning the solidus; he had learned that it could not be found anymore.

That solidus seems to have teased Dr. Baddeley as much as anybody else. He heard of it and pursued it, but in the end seems not even to have set eyes on it. I asked   Mr. Ernest Jones, who was born in Compton and lived here all his life, if he knew anything about it. He was 14 in 1901, he has a remarkable memory and would certainly remember if a namesake of his, possibly a relation, had found something as sensational as a gold coin. But he had never heard anything about it, not even a rumour.

It took quite a few letters, much questioning of my unfailingly patient and cooperative victims and hours with the notebooks to find out - so little. The Venus remains undetected and the trail of the gold solidus ends in an unspecified field of a 932 acre farm. Their ghosts should now be laid, but will probably continue to hover about the villa site, for rumours are well-nigh immortal.

As mentioned before, the existence of a villa in the Grove was no secret to local people, or, at least, to some of them. Mr. Irving, the Curator of Chedworth Villa Museum, told me, that the man who had lived in the gamekeeper's cottage in the Grove in about 1886 knew of it; he later became a woodman on the Chedworth estate and frequently met Dr. Baddeley and it is likely that he mentioned the site to him. Even so it does appear that Dr. Baddeley needed many visits to be sure at last (1925). It would have helped him, if he had had knowledge of a letter which Miss E. Crosse gave me in 1967. She had found it among the papers left by her sister, Miss D. Crosse, and thought it might be of interest because it deals with the Roman remains in the neighbourhood. The part relating to Compton Abdale reads as follows:

Haselton R.S.O. Gloucestershire Sept. 21st 1891.

Dear Sir:

In reply to your letter of the 16th Inst. about Roman remains I have sent you the following facts.

Compton Abdale Roman Villa is situated in a wood, called Compton Grove near the Withington road and the White Way (Roman), the situation is well suited for a Roman Villa, being sheltered from all points, and well supplied with water. It has been known to exist by a few people for years, I understand that about thirty years ago, when removing a wall, in the field called Sourmoor, adjoining the Villa 7 Pillae or supports of Roman pavements, were found, and for years were used as steps to a summer house, at the Lower Farm Compton Abdale, I also understand that pieces of Roman vases and other pottery were found, and also a lot of curious shaped pieces of bronze, which were taken to be trappings of horse harness. In the year 1883 when I lived at Compton Abdale I found several pieces of Roman Pottery of the Common grey and red sorts, but no Samian, also a lot of red, blue, and white painted wall plaster, and pieces of flue tiles in great abundance, and in one instance when digging out rabbits, I came to a sort of white concrete about 1 foot thick.

I was once told by a friend, that he saw in the British Museum London a piece of Roman pavement that .... at Compton Abdale, near .... Withington road in the .... I think he must have m.... mistake, can you tell m... such is correct?

The letter is signed W. H. Hewer and is written on pages of an exercise book. One eighth of one leaf is missing, hence the gaps towards the end. It is not known to whom the letter was addressed or how it came into Miss D. Crosse's possession.

The summer house at Lower Farm vanished long ago, but one pillar and the head of another have been located in a retaining wall of a flower bed close to the house. This may be the only survivor of the original seven, but after a hundred years one could hardly expect to find all of them; even so it confirms the rumour about the pillars which Mr. Hewer heard so long ago. Dr. Baddeley mentions another pillar in Mr. Maddy's garden, now called the Manor Garden

Hypocaust Pillar. A stray from the Roman Villa site in the Grove. In 1891 seven were known to be in the Lower Farm garden; they have since disappeared.

and it is still there, supporting a bird bath. Other hypocaust pillars stand on the terrace of Grove House.

Dr. Baddeley must have spoken of the site to a few archaeologists, for a small party of them visited it in March 1931. Mr. Key, Senior History Master at Cheltenham Grammar School, was one of them. He was keenly interested in the Roman period and the year before had been digging at the Roman site at Listercombe with a party of boys from his school. Dr. Baddeley saw them there when he made one of his rounds of inspection. He does not seem to have been favourably impressed by their method, for he remarks in his Notebooks that the diggers needed care. When he visited the Grove in May '31, he found that excavations had taken place there and learnt from the postman in the village that Mr. E. Turner (of Shipton, who then owned the Grove) had allowed Mr. Key and his boys to dig on the site. In those days apparently it was not necessary to notify anybody or to get permission from any authority to start a dig, so that the County Archaeologist himself was surprised at what he discovered at Listercombe and in the Grove. The owner, too, was free to invite whom he liked to investigate a site, as Mr. Turner invited Mr. Key and his boys to Compton at Easter to find out once and for all whether there really was a Roman Villa in the Grove.

They came and they dug, and they must have had a wonderful time, let loose on a promising and exciting site, unhampered by supervisors and their insistence on measuring and recording, innocent of stratification and other refinements. If a plan of the site was made, it must have remained in the private possession of Mr. Key. I could not discover anything more than the finds which are in Cheltenham Museum and the report of the excavation in the School magazine, "The Patesian". This report was not published anywhere else and the secretary of Cheltenham Grammar School very kindly copied it for me and gave me permission to reproduce it.

Extract from "The Patesian", the Cheltenham Grammar School Magazine, July 1931.

Excavations at Compton Abdale   Easter 1931

Some years ago a gold coin of the Emperor Gratian and a statue of Venus were found in Compton Grove, near Withington. Mr. Key (senior History master) was asked by Mr. Turner, owner of the site, to make investigations with a view to ascertaining if there was a villa in this beautiful valley. Since Easter was early it was decided that excavations at Listercombe would be probably hindered by rain and, therefore, the School archaeologists decided to accept Mr. Turner's kind offer of a house on the site and excavate at Compton. The number of excavators - twenty eight - was larger than ever and not only did the expedition prove enjoyable but the results obtained were most interesting. It was immediately noticed that the top of the valley had been artificially terraced like the Chedworth valley and the remains of two old walls could be discerned on the surface. Excavations were commenced along these walls and before long all kinds of evidence of Roman occupation were found. Much to our surprise however, it was noticed that the level of Roman objects extended below the level of the wall foundations and moreover no side walls were found. After a week of trench digging it was noticed that the wall, although built of Roman materials, was in fact, a post-Roman wall built by some Cotswold farmer. At one point a number of stone pillars from the veranda of the villa had been inserted endwise to act as wall stones, and elsewhere the interior of the wall had been filled with tiles and wall plaster. During the digging of the trial trenches much Roman wall plaster in a very good state was found. This plaster formed a design showing panels of red, white, green, yellow and blue.

It was decided to carry the investigations to a lower level and in a short time the actual Roman foundations were found at level of four feet depth - Mr. Cheney's "gang" being responsible for the discovery. Almost immediately other walls were found at the same depth and the work then went forward rapidly. It was discovered that the floor of the room was covered with soot to a depth of three inches and the pillars which were in situ were burnt to a bright red. During the remaining day or two enough was excavated to show that the room was a hypocaust and that it connected by a narrow passage way with a stoke hold. We had not only proved the existence of the villa but had also found the key to the whole plan of the establishment. The objects discovered were handed over to the keeping of Mr. Herdman (then Curator of the Cheltenham Museum) where the work of sorting and cleaning was completed. The objects include two practically complete omelette dishes in black pottery, a large fragment of mortarium, pieces of beautifully made Castor and Samian ware, a quantity of common red pottery, large quantities of wall plaster, roof tiles and nails, tusks of boars, bones, a finely preserved coin, fragments of glass and iron. Several fragments of pottery and a coin have been found on the neighbouring "Bell Tump". As usual we had a number of press reporters to see us. We were informed by Fox Photos representatives that pictures of our work were published in books and papers all over the world.

December 1931

The excavations of Compton Grove were started during the Easter holidays and the discoveries made then gave reason to hope for more interesting discoveries later. Thus the beginning of the summer vacation found a party of seventeen boys, with Mr. Key, Mr. Porter and Mr. Edwards, continuing the task of uncovering the remains of a Roman house which was built about sixteen hundred years ago. Although soil and vegetation has covered the remains to a depth of more than four feet and thus made the work difficult, great progress has been made. Already one wing of three small rooms has been uncovered, and it is hoped that further digging will bring to light some tesselated flooring.

The discovery of the pillars which supported the flooring was very interesting and this was made even more interesting when the position of the furnace which heated the rooms was discovered. The foundations of this furnace were in excellent condition and a large quantity of soot was removed. The heating arrangement was such that the floor supported on pillars had to have a hot draught of air from a furnace outside the house drawn under the floor, thus heating the room.

Nine Roman coins, making a total of sixteen for the site were discovered, and some of these are in excellent condition. The one of Allectus, A.D. 293-6, minted at Colchester, is the best preserved of all the coins. The mint mark, C, can be easily seen without the use of a glass. One of the coins is made of bronze being as big as a penny, but much heavier. It is is of the Antonnine period, and on one side a galley is depicted. A bronze earpick, or tooth-pick, is the best preserved discovery. It is ornamented and has a two-pronged end.

Many Roman nails - many of them still in the slates in which they were used - have been found in good condition. A large quantity of pottery has been found. Some of it is black and of a good quality showing by its shape that it is of round objects such as bowls. A portion of a quern, or millstone, was found. It is made of stone which is not found in the neighbourhood. There are fragments of sharp flint in the inside of the bowls, and grooves cut to allow the crushed grain to filter out are to be seen.

It is hoped that the site of these excavations will be revisited in the near future, when it is confidently expected that more important and interesting discoveries will be made.

C.F. Dale

But their hopes were not fulfilled; the Grove changed hands and permission to dig was withdrawn. They had been so confident that they would return, they had not filled in the trenches or tidied up the site. Cpt. Mayall, later owner of Grove Farm, utilised the biggest hole by building a swimming pool into it. A swimming pool in the ruins of a Roman villa could anything be more romantic? Actually, it is a tank-like concrete affair and the water is horribly cold, coming as it does from the spring which provided the villa with its water. Grass covers the scars of the excavation again and the site is but an open space amongst the trees of the Grove. It is now scheduled as an Ancient Monument and safe from amateur diggers until it can be excavated expertly. Only then will its extent and possibly its history and the stages of its development be known. For the time being, we have to be content with what we learn from the finds mentioned in Mr. Hewer's letter and the results of the 1931 dig. From these it appears that the Grove villa was one of the comfortable, luxurious houses with underfloor heating, plastered and painted walls, as well-appointed as the Chedworth villa. The mosaic floors will no doubt come to light in due time. The coins show that the house was occupied until at least A.D. 395, the minting date of the latest coin, but probably longer. The general state of the site suggests that the house was abandoned and by and by collapsed into a ruin. There are no signs that it was destroyed and set on fire.

While we know enough about the villa to make valid comparison with others and to gauge its character and importance, we know next to nothing about the ordinary members of the tribe, their life and their habitation. The workers on the home farm lived in the villa complex which consisted of the villa itself, the workers' living quarters and the farm buildings, and we can assume this for Compton, despite, so far, insufficient evidence, as it is the usual arrangement at other villas, but for knowledge of the tenant farmers we depend on local finds. Only a few finds of the Romano-British period have so far come to light outside the villa complex. There are the Venus and the legendary solidus, both stray objects unconnected with a possible habitation site, two Roman coins, one found in the vicinity of the Venus, one in the garden of the Old Post House near the Square, and a Romano-British burial at Spring Hill. This reveals nothing more than that a woman of forty years was buried there in a cyst grave, that she suffered from rheumatism and had lost only one tooth during her lifetime. There were no grave goods which could have told us more about her. Until more discoveries are made we do not know whether this grave indicates a cemetery or a homestead, or if it is just a solitary grave in the fields.

Dr. Baddeley mentions that Capt. Green from Chedworth took him "up to Maddy's farm" where he had found several 3rd century coins and four varieties of Roman pottery. He refers to "worked ground" and "terracing"; and it seems "Maddy's farm" here means the Manor House and Homeground, the pasture next to it which looks terraced and "worked". It has not been ploughed within anybody's memory. Dr. Baddeley thought it a good place for a villa because of the proximity of the spring, (the Crocodile). The handwriting of the Notebook is difficult and the text somewhat ambiguous.

21

The land of the Dobunni became one of the richest cantons of Roman Britain, and the Grove villa (and its land) was one of the many prosperous estates around Cirencester and along the White Way. The source of all this wealth was probably, then as in later times of prosperity, sheep farming. This was well established before the Romans came and was intensified as the demand for wool and leather increased. The army alone provided an immense market and wool was also exported to other parts of the empire. It was the only British product to be mentioned by the Emperor Diocletian in his price fixing edict of A.D. 309.

The Roman army was withdrawn from Britain in A.D. 410, and the province was left to fend for itself. The central administration broke down, the towns had decayed, and the villas, dependent on towns and good communications, were abandoned and fell into ruins. Rome had to yield to the relentless pressure of the barbarians and had to abandon the outlying provinces to concentrate on the defence of the homeland. But it was to no avail, Italy was invaded, the Lombards settled in the north of the country, the Goths sacked Rome, "...and never since have the Romans reigned in Britain", adds the Anglo-Saxon Chronicle for the year A.D. 409.

RÓSA CANÍNA
(Dog-Rose)

The Saxon Settlement

Barbarian raids on Britain had started long before the Romans left. In fact, the Romans are thought in the end to have made use of these invaders by settling them in the North-east and charging them with the defence of the frontiers against the Picts and the Scots.

Vortigern, the British king, later tried the same device of turning poachers into gamekeepers, but with catastrophic consequences. "...Hengist and Horsa invited by Wurtgern, king of the Britons, to his assistance, landed in Britain in a place that is called Ipswinesfleet; first of all to support the Britons, but afterwards fought against them. The king directed them to fight against the Picts; and they did so; and obtained victory wherever they came. They then sent to the Angles to send more assistance. They described the worthlessness of the Britons and the richness of the land. They then sent them greater support. Then came the men from the three powers of Germany: the Old Saxons, the Angles, and the Jutes. From the Jutes are descended the men of Kent, from the Old Saxons came the people of Essex and Sussex and Wessex. From Anglia...came the East Angles, the Middle Angles, the Mercians, all those north of the Humber..."

Thus the Chronicle tersely describes the beginning and the end effect of the invasion and then proceeds to fill in what happened in between, namely a century of battles. "The worthlessness of the Britons" is not very apparent in this record; every advance of the Saxons has to be fought for and to be consolidated before the next move. The occupation of the island was a slow process and it was only in A.D. 577 that the battle was fought which delivered the Cotswolds into Saxon hands.

What had happened here in the 160 years since the Roman departure? The short answer is that we do not know. It used to be believed that chaos and misery reigned after the Romans left, but this view is being modified. True, the cities fell into ruins and the villas which depended on them, too. The Roman way of life ceased, but the native life had to go on. People had to be fed and clad whatever happened. The economic pattern had to change drastically, but the estates need not have ceased to exist even if the Big House was left and, uninhabited and uncared for, fell into ruins.

Cirencester, which was the dominant factor for the villa estates in Roman times, cannot have disappeared altogether because it is mentioned as one of the towns taken by the Saxons in A.D. 577. There were kings of Cirencester, Bath and Gloucester, and where there are kings there must be some sort of social order. Had the Britons been as helpless and disorganised as was once thought, they could not have put up so much resistance against the advances of the Saxons, and they have a very creditable record against an enemy whom the Romans themselves could not defeat.

But finally "Cuthwin and Cutha fought with the Britons and slew three kings, Conmial and Condida and Farinmail on the spot that is called Derham (Dyrham) and took from them three cities, Gloucester, Cirencester and Bath", and certainly not only the cities, but the land as well, for the Saxon conquest was different from the Roman one. It was not a military occupation under which the subject people could go about its business, neither was it a campaign of raiding, plundering and departing again, the Saxons took the country for their own and settled there.

The Cotswolds were a rich prize, there had been peace and prosperity for more than half a millenium and it would not have been in the victors' own interest to destroy and despoil the land which they wanted for themselves, once resistance was broken and the leaders of the Britons defeated. The people who took possession of the Cotswolds were a West Saxon tribe called the Hwicce. They settled in what is now Gloucestershire, Worcestershire and Warwickshire, but they did not remain united with Wessex, the West Saxon kingdom to the South, for long.

For the conquest of Britain did not end in peace, it shaded off into wars for supremacy between the kingdoms of the tribes who had crossed the sea in search of land. One episode in that struggle was the battle of Cirencester in 628, when Penda of Mercia fought with Cynegils and Cwichelm, kings of Wessex, and made a treaty by which the Hwicce and their lands passed into the dominion of Mercia. The Hwicce had their own kings, under the overlordship of the kings of Mercia, and their territory was known as the land of the Hwiccans till the 11th century. It is only in 1016 that Gloucestershire is mentioned by name for the first time.

What became of the Britons who lived there when the Saxons came? We have no certain knowledge of their fate. Whoever could, and it would have been the wealthy, probably escaped to Wales. The poor had to stay and accommodate themselves as best they could to their new masters. The (villa-) estate owner, if he had not been killed in battle, certainly would have been deprived of his property which might have been given as a reward to some Saxon warrior. He, in turn, would have settled his people on the tenants' farms, and the Britons would have been reduced to the lowest levels of the social scale.

It is unlikely that they were slaughtered wholesale; the new owners would have deprived themselves of labourers, of people moreover, who knew the land and how to farm it to its best advantage.

It was thought that the Saxons must have exterminated the Britons altogether, because their language disappeared almost totally. apart from the names of hills and rivers, no trace is left. But this seems a hasty conclusion. The Saxons were the masters, they had no need to adapt themselves and learn the difficult and alien language of the conquered; it was natural to retain the names of rivers and other local landmarks, and once used, there was no point in changing them, as this would only have caused confusion. North America provides an exact parallel; the European invaders took over the names of rivers and mountains from the Indians and many of them are still used today.

In everything else the subjects had to adjust themselves to the masters. Whoever learnt their language first had the best chance to survive and improve his lot. For the old this would have been difficult, if not impossible, but the young, always adaptable, would have been bi-lingual very soon. Their children might perhaps understand, but would no longer speak the language of their fathers, and in three or at the most four generations it would have disappeared altogether, though the descendents of the Britons might still be numerous.

All this is, and must be, speculation, for lack of evidence. All that is certain, is that Romano-Britons, once the Dobunni, disappear from history after the Saxon conquest although many may have survived, eventually merging with their conquerors. With them disappeared the name of the villa and its estate; the Saxons were not interested in keeping the names and traditions of their predecessors alive, and, therefore, our village, with thousands of others, is known by its Saxon, if not altogether Saxon, name. Even if the Roman house had not been in ruins, no Saxon would have lived there, for they regarded Roman-built places with fear and superstition. So the new village grew up at a distance from the villa, in the valley by the spring and its brook. Grass and scrub grew over the deserted site of the Roman house, and over the years it faded from memory.

LONICÉRA PERICLÝMENUM
(*Honeysuckle, Woodbine*)

Mercia

After having established itself as a Saxon village, Compton disappears into complete obscurity, but certainly not out of existence, for when we next hear of it, it is worthy to be the gift of a queen. Until this happens however, more than three hundred years pass without a glimpse of it or a word about it. In A.D. 909 Compton is part of the Barony of Churchdown which Queen Aethelfleda, the Lady of the Mercians, bestowed on the Priory of St. Oswald in Gloucester, but how and when it became her possession we do not know.

Under King Penda (A.D. 626-655) Anglian Mercia became the most powerful and the largest of the Teutonic kingdoms. When the Hwicce were incorporated into it they were removed from the orbit and the influence of the South and oriented towards the North. Christianity, too, came to them from the North and this is important for the later history of the Barony of Churchdown and, with it, of Compton.

The Venerable Bede tells a story which illustrates the process; it is the story of Prince Peada's courtship. He went to Northumbria to ask King Oswy for his daughter - that his father, King Penda, had slain Oswy's elder brother in battle, that two years later Oswy would revenge his brother and defeat and kill Penda, made no difference, there were no hard feelings on account of politics. Here is Bede's story: "Being an excellent youth, and most worthy of the title and person of a king, he (Peada) was by his father elevated to the throne of that nation (Mercia), and came to Oswy, King of the Northumbrians, requesting to have his daughter Elfleda given him to wife; but could not obtain his desires unless he would

embrace the faith of Christ, and be baptised with the nation he governed. When he heard the preaching of truth, the promise of the heavenly kingdom, and the hope of resurrection and future immortality, he declared he would willingly become a Christian, even though he should be refused the virgin; being chiefly prevailed upon to receive the faith by King Oswy's son Alfrid who was his relation and friend, and had married his sister Cyneberge, the daughter of King Penda. Accordingly he was baptised by Bishop Finan, with all his earls and soldiers, and their servants that came along with him...And having received four priests, who for their erudition and good life were deemed proper to instruct and baptize his nation, he returned home with great joy".

King Penda, whom it is customary to regard as a wicked heathen and persecutor of Christians, surprisingly, did not object to the preaching and baptizing that started immediately in Mercia, when "many as well of the nobility as the common sort renouncing the abomination of idolatry were baptized daily."

This story shows not only how close were the ties between Mercia and the North, but also how firmly the Hwicce were embedded in Mercia, for nearly everybody who is mentioned in this story had later some connection with them: King Peada himself was made King of South Mercia by King Oswy, his Northumbrian father-in-law, who took over Mercia after the defeat and death of Penda. One of the original four priests, Diuma the Scot, became the first bishop of Mercia. Queen Cyneberge, Alfrid's wife and Penda's daughter, became the first abbess of the monastery which her son Osric founded in Gloucester. He was viceroy of the Hwicce until he was recalled to Northumbria to be king. King Oswy's elder brother, who had been killed in battle by Penda, is St. Oswald, King and Martyr, to whom the church in Compton is dedicated.

St. Oswald, King and Martyr

Oswald must have been a truly remarkable man to impress his contemporaries so much that he became a very popular saint soon after his death. A king he certainly was, and a very successful and powerful one who, having inherited a poor and war ravaged country in his short reign of only eight years (A.D. 634-642), became the mightiest king of Northumbria yet. That he was a martyr could fairly be doubted. True, he was killed in battle by the pagan King Penda of Mercia, but he was not the only, or even the first Christian king to fall victim to the Mercian warrior. Penda slew no fewer than five of them at one time or another, not to persecute Christianity, but in the course of ordinary political warfare, simply because he could not avoid them. Christian kings had become the majority. Penda, in fact, was the only one who remained a heathen.

But if not a martyr, Oswald was a devoted and active Christian and spared no effort to further and strengthen the Church, giving money and land to build monasteries and churches. He called his old friend Aidan from Iona and made him Bishop of Lindisfarne. Yet - does all this make him a saint? Perhaps not in our 20th century eyes. We might even suspect that his highly successful political activities could not have left much room for saintliness. Here the Venerable Bede comes to help our understanding. A near contemporary, and a Northumbrian himself, he writes at length about the Saint and the many miracles that followed in his wake. "Wonderful to relate", says Bede, "he always continued, humble, affable and generous to the poor and strangers" though he had obtained larger earthly kingdoms than his ancestors. He helped Bishop

Aidan, acting as his interpreter, as the Scottish bishop's English was weak, and once, at Easter, he not only ordered his servants to feed the multitude of needy people who begged for alms, but he broke a silver dish which happened to stand on the dinner table and distributed the pieces among the poor. Bishop Aidan, much impressed by such an act of piety, took hold of the king's right hand and said: "May this hand never perish." And, Bede reports, so it happened. The hand and arm cut off after the king's death "remain entire and uncorrupted to this day and are kept in a silver case as revered remnants in St. Peter's church in the royal city of Bamburgh."

Another source of miracles was the cross which Oswald raised before his very first battle against Cadwalla, King of the Britons, who, as Bede says, though a Christian was "a barbarian and more cruel than a pagan". He was a powerful enemy who had slain many kings, Oswald's predecessor among them, and the young king must have seemed an easy prey. Oswald could raise only a small army, but he defeated Cadwalla in an epic battle, rallying his men around the cross and praying to "the true and living God Almighty For he knows we have undertaken a just war for the safety of our nation". "No day was ever more disastrous for the Britons", says William of Malmesbury, "or more joyful for the Angles" "through the effects of faith and the accompanying courage of the king". Miracles soon began to happen at that place "as a token and memorial of the king's faith" and Bede tells many stories of the wonderful healing power of chips from the cross on the battlefield.

This early victory brought peace for eight years until, in A.D. 642, Penda of Mercia made war against Northumbria, and Oswald lost life and battle at Maserfield on the 5th of August. After Oswald had been killed, Penda, according to the custom of the time, ordered the fallen king's head, arms and hands to be cut off and displayed on stakes on the battle field. There they stayed until King Oswy, Oswald's brother and successor, took them down a year later. The head was taken to Lindisfarne and placed in St.Cuthbert's coffin, the hands and arms to Bamburgh. The body was buried at Maserfield and remained there until Oswy's daughter, Ostritha, translated the bones to her favourite monastery of Bardney in the province of Lindsey. There they remained until Queen Aethelfleda rescued them from the ruins of the monastery, which had been devastated by the Danes.

The early victory of faith and courage, two examples of royal grace and compassion and his death in battle - this is the sum total of what we learn from Bede about Oswald himself. But in his time he stood out brightly against the dark background of barbarity, so that even the virtues and achievements which he shared with others seemed his alone, and he became Saint Oswald, King and Martyr. His veneration spread quickly and far beyond the British Isles. He is the patron saint of Zug in Switzerland and is well known as far away as Italy and Hungary.

St. Oswald has four emblems, the attributes by which the illiterate worshippers could recognise him among the multitude of saints: the cross, the silver dish, a raven and a hunting horn. The last two are not related to any incidents in the Saint's life and seem secondary and later additions. The raven is said to have been a messenger between the king and a

St. Oswald and his hunting horn. Sculpture over the arch of the west window of the church tower. One of the rare representations of the saint.

pagan princess whom he wished to marry. The hunting horn seems to originate in Durham, where St. Oswald's head had found its final resting place, still in St. Cuthbert's coffin which had been taken from Lindisfarne to save it from the Danes. A silver horn was kept in Durham near St. Cuthbert's tomb and, though it may originally have had nothing to do with either saint, was in time associated with one of them, the royal St. Oswald. So we see him represented on the west side of the churchtower in Compton Abdale as a youthful head wearing a crown and his hand raising the hunting horn to his mouth.

31

Queen Aethelfleda

The year 909 is an important date in Compton's history. It was then that Queen Aethelfleda brought the relics of St. Oswald to Gloucester and founded the Priory of St. Oswald on which she bestowed the Barony of Churchdown, of which Compton Abdale was a part. This determined Compton's fate for 650 years; it remained in the possession of the Priory and later, with the Priory, in the possession of the Archbishop of York till the middle of the 16th century.

We have no knowledge of what Compton was like in A.D. 909 or how the village in the valley had fared during the centuries of Mercian power. When the Mercians became Christians, the Hwicce were included, and Peada, who brought the priests from Northumbria, was king of South Mercia. But the message of the preachers may not have been altogether new and strange to the people, if, as we assumed, a considerable number of Britons survived and lived among them. The Britons had been Christians in Roman times and would certainly have kept their faith, even if they had to keep it secret from their pagan masters. This, however, may not have been necessary, for persecution of the Christians does not seem to have been a pre-occupation of the Mercians, according to Bede's record of Penda's, the arch-heathen's, attitude to the new faith: "Nor did King Penda obstruct the preaching of the word among his people the Mercians, if any were willing to hear; but, on the contrary, he hated and despised those whom he perceived not to perform the works of faith, when they had once received the faith, saying: 'They are contemptible and wretched who did not obey their God in whom they believed".

So Christianity may have survived in Compton, as elsewhere, as the faith of the depressed and the poor, which indeed it had been in the beginning, long before it became the religion of bishops and kings.

If we know, or at least can infer, something of the spiritual life of Compton, we know almost nothing of its material circumstances. Very little is known of Saxon economy. But there is one hint that the kind of farming that made the Cotswolds prosperous in the Roman days and before was carried on under the new management; export of wool is mentioned in the correspondence between King Offa of Mercia and Charlemagne, and the field name of Sheppey in Compton, as well as the name of the neighbouring village of Shipton, confirm that sheep had remained an important part of farming.

King Offa was the last powerful king of Mercia. After the reign of his successor Kenulf "the kingdom of the Mercians sank from its prosperity, and becoming nearly lifeless, produced nothing noteworthy to be mentioned in history" until in A.D. 875 Alfred, King of Wessex, added it to his kingdom. This decline of Mercia and the rise of Wessex were, however, not just another phase in the fight for supremacy in the old style. The great calamity which felled Mercia, as well as her neighbours, had begun with the first landing of the Danes, still in Offa's lifetime. The Danish conquest completely altered the pattern of power in the land. King Alfred's desperate struggle and his eventual ascendency over the Danes is one of the best known chapters of history, and every English child knows the story of the burnt cakes.

But when Alfred died, the war was by no means over and his son Edward had to take on the task of pushing the Danes back to the north-east and to contain them there. "And here indeed Aethelfleda, sister of the king and relict of Ethelred ought not to be forgotten", says William of Malmesbury, "as she was a powerful accession to his (Edward's) party, the delight of his subjects, the dread of his enemies, a woman of an enlarged soul, who, from the difficulty experienced in her first labour, ever after refused the embraces of her husband; protesting that it was unbecoming to the daughter of a king to give way to a delight which, after a time, produced such painful consequences. This spirited heroine assisted her brother greatly with her advice, was of equal service in building cities, nor could you easily discern whether it was more owing to fortune or her own exertions, that a woman should be able to protect men at home and to intimidate them abroad."

34

"This woman of an enlarged soul, this spirited heroine", was the Lady of the Mercians, King Alfred's eldest child. She was married to Ethelred, whom Alfred had made viceroy of Mercia, and her title, Lady of the Mercians, was the exact equivalent of her husband's. In fact, after his death she ruled over Mercia in her own right.

35

Though a capable ruler of considerable power, Aethelfleda never tried to rival her younger brother, but became his loyal helper and ally. Together they devised a new and effective way of fighting the Danes and containing them by building a chain of fortified towns as bases for their operations. By this method they succeeded in retaining the land they had won and sealing it off against further raids by the enemy. Edward could not have carried out this far-flung scheme without the dependable and able collaborator he found in his sister.

It was as commander in the field that the Queen came to the ruined monastery of Bardney in Lincolnshire, which the Danes had sacked in A.D. 870. Here she found the relics of

St. Oswald that Queen Ostritha had brought from the battlefield more than 200 years before. Aethelfleda rescued them from the ruins and translated them to Gloucester, where she and her husband, Ethelred, had built a monasterium a short while before (or, according to another version; which they had built specially in honour of St. Oswald and his relics.). This monasterium was not a closed monastery for monks, as was customary in later centuries, but a so-called minster, which was the usual form of religious foundation in the 10th century. These minsters were communities of secular priests, whose duty was the spiritual care of the people on the lands of their founder.

When Ealdorman Ethelred and Aethelfleda, the Lady of the Mercians, elevated their minster into a shrine for St. Oswald's relics, they endowed it with a rich gift of land from the royal domain, later known as the Barony of Churchdown, consisting of Churchdown, Hucclecote, Norton, Shurdington, Witcombe, North Cerney, Compton Abdale and Oddington. How long these lands had been in royal possession it is impossible to say, at least for Compton Abdale, because there is no documentation. Perhaps its very absence indicates that this state of affairs was taken for granted. When Penda of Mercia in A.D. 628 acquired the land of the Hwicce, he took a considerable risk in incorporating a large West Saxon tribe into Anglian Mercia. He would certainly not have done so if he had not thought the risk worth taking, if the richness of the land had not justified it. He would not have been interested in waste land, and as was customary elsewhere, the best would have been held by the rulers, the kings or viceroys, the best being the estates which had been flourishing in Roman times and can be expected to have retained their relative prosperity through the following period of change.

In Withington, Compton's neighbour in the West, a minster was founded in A.D>692; it was endowed by Oshere, grandson of Penda, and then viceroy of the Hwicce. He presumably owned the estate he donated before he gave it away. There was no religious foundation in Compton and therefore no charters, so we hear nothing of its ownership until A.D>909 when it, too, was given away by a viceroy - a viceroy no longer of the Hwicce under Mercia, but of Mercia under Wessex, - on whom nevertheless the ownership of the estate may have devolved, perhaps through Aethelfleda, for her mother was a Mercian princesss.

Both, Ethelred and Aethelfleda, were buried in the minster church of St. Oswald. The Ealdorman died in A.D. 911, the Lady of the Mercians in A.D. 918 at Tamworth, which was one of her fortresses against the Danes.

PRIMULA ACÁULIS
(*Primrose*)

The Priory of St. Oswald in Gloucester and the Archbishops of York

The minster, generously endowed, enriched by the relics of the saint and honoured to be the chosen burial place of its royal founders, was the principal religious house in Gloucester. But St. Oswald's did not enjoy this eminent position for long. A little more than a century later its fortunes changed, and the causes of this change lay quite outside St. Oswald's itself: the ancient ties between Gloucestershire and the North now proved adverse to the fate and fortune of the Lady of the Mercians' minster. From being rich and prominent, it became poor and part of an isolated enclave in Gloucestershire of the Archbishop of York's province and jurisdiction .

The connection between the Archbishops of York and Gloucestershire began in A.D. 972, when Bishop Oswald of Worcester became Archbishop of York without giving up his see. The two sees were held together by his two immediate successors until 1062, when Pope Nicolas II objected to this arrangement. Archbishop Ealdred then resigned from the bishopric of Worcester, but retained 12 vills of the estates of the bishopric for himself and his successors to help York, which had not yet recovered from the devastations of the Danish wars. These 12 vills are not named and, therefore, cannot be identified with certainty. As this happened only twenty-six years before the country was thoroughly surveyed for King William, one would expect a record of this transaction in the Domesday Book. Though it lists the possessions of the Archbishop of York in Gloucestershire, his vills do not number twelve and there is no reference to Archbishop Ealdred's acquisition.

Domesday Book produces more surprises in regard to the Barony of Churchdown, for we find that it is the Barony that is the main component of the Archbishop of York's lands in Gloucestershire, while St. Oswald is not mentioned, not even as its previous owner. If we had no other source of information but Domesday Book, no one would guess that St. Oswald's ever had anything to do with the Barony at all.

It is Stigand, Archbishop of Canterbury, who is registered as owning the Barony in King Edward's time, and no further explanation is given; historical enquiries were not the survey's business. Stigand lost the Barony together with all his other temporal possessions when he was deposed in 1070. He was succeeded by the Norman, Lanfranc, and it could be expected that Lanfranc would succeed Stigand in the ownership of the Barony as well. But King William held it and gave it neither to Lanfranc nor to its one-time rightful owners, St. Oswald's, but to Thomas of Bayeux, when he became Archbishop of York in the autumn of 1070. The king thus acknowledged and confirmed York's claim to land in Gloucestershire, whatever the original twelve vills may have been and whatever had happened to them since 1062. Since then the Archbishops of York were the lords of the manor of Compton, holding it in chief from the King for a fourth part of a Knight's fee. until Archbishop Holgate sold it to the crown as part of the Barony of Churchdown in 1544. To the people of Compton these changes in lordship probably made very little difference. They had to pay taxes and tithes and give of their services whoever the lord of the manor was.

Meanwhile St. Oswald's, with its church and chapels, shorn of most of its lands, remained a free chapel of the king, not subject to the Bishop of Worcester, in whose diocese they lay, until in 1095 the Archbishop of York acquired the spiritual jurisdiction over it and its dependencies from William Rufus in compensation for relinquishing claims in Lincolnshire. From then till the Reformation he was the temporal lord of the Barony, as well as the spiritual head of the erstwhile Minster and its chapels, and Compton belonged to York, body and soul as it were.

St. Oswald's independence was severely curtailed under York and the Archbishop determined its fate and its very nature. In 1153, Archbishop Murdac replaced the secular priests with Austin monks and, strictly speaking, it is only now that the Minster becomes a Priory. The Prior is appointed by the Archbishop, not elected by the canons, and he as well as the priests of St. Oswald's chapels are responsible to the Dean of the spiritual jurisdiction. To help the new house to establish itself, the Archbishop gave it his manor of Compton - Cuntun super montes - for four years or until such a time when he could come to Gloucestershire and see for himself how the new foundation fared. But he died in the same year and never came to Gloucester and Compton presumably reverted to the archbishops in 1157.

In the next century the archbishops sublet the manor to the Despensers. Thurstin Despenser is mentioned in 1266 as holding it from the Archbishop of York, and in 1284 Adam le Despenser held Compton in the same way for $1/4$ knight's fee.

This family was descended from Robert le Despenser who was Steward to King William and had come over with him from Normandy. He was "a great man in those days...and seized of 17 Manors in Leicestershire, 15 in Lincolnshire, 4 in Warwickshire and of the Manor of Child's Wickham in Gloucestershire". The Despensers also held King's Stanley and the serjeantry of Leckhampton. At least four generations held the office of Despenser or Royal Steward and the family possessed great power and wealth for centuries. The small manor of Compton was only one of many in their possession and it is unlikely that any of the Despensers ever set foot in it. They enjoyed the income from the manor, but they also had to take over the archbishop's obligation to the king.

Tenure of land in terms of military service was the essence of early feudalism, and the ecclesiastical barons, the archbishops, bishops and abbots who held land of the king were not exempted; they had to provide knights in the same way as temporal lords. The Archbishop of York owed a total of 60 knight's fees, $4 1/4$ of these for his barony in Gloucestershire.

It had become apparent very early that it sometimes was not possible to render knight's service in person and a payment in money to provide a substitute had become acceptable. This commutation of service into money enabled whole knight's fees to be split up into fractions when the land in question was thought too small to support a whole fee. Compton for instance was assessed for only a $1/4$ fee, while for Churchdown the Archbishop had to render two.

It is not known when the connection between Compton and the Despensers began or when it ended; but in 1290 Archbishop Romeyn visited Compton twice - would he have done so if the manor had still been let to Adam le Despenser?

Apart from the time when the Despensers held Compton, the manor seems to have been administered from Churchdown. The reeve of Compton had to render account to the bailiff of Churchdown, the last of whom was appointed in 1465. Thereafter the manors were probably let, this being the tendency in ecclesiastical property at the time. When in 1544 the Barony became crown property, Thomas Lane was the tenant.

Once an ecclesiastical body, be it a monastery, a bishop or an archbishop, had come into possession of land, it held on to it till deprived of it at the Reformation; therefore Compton, as part of the Barony of Churchdown, had one lord only from 1070 till 1544. "Parishes thus held have no history. Their inhabitants lived and died in peace." This was the opinion of a President of the Bristol and Gloucestershire

40 Archaeological Society, surely a trustworthy authority, referring to another of the Archbishop's manors. If history is taken to be a matter of great events and great men, of states and wars, battles and other spectacular happenings, then Compton indeed has no history. But even if its inhabitants lived and died in peace, we should like to know how they lived, how the descendents of the 22 villeins and 5 cottagers fared under their lord, the Archbishop of York.
We should like to know - but it is difficult to find information about a small place like Compton for the next centuries. Writing was a rare art and the few that mastered it used it for the tasks that they and their time deemed important: the monks in their cells were busy with chronicles and the lives of the saints, the clerks of the king and the great men of the realm with the business of governing the land and administering their estates. What we know about the unremarkable lives of ordinary people we know incidentally. Nevertheless, there is much and manifold information to be found in royal inquests, Domesday Book though unique in its way was only one of them, in other State papers and monastic records. But, this

Minster arches in Gloucester. The only remnants of the Priory of St. Oswald, once Queen Aethefleda's (d.918) minster.

information is ₁scattered throughout an enormous mass of documents and it refers to many different places. The general

41 composite picture of medieval village life that can be built up from these fragmented pieces would be valid for Compton as well. Though no two manors were alike, they had so much in common that a general description fits all of them. We may not know how much ploughing service was due in any one manor, or how much merchet had to be paid, but we do know that every villein in every manor had to serve the lord before he could think of his own affairs, that he had to suffer personal bondage and oppression.

Domesday Book

20 years lie between the battle of Hastings and Domesday Book, 20 years of almost continuous warfare against external enemies, of internal upheavals and campaigns against rebellious uprisings. The English nobility had been almost completely wiped out, either killed in battle or forced into exile, and their estates had been given to King William's Norman barons. English archbishops, bishops and even abbots had been replaced by foreign churchmen. The king himself had been out of England most of the time and now, in 1085, had once more to reckon with having to defend his kingdom in England and his duchy in Normandy against a combination of his enemies, in the North and South. It was imperative for him to know the state of England, his own royal possessions, the ownership of land by his barons and the Church, how much tax he could impose for the expected war, how much knight service was due to him. In short, he wanted a thorough survey of his kingdom of England.

So it came about that, when the king held his court and wore his crown in Gloucester at Christmas 1085, "he had much thought and deep discussion with his council about this country - how it was occupied and with what sort of people." To find this out the country was divided into circuits for the king's commissioners who collected the information "according to the oath of the sheriff of the shire, and of all the barons and their Frenchmen, and of the whole of the Hundred court - the priest, the reeve and six men from each village. They inquired what the manor was called, and who held it in

the time of King Edward; who holds it now; how many hides there are; how many ploughs in demesne, how many belonging to the men; how many villeins; cottars, slaves, freemen and sokemen; how much woodland; meadow and pasture; how many mills and fisheries; how much has been added to, and how much taken away from the estate; what it used to be worth altogether; what it is worth now; and how much each freeman and sokeman had and has. All this to be recorded thrice: to wit as it was in the time of King Edward; as it was when King William gave the estate, and as it is now. And it was also noted whether more could be taken from the estate than is now being taken."

The survey was so thorough that the Anglo-Saxon Chronicle complains: "So very narrowly did he have it investigated that there was no single hide nor a yard of land nor indeed (shame it is to relate but it seemed no shame to him to do) was one ox or one cow or one pig left out, that was not put down in the record. And all these writings were brought to him afterwards".

This is Domesday Book, a tremendous achievement for that or, indeed, any other time and a record unique in European history. Fortunately for us it still exists and we can see the state of England in 1086 and learn all King William wanted to know. Unfortunately, however, this knowledge is now less meaningful than it was then, and Domesday Book and its interpretation has been the subject of study and controversy for generations of historians. For our purpose we can disregard the controversial things and still see Compton as it was recorded for King William 900 years ago.

Stigand archieps tenuit *Cvntvne* .Ibi erant . ix . hidæ.
Ibi funt . ii . car 7 v . ac pti .7 xxii . uilli 7 v . bord cu . xi . car . Ibi . v . ferui .7 molin de . v . folid.
T.R.E . ualb . ix . lib . Modo: vii . lib . Thomas arch tenet.
Vn ho Rog de Jurei ten un ꟽ de . iii . hid ptin huic ꟽ.

43   Hoc ipfe arch caluniat.

"Stigand Archbishop (of Canterbury) held Compton. Here were 9 hides. Here are 2 ploughteams and 5 acres of meadow, and 22 villeins and 5 bordarii with 11 ploughteams. Here are 5 serfs and a mill worth 5 mark. In King Edward's Time it was worth £9, now £7. Thomas Archbishop (of York) holds it. Roger de Ivri's man holds one manor of 3 hides belonging to this manor. This the

44   Archbishop claims also."

This is what the priest, the reeve and the six villeins answered on oath for the manor of Cuntune, and the key to these laconic statements is the King's commissioner's questionnaire. Stigand, the Archbishop of Canterbury, is recorded as the previous owner without comment. Explanations were not called for, so we learn nothing more than that "on the day King Edward was alive and dead" Stigand had somehow acquired Cuntune as part of the Barony of Churchdown and other manors as well, Cheltenham among them.

"here were 9 hides": this is the tax assessment, the rateable value of the manor. The hide, originally the land which could support one family and reckoned at 120 acres, developed early into a fiscal unit for levying taxes and, as such, had no longer anything to do with land measurement. Tax had to be paid at so much per hide. But the hidation for tax purposes was so erratic and exemption, privileges and similar causes had intervened so much, that we can draw no conclusions as to size or value for any manor from its hidation. We can only accept the statement, that the manor of Compton had to pay tax for 9 hides, as for instance in 1084 when King William imposed the very heavy tax of 6s. per hide. The lord of the manor was responsible for the tax to the king and he actually paid it, but he recovered it from his manor and his tenants and so it was the peasant who ultimately paid it.

The taxable value was followed by the statistics of the manor: "There are 2 ploughteams in demesne", that is, belonging to the lord and the home farm. 8 oxen are reckoned to make one team. For practical purposes this seems a good deal of oxen, too many for one plough. Mr. E. Jones, who lived in Compton and started his working life with oxen,

45   thought so too; 4 oxen were a ploughing team in his opinion. Whether 4 or 8 to the team, 2 teams of oxen do not seem to indicate great wealth on the demesne farm. But the Lord's teams were not alone in working on his land; his tenants and theirs owed him help and service.

"There are 5 acres of meadow": this entry comes after the demesne plough teams and before the villagers and their teams, so it seems that the meadow was in demesne as well. In each of the 20 entries that follow the one for Compton in Domesday Book, the meadow is grouped with woods etc. at the end of the list for the whole place; grouped as it is with the Lord's teams indicates that it, too, belonged to the lord.

Meadow is not just pasture, which is a separate item, but not enumerated for Gloucestershire; it is grass land for making hay which was the only winterfeed available and therefore important and valuable. Because grass-land management was unknown until comparatively modern times, only riverside meadows where the grass grew lush enough naturally were suitable for making hay. In Compton we have to look for the 5 acres of Domesday Book meadow in the valley of the brook, west and southwest of the village. Samuel Rudder illustrates the value of meadow land in the age of common fields when he mentions some prices for land in Chedworth for the year 1298 (26 Ed I): "Guy de Beauchamp had in demesne 200 acres of arable land worth 2d an acre, and no more, because it was hill country land, eight acres of meadow, worth ls 6d an acre, and 200 acres of wood, the underwood was worth 30s. and no more, because it was common. This abstract from the escheator's inquisition serves

46 to shew the value of land at that time." There was very little meadow land in the manor of Compton because the river valley is narrow; the rest is "hill country land".

After the demesne, the village: "There are 22 villeins and 5 bordarii with 11 ploughteams".

Domesday Book mentions five classes of rural inhabitants: freemen, sokemen, villeins, bordarii and cotarii, and serfs. There are no freemen or sokemen in Compton; every man holds his land in tenancy from the lord of the manor and the villeins are here as everywhere else in the majority.

A word about the nomenclature may not come amiss, because the terms used are strange and difficult to translate. Translation is indeed the root of the trouble, not only now but right at the beginning, when the information was written down. Domesday Book was written in Latin by Norman scribes and their subject matter was Anglo-Saxon land and people. The reeve and the six villeins would certainly have given their answers in English, a foreign language to the Normans . There would be no shortage of translators, from the priest up, but still room for misinterpretation, for it is not only a question of language but of the complexity of social order, land use, economy, etc. The word villein is a good illustration of the difficulties. The Latin for it is villanus: a man belonging to a villa. But this villa is not what comes to our mind when we use the word; it is the scribe's translation for the Saxon word tun, the settlement, the village, and a villanus is a tunsman; a villager. To avoid the confusion which the use of the word villa inevitably brings with it, historians have agreed to call a medieval village a vill and its inhabitants villeins. To call a vill a village would again be misleading, for a modern village just is not a vill any more. Villein is used in this general sense of villager when it is said that six villeins give information to the king's commissioner. But it acquired another, specific meaning and then it expresses a social grade: a man who holds his land in tenancy from the lord of the manor. Later on, when the principle and uses of feudalism are established and well-documented, villeins are sometimes called virgaters and are thought to have had a share of one virgate, estimated at 30 acres in the common fields. They owed service and rent according to the size of their holding; the more land, the greater the amount of work for the lord. Domesday Book gives little information beyond the bare answers to the questionnaire and says nothing about rents and services, or the mutual relations between lord and tenants. The manor is assumed as the customary unit, but how far assumption and reality coincide or are in conflict has been a matter of controversy ever since Domesday Book has been studied.

The bordarii and cotarii are the smallholders of the vill; their share in the fields is only 5 acres each and they owe little service for their land. Thus they had time to do other things beside work their fields and they probably provided the craftsmen, the smith, the carpenter or the shepherd, and worked for the virgaters. There were only five such cottagers in Compton, while there were 22 villeins.

The reeve was chosen from the villeins. He was reeve for a year and was responsible to the lord or his bailiff for all matters concerning the work and the men. This was an office that demanded much time and carried great responsibility and was not always accepted very willingly. A reeve had to act in the interest of the lord, but at the same time be a spokesman for his fellow villagers; this could lead to unpopularity in the village or to difficulties with the lord. In Compton the reeve was an important man, for the lord of the manor was far away and his bailiff had to look after the whole of the Barony with its seven manors, and the day to day running of the manor was in the hands of the reeve.

Lastly, there are the 5 slaves, the lowest category of men. They have no rights whatsoever; they cannot hold land; they are the property of the lord and can be bought or sold. Slavery, unknown to the Normans, was an old established custom in England. Bristol had been notorious for its slave trade for centuries before the Conquest and Gloucestershire had the highest number of slaves of any county. 25.% of its population were slaves, 23.2% were bordarii, 46.2% were villeins; Compton had a much higher percentage of villeins than the county average. Slaves disappeared quickly under the Norman kings, but, on the other hand, all other classes of the rural population were increasingly depressed and their servitude grew so much that in the end villein was but another name for serf.

This, then, is the male population of Compton in 1086: 22 villeins, 5 bordarii and 5 slaves. The villeins and bordarii would be the heads of families, while the slaves are thought to have been numbered individually , and if we assume that the average household had five members, Compton would have had about 140 inhabitants, 27 families and 5 slaves. This can, of course, be only an estimate. How does it compare with later population figures? In 1608 Compton had 29 men (*Men and Armour in Gloucestershire*).

In 1650 there were 12 families
In 1779 there were 130 inhabitants (according to Rudder)
In 1901: 159, in 1911: 142, 1969: c. 105

The population of Compton has been remarkably steady through the centuries, apart from the very recent decline in numbers, and at the other end of the scale, the increase during the middle of last century, when the peak was reached with 258 inhabitants in 1861.

The villeins and bordarii together had eleven teams of oxen; they had to do ploughing service on the lord's land to help the two teams in demesne. Many attempts have been made to calculate the area of arable from the number of plough teams, but this had proved a hazardous undertaking owing to the brevity of Domesday Book and the many unknown factors involved. Even comparative figures are misleading; statistically the density of plough teams on the Cotswolds was slightly higher than in the Severn plain. Can one deduce that there was more arable on the hills, or could it be that more teams were needed to plough the hilly fields? I asked Mr. E. Jones, who worked with the twenty-two oxen at Hill Barn, whether one team of oxen could plough one acre in one day, and he at once made stipulated: "That depends on the field, on most of ours you could not".

By listing ploughteams, but no other stock, Domesday Book gives a picture of England as a highly, and, moreover, uniformly cultivated land, the arable of which has been thought comparable to modern times. Had the king's wise men formulated a different questionnaire, and had the statistics of sheep, pigs, etc., not been omitted in the final redaction, we should perhaps have a different impression.

All we can deduce for Compton with certainty is, that it was not a poor place; there are 22 virgaters and only 5 bordarii, and in the Barony, Compton, in size and value, came second only to Churchdown which was worth £13 in King Edward's

time, and £12 in 1086. The manor had 18 villeins, 5 bordarii and 7 radmen (riding men) with thirty teams, and was assessed at 15 $\frac{1}{2}$ hides.

"There is a mill, worth 5s." Out of a total of 363 villages in Gloucestershire 178 have one or more mills. Their value ranges from 6d. for the mill in Saintbury to 15s. for the Hatherop mill, and 35s. for the two at Kings Stanley. A mill was a valuable asset to a manor and a very profitable one for the lord. Nobody was allowed to have his corn ground anywhere but at his lord's mill, and heavy fines were imposed if anybody was discovered grinding corn at home with a handmill. The villagers naturally had to pay for the grinding, usually with a portion of their corn. On average this was one

The Mill has since been converted into a house so sensitively that the change is hardly discernible.

sixteenth of the weight, but the amount varied from manor to manor. The miller who rented the mill from the lord had ample opportunity of cheating and extortion, of substituting bad grain for good, of feeding his animals at the expense of others, and he often made use of it. In consequence, there was little love for him in the village.

It is very likely that the mill mentioned in Domesday Book stood in the same place which the present building occupies now. A mill is an expensive and complicated piece of machinery and, once installed, would not be moved. If the mill lies on a stream, it may be just conceivable that one situation is given up for a more favourable one, but the Compton mill has no stream; it depends on a spring at the eastern end of the valley. So a mill pond and a mill race had to be constructed to provide the power for the wheel. This spring is higher up the hill-side than the much stronger "Crocodile" and therefore has a better fall at the mill. The terrain has been used very skilfully and one could not find a better place for a mill in the whole of Compton valley. When, in 1965, a trench was dug at the eastern end of the mill buildings, potsherds of the late 12th or early 13th century came to light. They indicate that the site was occupied then, a hundred years after Domesday Book, even if they do not prove the existence of the mill itself.

50

The mill, like Compton, existed long before Domesday Book and was a vital part of the village for at least a thousand years. Now that the village is no longer a self-sufficient community, the mill has come to the end of its useful life. But, unlike the smithy and the carpenter's shop which share this fate and have disappeared altogether, the mill is still there, one of the few that survived the economic changes of the last century. Though it has been out of use since the early twenties and is now used as farm buildings, the machinery is still intact.

In a Sales catalogue of 1911 it is described as "a water mill of 3 floors, a substantial stone building with stone tile roof, overshot wheel of 26ft. diameter, driving 2 pairs of stones, 4 bins on the top floor, 1 bin over the porch entrance, with pulleys and driving belts, toolhouse and coalhouse. In the rear of the cartshed is the (sheep) washpool with an unfailing water supply and pond and basin for the mill." The equipment inside is still in working order, but the outside is in a sorry state of decay. The big cast iron wheel lies askew in its trough, the "basin" and the sheepwash are overgrown and crumbling, and the water dripping from the leaking runs adds a melancholy note to the scene. It is hoped that it may be possible to repair and restore the outside before it decays much further and gets beyond repair. The old mill deserves as much as any castle to be preserved, especially as there are many more castles than mills in existence.

The mill-pond used to share the general air of neglect and decay, but it has lately been cleaned and repaired and a solitary swan lords it over its waters. It is a lonely place, hardly visible behind its wall and trees. Mr. E. Jones, who was the last miller, told me that in days long gone the pond had a boat and a boathouse, and that Mr. Morgan, who was vicar from 1873 till 1893, had a shelter made on the artificial island and that he went there to prepare his sermons in peace. At one time wild ducks were reared on the pond; caught after dark, they were later released on the hills for the hunters to shoot. Mr. Jones remembered collecting duck eggs, as many as forty at a time.

"What was the manor worth in King Edward's time and what is it worth now?" "It was worth £9 and is now worth £7". As usual, no reason is given for this devaluation of the manor, the questions are answered and the facts are stated and that is all.

This loss of value is recorded for the majority of manors; the upheaval of the Conquest, the wars following it and the heavy taxation could explain it, though Gloucestershire was relatively quiet. There was no rebellion and, therefore, no retribution as there was in the North, where Yorkshire in particular suffered terrible devastation in punishment for revolt. There were no wastes owing to war on the Cotswolds, nevertheless Compton lost nearly a quarter in value.

"Who holds Cuntune?" "Thomas, Archbishop of York". We have already seen how the Barony of Churchdown passed into the possession of the Archbishops of York. The Norman, Thomas, inherited the claim to lands in Gloucestershire from his English predecessor Ealdred. Ealdred, who had crowned the Conqueror, died in 1069. The man chosen to be the next archbishop was a protégé of King William's half-brother, Odo, Bishop of Bayeux and Earl of Kent; he was Thomas, at the time, treasurer at Bayeux. Thanks to his royal patronage, Thomas rose quickly. He was only twenty-five when he became Archbishop of York and held one of the most powerful positions in the Church. His brother, Samson, followed him as treasurer and later became Bishop of Worcester. Samson's son, Thomas, became Archbishop of York after his uncle.

The first Thomas, powerful though he was, was soon put severely in his place by Lanfranc, the Archbishop of Canterbury, who asserted the primacy of Canterbury over York. Thomas naturally protested, but Lanfranc was upheld by the king, who had reasons to hold York in check, so York had to submit. It would not be surprising if one of the motives of the Archbishop of York to acquire the spiritual lordship over his temporal possessions in Gloucestershire (in 1095) had been animosity against Canterbury, in whose province they lay. If Thomas intended to annoy Canterbury, he certainly succeeded.

Strenuous efforts were made to bring the Priory back under the jurisdiction of Worcester and so into the province of Canterbury. The ban was laid on it repeatedly, the Priory invoked the king's help, reviving the claim to be a free chapel of the king, and even the Pope had to interfere in the quarrel. It was not until 1308 that these attempts on Canterbury's part ceased.

One final question, and the Commissioners had done with the men from Cuntune: "Has anything been added or anything been taken away?" Nothing had been added, but something had been taken away: A man of Roger de Ivri holds one manor of three hides belonging to this manor. The archbishop claims this also.

Roger de Ivri as the king's butler, was a member of his household and one of the big Norman landowners. Most of his estates were in Oxfordshire, but he had some manors elsewhere, among them Hampnett, bordering on Compton, where this man probably was the bailiff. We do not know the name of this small manor of three hides or where it lay, or if the archbishop succeeded in his claim against the baron. There is a faint echo of a quarrel between Hampnett and Compton: a field on the boundary of the two parishes is called Flitgo. Flit is a Saxon word meaning strife, and fields with this component in their name are found on parish boundaries. But one field does not constitute a manor, however small, and Flitgo may immortalise yet another boundary quarrel. Perhaps this manor was at Hampen which was a hamlet of Compton until 1883. Rudder, after dealing with the two Domesday Book manors there, says: "But there was another estate at Hampen dignified with the title of manor, held (at the dissolution) of the Archbishop of York by Thomas Lane." The Priory of St. Oswald's held some land in Hampen too. If this estate is the disputed manor, the archbishop's claim had succeeded.

This, then, is Compton according to Domesday Book; it looks a model manor - but does Domesday Book give a true picture of the place or does the rigid grid of the questionnaire obscure the individuality of villages and their economic state? It is hard to believe, for instance, that sheep can have disappeared from the Cotswolds, yet they are mentioned only twice, for Cirencester and Kempsford, and the apparently high density of ploughteams elsewhere hardly leaves room for them. But this is the problem of Domesday Book: "It is hard to interpret and easy to misunderstand. It is not always accurate. It baffles all attempts to make a satisfactory estimate of the population upon the basis of the data that it supplies. But, in spite of these defects, Domesday Book tells us more about the human geography of the country in the eleventh century than will ever be known about the condition of any other part of the world in that early period." And there we have to leave it - baffled, but grateful that it exists at all.

Should we recognise Compton if we were transported back in time to 1086? Perhaps not at first glance, because so many familiar features would be missing, but after wandering around for a while we should realise that it is the same place we know so well in its 20th century shape. Instead of the present trim stone-built houses there would be timber or wattle and daub one-roomed hovels without chimneys, roofed with turfs or at best, thatched with straw. If they had windows at all, they certainly were not glazed. Each house would stand in its yard and plot, called a toft, with housing for pigs, chickens and other livestock at the rear. But we should find the houses in roughly the same places their successors occupy now, for the hills determine where men can build in this narrow valley along the brook. The brook and its spring might puzzle us, for we should not find them where we are accustomed to see them, namely, close under the bank of Church Hill. This channel and the Crocodile are no older than about 130 years. The spring which really rises east of the White Way used to send its brook across what is now the Square and then along the bottom of the valley until the hills deflect it to the south to join the Colne at Cassey Compton.

The mill, as mentioned before, would be where it is now, and so would the church. Domesday Book does not mention the church, but this does not signify that none existed. It gives only ten places with churches in the whole county, and only four priests in connection with them, there are forty-four places with priests but without churches, sometimes more than one priest per place. This information is more or less incidental; churches as such were not asked for. The dedication of Compton's church to St. Oswald indicates the close tie with St. Oswald's in Gloucester, a tie that would have been strongest in the early days before 1070, when St. Oswald's was a minster charged with the care of souls on its land, and a place of worship would then have been erected, even if it was only a small timber edifice. We can therefore safely assume that there was a church on the hill side, though Domesday Book does not record it.

As soon as we leave eleventh century Compton by one of the tracks, we should hardly call roads, we are in open country, country without the chequerboard pattern of fields and pastures and without the boundary walls which for us are an almost natural part of the Cotswold landscape. There are no fields as we know them; the tilled ground is concentrated in two or three areas, only one of which is cultivated at one time. This big field, fenced against the roaming animals, is made up of one acre strips, each man's acres dispersed over the common field. Around the fields lie the "waste" and common pasture which stretch to the boundaries of the manor.

This is Compton as it was in 1086 and as it had been for

centuries before it was recorded, and ass in broad outline, it will be for another seven hundred years. Not that it will be, or ever has been, static and unchanging, but all changes will occur within the framework of the common field system, until 1805, when with the Enclosure Act this ancient pattern will be broken, then the Common will be shared out among individual owners and the walled fields which are so familiar to us now will appear.

The Millpond. Now deprived of its purpose the pond is a place of hidden beauty and tranquility.

The Manor and its Lord

Even if we know next to nothing about the villeins on the manor of Compton directly and at first hand, we can infer a good deal from "the manner and form" in which the archbishops held the Barony of Churchdown The document which sets this out with great care for the Chamberlaynes, the successors of the archbishops, fortunately survived and was handed over to the County Record Office by the last of them, Miss Ingles-Chamberlayne in the early 1950s.

Thomas Chamberlayne acquired the Barony of Churchdown in Henry VIII's time and Edward VI confirmed the grant to hold it "in the same manner and form as the Archbishop of York held it". All rights and privileges are listed at length and in detail and we get a clear picture of the archbishops as feudal lords and, correspondingly, of the conditions of life on the manor.

How far the reality of Tudor England diverged from the feudal claims of the grant is at the moment not our concern; we are interested in the time when the lord of the manor did exercise his rights and when his claims had to be met, when they were the rules of life, not mere rhetoric.

"Edward the Sixth by the grace of God of England, France and Ireland King..." in rolling phrases and with many words "gives and concedes to Thomas Chamberlayne, Knight, the whole of the Barony of Churchdown...with all manors...with all dues, jurisdictions, liberties...and privileges, with all and every demesne, manor, messuages, houses, edifices, granneries, stables, dovehouses, ponds, vineyards, orchards, gardens, tenements, mills, tofts, cottages, meadow, common pasture, waste...woods and underwoods, warren, rents, revisions and service, ward, dower and estreat, reliefs, heriots, fines and amercements, Court leets and view of frankpledge, waifs and strays, goods of felons, fugitives, outlaws and suicides, bondmen and bondwomen, villeins and their belongings, markets, tolls and any other dues, privileges etc. whatsoever."

This is a very short (translated) abstract of the grant which with many repetitions runs to three full foolscap pages. It could be put into even fewer words: the archbishop owned the land and everything on it, including the people. He, of course, did not own it outright, but held it in barony of the king and could be deprived of it, if he did not fulfil his obligations or committed some crime against the king, as barons in revolt did.

This long list of the archbishop's rights and claims is a blueprint of feudal practice, exceptional perhaps only in the range of privileges, and shows us how all-embracing was the power which the lord of the manor had over his villeins - from the moment they were born to the grave.

"Bondmen and bondwomen, villeins and their belongings" are mentioned towards the end of the list. The Latin for bondman and bondwoman in the grant is *nativus* and *nativa*, which does not mean just natives, but persons born into serfdom and inheriting the rightlessness of their parents. They literally belonged to their lord; bound to the soil, they could be - and were - sold with the land; they could not leave the manor or choose another lord. Their personal affairs were the lord's business, for what they did or what happened to them was his profit or loss. They could not marry without asking, and paying for, permission. Their son could not join the Church, should he wish to, but the lord had to agree to it and be recompensed for his loss of a man. If a daughter married, her father paid "merchet"; if she strayed from the path of virtue, the lord had to be recompensed, for his property had lost in value. Lastly, at the villein's death, the lord claimed the man's best beast as heriot.

It was not only on the great occasions of life that the lord's hand made itself felt; the villeins were not allowed to forget their servitude for a single day. They were the lord's and his interests came first. His acres had to be ploughed first, his harvest to be brought in, additional "boon work" could be asked, irrespective of the villeins' own need. His mill ground their corn and woe to anybody found with a handmill. The pigeons in his dovehouse provided fresh meat in winter exclusively for the lord's table, but they could devastate the sown fields or the gardens without hindrance or redress. Here and there, as in Quenington and Naunton, a medieval dovehouse has survived, and substantial buildings they were. Compton's columbarium has disappeared, only an old fieldname may indicate where it once stood. It is "Pigeon Close", a small field behind the village hall. The lord had right of warren, too, and so the wild creatures, the hares, the fish, the deer, were his and poaching carried heavy fines.

Though the rightlessness and oppression under which the villeins lived seem absolute, the power of the lord was not quite unlimited and arbitrary. He was bound by the Custom of the Manor in the same way as the villeins were. If it was the Custom to pay 6d for merchet, the lord could not suddenly demand 2s 6d, but, on the other hand, the villein could not pay only 4d or refuse it altogether. These Customs varied from manor to manor and were eventually written down in the Custumals. Unfortunately, Compton's Custumal has not survived - unless it is somewhere in the archives in York - and

so we do not know the conditions of life on the manor in detail, though we learn a little from a few Court Rolls and Reeves' Accounts which are preserved in the Gloucester Record Office.

Court Rolls are the records of the proceedings of the Manor Court. This court and the Custom of the Manor ruled the lives of the tenants. It took place at regular intervals, from three weeks to six months. Of four court rolls of the Barony two are dated April and two September, so it seems that the business of the manors came before the bailiff twice a year.

The bailiff presided at the court assembly, at his side the clerk who took notes for entering the proceedings on the court roll. After the beadle had called to attention with an "Oyez!", the sitting began with the roll-call and excuses for absence. Attendance at court was compulsory and unexplained absence was fined. Then the reeve gave his account of work done since the last sitting, future work was planned, the labour service on the demesne set, the working on the common fields was agreed on, any trespass or straying animals dealt with, rents and fines were paid, changes of tenure had to be applied for and were registered, not without payment of course, in short, the working life of the manor was the business of the Manor Court. Misdemeanours which interfered with the smooth running of the manor were dealt with also, but any civil crimes affecting the village community came before the Court Leet, that is, the court of view of frankpledge. In a village which was practically identical with the manor, as Compton was, the distinction between Court Leet and Manor Court was more or less theoretical, but when a village was divided between several manors, the difference was important; the village community as a whole was subject to the Court Leet, irrespective of the functions of the various Manor Courts.

View of frankpledge was, strictly speaking, part of the

king's jurisdiction and could only be exercised if it had been
52 granted by the king. It was closely bound up with the system
of tithing, by which the village was divided into groups of
originally ten men, headed by the tithingman. The members of
each tithing were mutually responsible and liable for each
other's good conduct and lawful behaviour. Every villein had
to be enrolled in a tithing; freemen, women and clergy were
excepted. As soon as a boy reached the age of twelve, he had
to join. At his first court attendance he would put his hand on
the Book and repeat: "I will be a lawful man and bear loyalty to
our lord, the king and his heirs, and to my lord and his heirs,
and I will be justifiable to my chief tithingman, so help me God
and the saints." He swore, too, neither to be a thief nor a
helper of thieves, and was thus sworn in to the duty of keeping
the peace. He then kissed the Book, paid his penny and was
enrolled on the tithing list.

Keeping the peace did not mean just to be of good
behaviour, but actively to assist, to raise the hue and cry on
discovering a misdeed, to help with pursuit if it was raised by
another, to help the constable in keeping order and not to
harbour or succour strangers.

At the Court Leet each tithingman had to give account
of his tithing and any wrong doings were then dealt with. In a
community as close as a medieval village, where so much was
forbidden, the scope of breaking the law or of usurping a right
was wide. Using a handmill, snaring the lord's game, brawls,
trespasses, taking another man's beasts or crops, false measures
and weights, illegal brewing and baking, all these every day
crimes came before the court at one time or another. The jury
considered each case and gave its verdict. The lord or his
bailiff imposed the fine (amercement), though here, too, he was
restrained by the custom of the manor. Nevertheless, view of

frankpledge was profitable business and lords were eager to
lay their hands on this additional income.

Graver crimes against the king's peace were the concern
of the Hundred and the County Courts. But the list of the
Archbishop's privileges and liberties shows that he had the
most extensive jurisdiction possible, especially after 1267, when
he and his tenants in the Barony were granted quittance of tolls
and from suits of Shires and Hundreds. So the Barony was
53 almost an extraterritorial complex within the shire of
Gloucester just as the spiritual jurisdiction of the Archbishop of
York over the Priory took it and its dependencies out of the
domain of the Bishop of Worcester.

The only liberty that is not mentioned is the right to
execute criminals, so we do not know if the Archbishop had his
own gallows or not. Though many crimes were punishable by
death, executions were under strict control by the king through
the coroner. The coroner had to be notified of a pending
execution and he recorded the circumstances. It was his
record, not the sheriff's ,which had weight with the king's
justices.

As well as being present at executions, the coroner had
to be called at sudden deaths, at the finding of treasure trove
and valuable shipwrecks. He also had to release fugitives from
sanctuary. We may wonder if ever a felon pounded up the hill
to reach our church and so to be safe from his pursuers? If he
reached it, he had to stay there until the coroner came and the
village had to feed and guard him. If he escaped and was
caught he could be beheaded at once. If he got away, the
village was fined, but if he put himself into the hands of the
coroner, he could abjure the realm and was solemnly sent out
of the country. He then had to walk to the nearest port, bareheaded and barefoot, staff in hand, keeping to the king's

highway where he would be safe. Once overseas, he could not return, unless pardoned. In any case, whether he went or was hanged, his goods and chattels were forfeited, ordinarily to the king, but in the Barony, to the Archbishop of York.

All these rights and privileges were profitable in fines and confiscations, they carried, however, the responsibility of the office, for the king expected the duties of the courts to be carried out whosoever exercised the jurisdiction.

This, then, is the manner and form in which the Archbishop of York held the Barony; as lord of the manor he owned the land and the villeins, as holder of the jurisdiction he, or his steward, could deal with every crime and misdemeanour bar executions. His power seems nearly absolute and the subservience and rightlessness of the villeins total. But self-interest will have tempered the despotism, for in the end the lord depended on his villeins for his income. The king demanded his taxes of him, not of the villeins, and he had to pay and recover them from his manors. In his own interest he might stop short of oppression, he could hardly afford to be lenient even if it had occurred to him to be so. But it did not, for pity and compassion were for the saints, not for the lords of land and men, be they king or barons, monasteries or archbishops.

The villeins on their part never ceased to struggle against their servitude and tried again and again to rid themselves of the stigma of bondmen, of the impositions on their personal life and of the labour service on the demesne. It took centuries and the force of changed economic circumstances, the Black Death and the rise of towns and commerce before the manor and its laws gave way. The Compton Court Roll for 1547, the last year of Henry VIII's reign, is far more akin to the archbishops' feudal manner than

to what we mean by the Elizabethan Age and which was then only a few years in the future. Even in 1608, when Compton was sold, the tenants had had to pay the customary tribute on "the first coming of the lord", as tenants had to do since "time out of mind", as we find it recorded on a Court Roll for 1534. True, in 1608 it was a token payment of 2d and 3d, nevertheless they did pay "in way of atturnamt. and did in full court atturne tenants to...Sir Richard Grubbam, Knight, for all lands, tenements and Hereditaments in their Occupation". And as late as 1789, William Marshall, reviewing the state of agriculture, remarks that on the Cotswolds the Manor Courts fell into disuse through Enclosure and adds: "A circumstance which the country may have reason to regret", but he does not say which reason.

As the Hundred Court has been mentioned several times, this may be the place to deal with the Hundred. The Hundreds are ancient pre-Conquest units, sub-divisions of the shires, though older than these. Originally, they probably consisted of 100 hides, but hideage became erratic quite early on and a Hundred and its hides soon did not correspond any more. Compton together with Northleach, Farmington, Stowell, Coberley, Turkdean, Hampnett, Salperton, Winson, Hazleton, Yanworth and Coln Rogers belong to the Hundred of Bradley (Bradelege, broad meadow). This is one of the Seven Hundreds of Cirencester, of which the Abbot was lord. Lordship of a Hundred carried no prestige; it was purely a source of income from fines imposed by the Hundred Court. This court dealt with minor matters of lawbreaking like battery, brawls, trespasses, slander, debts below 40s. and similar crimes. Most of them could just as well have come before the Manorial Courts and lords did not like their tenants to go to the Hundred Court, again mainly for financial reasons.

But when the litigants belonged to different manors, the Hundred Court took over. It met every three weeks, and the reeve and four men from each vill had to attend, if not regularly, then, at least at the Great Hundreds at Easter and Michaelmas.

The Hundreds met at traditional places in the open, and it has been suggested that Hangman's Stone, at the junction of the A40 and the Salt Way, was the meeting place of Bradley Hundred. This place obviously has some ancient and obscure significance. There is nothing remarkable about it now and the story about the man who hanged himself while carrying a stolen sheep over a stile is too pat and too tailored to make it fit the name. Besides, it is told of quite a few other places.

PRÍMULA VÉRIS
(*Cowslip, Paigle*)

The Lord visits his Manor

The "12 vills in Gloucestershire" which were so important to the see of York in the 11th century, were soon only an insignificant part of the Archbishop's wealth. In a valuation of 1322 the Barony of Churchdown was assessed at £37 6s 4d out of a total of £964 3s $9^1/_2$d for the Archbishop of York. But the archbishops did not lose interest in their small distant domain and visited Gloucestershire fairly regularly at least up to the beginning of the 14th century. Of course, they did not undertake the journey from York to Gloucester for the sole purpose of supervising eight manors and looking after the spiritual well-being of seven canons and a handful of parish priests. They travelled south, to London or to the king's court on government business, for they were not only dignitaries of the Church but high officials of State and the King's Counsellors; the Archbishop of York was, for instance, one of the three members of the State Council who reigned in England after the death of Henry III, until his successor, Edward I, came home from his crusade (November 1272 - August 1274).

When the archbishops came to Gloucestershire they stayed mainly in Churchdown, the chief manor of the Barony, and also at Oddington where they had a house and stables, so large and well-equipped that even the king stayed there occasionally. Archbishop Romayn was in Gloucestershire in Spring 1290; he stayed at Churchdown and left for Nottinghamshire on May 30th. This was a great day for Compton, for the Archbishop diverged from his usual journey not at Oddington, but here. As far as we know, this was the first time that Compton had been visited by its lord and this event must have filled every man, woman and child with excitement and awe. The bailiff of Churchdown who was ultimately responsible for the manor, the reeve, the priest, and the bailiff of the Priory who had to answer for Rectory Farm, must have been apprehensive, for it is clear from the injunctions which followed the Archbishops' visits to the Priory that such visits were not just courtesy calls, but inspections that went into every detail of the Priory's administration and the canons' conduct; and the manors of the Barony would have been scrutinised as closely as the Priory. The running of the manor and the cure of souls alike must prove themselves in the eyes of the lord archbishop. For the bailiff and the reeve the problems of hospitality loomed large, for needless to say, the Archbishop did not travel alone. Even on an ordinary visitation the bishops and archbishops, the deans and archdeans went about with a large retinue.

The Pope had found it necessary to counsel them to restrict the number of their attendants, for their visits were a ruinous burden on their hosts, the village clergy. An archbishop should not have more than forty to fifty men in his party, a bishop only twenty to thirty and they should leave their hounds and hawks behind. How to accommodate and feed such a multitude of officials, clerks and servants must have engaged all the reeve's and steward's ingenuity and resources. True, the Archbishop stayed only for a few hours on that first visit, but he returned in November, on his way to London and the Continent, and then he stayed overnight. Oddington was geared to the archbishops' visits, but did Compton have a house grand enough for the lord of the manor to stay even one night? Well, he did stay, so there must have been a house, moreover, a house substantial enough to be crenellated and fortified, for in the year after his visit the

58 Archbishop requested and received royal permission to fortify his mansion at Compton Parva with a wall of stone and lime.

Crenellation and fortification of mansion houses came into fashion in Henry III's reign (1216-1272). It was not so much a warlike measure as an attempt to make a great man's house look like a castle, in today's language, a status symbol. Royal permission was needed to fortify a manor house; Henry III made twenty such grants, Edward I (1272-1307) made forty four, one of them for Compton. The applications increased during the following reigns and quickly diminished *59* after Henry IV's accession.

Why the Archbishop should have wanted to confer such distinction on his manor of Compton Parva is hard to see, even if he liked the place which, of course, would not surprise us. Whatever his reasons, the bailiff of Churchdown and the reeve could be well satisfied with this outcome of the lord's visit, for he would hardly have considered such a step if he had found much amiss in the manor.

What of the priest and the villeins and their womenfolk in these tremendous days when the village was full of clamour, of liveried grooms and guards out numbering the villagers, not to mention the closer entourage of the Archbishop, his chaplain, the clerks and the crowd of various officials? The bare record that the Archbishop was at Compton on May 30th and November 16th - 17th, tells us nothing about the impact on the village of this onslaught of the great and - as it must have seemed - glamorous world. And lastly, the Archbishop himself, this near legendary figure, not only a great man of the realm, but their own spiritual lord. The priest and his flock lived in isolation among the parishes of the bishopric of Worcester, and they must have felt it, especially as neighbours of Withington, where the Bishop of Worcester had a big house.

Would they not feel that at last they had come into their own, having the Archbishop in their midst?

And when he had left, followed by his multitude, was everybody happy that the excitement was over and the village could settle back into its old calm life, to the everlasting work the land and the seasons demanded? Or were there some restless spirits who wished they could have gone away with the departing visitors? Did the girls dream of those men of the world who had come from far away and would go to foreign places? Alas, we shall never know.

The Priory of St. Oswald also had cause for satisfaction, for one Nicolas Russel, made them a gift of thirty acres of land in Compton at this time. This gift was probably another consequence of the Archbishop's visit, for Nicolas Russel could not alienate his land without the lord's sanction, and he may have obtained it from the Archbishop in person.

Compton and the Priory of St. Oswald

When the Priory lost the Barony of Churchdown, it lost the greatest part of its wealth and was reduced to a few possessions of land and to the income from its chapels. The income of a church consisted then of the tithes, the fees for baptisms, marriages and funerals and the offerings to the altar. There was also the glebeland with which the founder, as a rule the lord of the manor, had endowed the church for its upkeep and the livelihood of its priest.

The tithes were divided into the greater tithes which were payable on stock and crops and went to the rector, and the lesser tithes, payable on everything else, which were part of the income of the parish priest, in addition to the fees and the glebeland. But there were no rules about the division of the income of a church in the early days, and if a monastery or a priory was the rector, it often happened the rector took the whole and paid a chaplain for the cure of souls. This is what the Priory, being the rector, did in Compton; tithes and the glebe belonged to the Priory and therefore the canons had a considerable interest in "Cumpton super montes".

Priests who were paid in this way, the stipendiary chaplains, were the lowest paid clergy, the poorest of the poor, ill-trained village priests. Domesday Book lists the priest with the villeins and he stayed at that level for centuries. Pope Innocent III tried to improve the lot of the village clergy, which had become of considerable concern to the Church, and recommended that vicarages be created and the priest be given the freehold of the vicarage and security of tenure. Some bishops took the Pope's advice and raised curacies to vicarages. The Priory, poor itself, had to rely mainly on its income from tithes and glebes and probably could not afford to provide vicarages, so Compton among others has remained a Perpetual Curacy, to the present day.

Tithes, that is one tenth of all products, were the due of the Church; at first a more or less voluntary offering, they had been enforced by law since the tenth century , and were a heavy burden. To give up every tenth stook of corn, every tenth fleece, the tenth of their precious hay, of hens, eggs, milk, a tenth of any of the fruits of their labour was hard on the people, and they did not always render their due with a joyful and generous heart. But the Church extracted the tithes with great severity from its reluctant flock. She threatened the unwilling with hell-fire and eternal damnation and the parish priest was encouraged to excommunicate solemnly, with bell, book and candle, any one who was amiss in paying. Hell and damnation were far from being a figure of speech, they were as real as life to the people of the Middle Ages. Life hereafter lasts for ever, it is eternal bliss or eternal torment, according the one's deserts, and the chances of going to hell were great - who could say he was without sin? The Last Judgement was ever in people's minds and thoughts and the salvation of their souls their constant preoccupation. Every time they went to church they could see and contemplate the fate of the unrepentant and unpardoned, for hardly a church was without a painting of the Last Judgement with its torturing devils and its angels who carried the saved souls up to Abraham's bosom. To be excommunicated, to be deprived of the comfort and the forgiveness of Mother Church, to die, unshriven and certain to go to purgatory if not straightway to hell, held a terror for the sinners which we cannot imagine any more. They were ready to do anything to avoid this fate, they donated land, gave money and paid their tithes, hurt as it may.

But the Church was never quite sure that a man had paid all he should, despite all threats and curses, and so she gave him the opportunity to make up for any omissions: when he died the Church received a "gift", called a mortuary, usually the man's second best beast - the very best was claimed by the lord as heriot. Even when mortuary went out of use, the Church did not go short, as the will of William Midwinter of Northleach shows:... "To the high alter of Northleache, in recompense of offerings and duties forgotten, in discharge of my soul, 40s.".

Naturally, tithes caused much friction and bitterness between the parish and its priest when the lesser tithes went to him. This, at least, was spared to the priest of Compton; he had part neither in tithes nor in the glebe and they could not come between him and his flock, though he was much the poorer for having to do without.

As chapel of a minster, Compton Church probably never had any glebeland of its own. As long as the Priory owned the manor, it was not necessary to set land aside for the priest. Domesday Book at any rate does not mention a priest as owning oxteams. Later the Priory did acquire glebeland in Compton, as the 30 acres of Nicolas Russel show. There must have been other gifts, for in 1803 the Rectory farm consisted of 168 acres, then the third largest farm in the village.

We do not know in detail how the canons worked and administered their land in Compton, but we get some idea from Archbishop Gray's Injunctions of 1250. After his visit to the Priory, he wrote to the prior and canons to tell them what he had found amiss and should be corrected. Of the twenty-seven points on his list, four deal with life in the granges. We gather that if the canons did not work the land entirely by themselves, they did not mind lending a hand and the archbishop had to mention specifically that: "Canons are forbidden to leave the house (the Priory) in order to make hay or to do other rural work". True, the land had to be tended and the tithes collected, and some representative of the Priory had to visit their scattered glebelands frequently. However, the Priory had its bailiff who looked after the granges, and there were lay brothers who could assist him, if necessary. So the canons themselves need not have left the house unless they preferred the active to the contemplative life. The Archbishop's strictures though, make it clear that the brethren had taken to country life wholeheartedly and hay-making was not the only thing that aroused his displeasure. Lay brothers, too, left to themselves, had fallen to the temptations of the good life, but henceforth they "may not eat flesh-meat save in the presence of the prior or a canon". Not that this was necessarily a hardship, for another admonition shows that the prior and canons did not live by strict monastic rules either, especially when away from the Priory: "For repression of superfluous drinking parties and unhonest meals, the prior and canons are forbidden to brew in their granges. When they go there to the profit of the house, they are to take all necessaries with them from the priory. They must not stay in the granges in the vale of Gloucester for more than a night together, and only the urgent necessity or manifest profit of the house can excuse a longer stay at Compton Abdale or Eston (Cold Aston)". Long days in the country, making hay, superfluous drinking parties and unhonest meals - the list of sins is formidable, but not yet complete, for: "Women must not pass the night in granges where brethren are staying. Women, if necessary, may work in such places but only such as cannot give rise to suspicion."

It was a jolly life that the good canons led at their granges, and they must have been most reluctant to give it up and to return to the dull routine under the rules of their order. But the Archbishop forestalled any relapse after his departure with the final point of his Injunction: "The Injunctions are to be read at the beginning of every month in Chapter. If the prior or an obedientiary be convicted of neglecting them, he is to forfeit his office; while a heavy penalty, at the disposal of the Archbishop or his deputy, will be inflicted on disobedience upon a simple canon." Nor was this an empty threat, for in the following year the Prior was deposed and the benefices of the convent sequestrated.

Whatever may have come to the Archbishop's ears about "unhonest meals and superfluous drinking parties," it was surely unrealistic to expect the canons to bring up their provisions. Ale being the staple drink of the age, to prohibit brewing in the granges, would be equally vain. He did prohibit it and it would have grieved him, could he have seen into the future, that the malthouse outlived Rectory Farmhouse and that of all the buildings of the farm, only the tithe barn lasted longer.

While in 1250 the canons had been only too willing to look after their granges and Archbishop Gray had to restrain their enthusiasm for country life, 70 years later his successor found an entirely different situation. In his Injunction he had to recommend that "the houses, granges and manors of the Priory are to be diligently kept in repair, where it is needed and can conveniently be done. The demesne and other lands are to be tilled and sown at convenient seasons." Whether the brethren had taken Archbishop Gray's admonitions too much to heart, whether it was neglect and indifference, or sheer inability to look after their possessions, the affairs of the Priory and their manors and farms were in a bad state. This situation became even worse, when twenty-five years later, the Black Death struck the country and the Priory suffered severely. Two priors died in 1349; how many canons fell victim to the plague is not known, but in 1365 their number was so decimated that the extinction of the Priory was feared, and it never wholly recovered from this misfortune.

In 1417 the Bishop of Hereford made an enquiry into the financial affairs of the Priory in connection with the appropriation of the vicarage of Minsterworth. His commissioners found that "the various lands and possessions of St. Oswald's Priory were largely untilled and unoccupied, owing to default of tenants and lack of servants", and that "the negligence and wantonness of divers priors, pestilence, and murrain which fell with special severity on their sheep, had brought them into debt." The commissioners do not name or specify the lands, but there is no reason to exclude Compton from this general verdict. The small glebeland on the hills would certainly not be taken better care of than the lands in the vale which were easier to reach from the Priory, and the fact that the sickness of the sheep is included in this list of woes suggests that the hill lands were inspected too. It indicates also that wool was an important part of the Priory's income.

The Priory had its own troubles, but the difficulty of administering dispersed lands was not peculiar to St. Oswald's which, after all, was only a small house with few possessions. It was much more acute for rich monasteries who owned vast numbers of estates, and it seems a natural and inevitable development that the lands were let to tenant farmers. When the Priory lands were first let is not known; the Bishop of Hereford's survey mentions the default of tenants already in 1417. The earliest preserved rent agreement for Compton was made as late as 1530, but the tenants are to hold the farm "as other farmers previously held and occupied it", so they were by no means the first.

William Rogers and his wife Johanna, with whom this rent agreement was made, were more than just tenants, they were truly rectorial farmers and with the tenure took over all rectorial rights and duties, as the Indenture sets out in detail, as presumably their predecessors did. They hold Rectory Farm with all houses and buildings on the site, the (glebe -)land, arable, meadow, pastures, etc., and all tithes, profits and commodities due to the Rectory and Church. In return they have to repair, maintain and roof the chancel of the Church and to provide sufficient wax and wine for divine service. They pay 20s. towards the repair of the Rectory while the Prior and Convent undertake to safeguard it against water, wind and rain.

The rent is £9 per annum, and 3s. payable to the lord of the manor for the virgate of Cropthorne yardland, which the Priory holds of old and which is already mentioned in the compotus of 1400.

The Prior and Convent, however, have not relinquished Compton altogether; they apparently are still as fond of country life as were their predecessors nearly 300 years before, and the archiepiscopal fulminations do not seem to have had much effect. Or perhaps they had provided themselves with a retreat in the hills when strife and civil war made "the house of Sent oswald, king and martyr besyde gloucester" unsafe and downright dangerous. At any rate, they reserve "one chamber at the upper end of the hall, a buttery, one stable and a vault at the lower end of the hall, with free entry and exit, in case they want to come here." The Rectory farmhouse must have been a substantial and spacious building if it had a hall and enough

chambers to have one reserved for the canons, and room enough for the tenant, his family and servants. Two hundred and sixty years later, in 1793, this farmhouse which may well have been essentially the same building, will be called a "mansion and considerably too large for the property".

This agreement with William Rogers had been made by William Gylford, who was the last Prior of St. Oswald. Six years later, in 1536, religious houses of less than £200 value were dissolved, St. Oswald's among them. The survey and valuation had given its value as £90 10s $2^1/_2$d, the income from tithes and oblations of the chapel at Compton Abdale being £6 5s 4d. The glebeland is not mentioned at all.

So, St. Oswald's, once Queen Aethelfleda's Minster, ceased to exist. The Prior retired with a pension of £15, the canons dispersed, either joining other, larger monasteries (so far still undisturbed) or became secular priests. The spiritual jurisdiction of the Archbishop of York lapsed when the churches were transferred to the king, and were, in 1541, included in the new bishopric of Gloucester. The tithes and the glebeland were, however, dealt with separately, they were, in 1542, granted to Edmund Tame and his wife, Katharine. He cannot have enjoyed them very long for they were given to the new bishopric of Bristol in the same year, and henceforth the Dean and Chapter of the Cathedral Church of the Holy and Indivisible Trinity in Bristol are the owners of Rectory Farm and the receivers of tithes.

Stone

When digging your garden and your fork strikes yet another stone and jars your wrist, you are ready to believe, as the saying goes, that with an acre of ground you buy enough stone to build a house. That fragment of the limestone ridge which stopped your fork is probably no bigger than two or three inches square, though it may feel as if you had met with a boulder. The rock of the Great Oolite is never far from the surface and the fields are littered with its debris which is constantly coming to light. In fact, there is stone everywhere, and yet nowadays very few new houses are built of it. Cotswold stone houses are very expensive and the situation today resembles that of the early Middle Ages when only the very few could afford houses of stone and the majority had to content itself with wattle and daub - only today it is not wattle and daub, but reconstituted stone. Between the fifteenth and the early twentieth century, even the humblest cottage, the barns, the cattle sheds and pigsties were built of stone, built carefully and lavishly, with thick walls, beautiful cornerstones and shaped doors and windows. Today it would be out of the question to build a barn like Clayhill barn, though it is only a small and unpretentious building or the churchlike enormous structure of Rookshill barn built in 1863. (Since demolished) There is neither time nor manpower nor material. The local quarries have been abandoned, stone has to be bought at one of the big commercial quarries and transported from there at prohibitive cost, and the craftsmen have disappeared from the villages.

Much has been written about the beauty of Cotswolds villages and about their harmony with the surrounding landscape, with which they form such an integral whole that they appear to have grown rather than been built in their valleys. In a sense so they have, if not entirely without human help, for nothing alien intruded between them and the hills, each stone from the door sill to the very ridge of their roofs came from the soil of their own parish. Each village had its own quarry and only rarely required material from outside, such as stone for special purposes, like flagstones or rooftiles, which was available only at particular quarries.

The quarries disappeared when the villages ceased to grow and when the improvement in transport made substitute materials available. When the railways brought Welsh blue slate within reach it became fashionable to use it instead of stone tiles. The Old Vicarage which was built in 1885, was the first house in the village to be roofed with blue slate and a few cottages followed suit. There are even two red-tiled roofs in the village, a sin that cannot be committed any more, the planning regulations see to that, but it is debatable what looks worse, red tiles or dull, grey concrete tiles in dead straight rows.

Before being filled in, the quarries were used as rubbish dumps and will be mines of information for future archaeologists. Everything that was useless or even only old-fashioned, like oil lamps or old farm implements, was taken to the quarry. Mrs. Iles who came from Hazleton and lived there and in Compton all her life (she died in 1967), told me that she made her brother take the horses' equipment - brasses and all - to the quarry when tractors came in. "Well", she said, "the stuff was cluttering up the place and I did not know then that horse brasses would be something special one day".
Another place to look for "treasures" would be the old lime pit

in Mill Ground, just behind the cottages which are now called Cobbler's Hill, formerly known as Cats Abbey.

Compton's last quarry was filled in in the late fifties with surplus soil from the road when the A40, leading up from Compton Bottom, was lowered. It was a handy place just on the other side of the wind break. A layer of "limestones, *60* beautifully oolitic, flaggy here and there" was "seen for 15ft." in this quarry in 1933, now buried again and regretfully remembered by only the older men.

A quarry is first mentioned in the compotus for 1422. It *61* had been let to the church in Cirencester for a year at a rent of 4s. *62* The church in Cirencester - as most churches - had been rebuilt and enlarged ever since the first church was built there, but during the 15th century the masons hardly ever left the site. In 1416 the great tower was completed, the Chapel of St. Katherine was added in 1420, the Chapels of Trinity (1434) and St. Edmund followed. The magnificent South Porch, though no part of the church, was built towards the end of the century and finally the nave was rebuilt in 1515-30. The demand for stone was great and quarries as far away as Compton's contributed to the beautiful Parish Church of Cirencester. We do not know for how many years the quarry was let to Cirencester, because the compoti for the preceding and following years did not survive. In 1441, however, the tenants of the manor were in need of stone themselves and rented the quarry from the lord for 3s.4d. We know no more, but it seems reasonable to assume that they used the stone for building - a sign of the prosperity which enabled the tenants to replace their medieval hovels with stone-built houses. The quarry is now called Hollow Stone quarry, situated near the lord's wood. This name appears already in 1413 in connection with meadows and pasture below the wood. It is tempting to identify Hollow Stone quarry with the deepest

indentation of the hillside at the southern end of the Grove, particularly as perforated stones are a striking feature of the Long Barrow which is situated on the same slope, not far from the assumed quarry site. The compotus of 1450 and the following and last one record that Robert Oliffe and Robert Gryme omitted to pay rent. This indicates that the quarry is back in the lord's hands.

Limestone weathers well and quickly and it is very difficult to judge the age of a house from the appearance of its stonework. The walls of the chancel of the church which are about 500 years old look no different from the walls of the shop which bears the date of 1817 (though the house may be older). Both are random built, that is, of stones of varying size which are hewn, not sawn, as ashlars are. The resulting irregular surface of the walls where each stone casts its own crooked shadow, where tiny crystals and fragments of fossilised shells reflect and diffuse the light and yellow lichens settle, gives these houses a character which neither ashlars or much

Fossilised sea-urchins and sea-shells in great variety found in fields; reminders of the Cotswolds' maritime past.

less reconstituted stone can ever achieve.

A great deal of the charm and beauty of old Cotswold houses is also due to their stone-tiled roofs. These roofs become more precious as time goes on because stone tiles are not made any more. This, unlike dry-stone walling, is definitely not only a dying, but a dead art. In 1958, a Mr. John Slee wrote in "Country Life" that he had searched the Cotswolds for stone tile makers and that he had found only a single one in Naunton, and he was seventy then. Now there are none left. It seems almost incredible that this craft which flourished already in Roman times, as Chedworth Villa shows, could die out completely, but the fact remains that new stone tiles are not made any more. Secondhand tiles which are taken off barns or saved from demolished cottages are correspondingly expensive and precious. In 1789 a square (100 sq.ft.) of tiles on the roof, plaistering included, cost 26s., in 1910 they were £3 10s a thousand, in 1958, at Mr. Hughes', the Naunton tile maker's guess, £20-30, tiles only, of course, not on the roof. Now (1970), secondhand tiles are approximately £25 a square. When the price is prohibitive, as it only too often is, grey concrete tiles are used, as red roofs are not allowed.

How rigid and lifeless a roof looks when tiles of equal size march along in evenly spaced rows is not noticed so much when the roofs of all the surrounding houses are covered in the same fashion, but when there are stone-tiled houses in the neighbourhood, the deadening effect of this uniformity becomes immediately obvious. For it is not only the texture of the stone which gives a Cotswolds roof its distinctive look, but the grading in the size of the tiles which adds rhythm and harmony of proportions. Concern for effect and beauty was certainly not the reason for this grading. Purely practical considerations caused the builders to lay the largest stones in the lowest rows and to diminish their size towards the ridge. The colossal weight of the stone determined the manner of tiling and the pitch of the roof.

Rooftiles of various sizes are not defined by their dimension in inches, but by name. These traditional names vary slightly from place to place, but only slightly; not enough to make co-operation between slaters difficult. The list of names used in Compton was supplied by Mr. Sam Iles and is as follows: Sixteens, Fifteens, Fourteens, Thirteens, Twelves, Elevens, Whippets, Nines, Muffets, Becks, Batchelors, Cuttings, Long Cocks, Short Cocks. Sixteens are the largest; they are not 16" long but 24"; Cocks, used at the ridge, are 7" or 9". The terms are confusing to the uninitiated; a "slate" is a measure of one handspan across and one handspan in length. A slate may be one, two or more "slates". 1000 "slates" cover 2 squares, and this will be about 750 actual slates of various sizes.

Rooftiles were never "made" or manufactured, they are a natural product, they are about 80% Nature's work, and 20% man's, but, if the human part in the process is small, it is crucial, and highly skilled work. Not every kind of stone is suitable for slates, but only a certain laminated formation which occurs in a usually thin layer below the ragstone, from 12 to 15 or more feet below the surface. It is not accessible everywhere and Compton was fortunate to have a quarry which provided slates. This was not the quarry near the A40, but one situated half a mile east by south of the village, and there were other slate quarries in the neighbourhood between Shipton and Hazleton. All of them were abandoned long ago and are nearly forgotten. The Rookshill quarry was last used during the First World War, not for roof slates, however, but for road metalling.

The Cotswolds have been declared an Area of Outstanding Natural and Architectural Beauty and strict regulations govern materials and style of building. In the endeavour to preserve the appearance of the villages, red brick and tiles are prohibited; only reconstituted stone and grey roofs are permitted. Reconstituted stone is an artificial product, a mixture of cement and ground stone, it comes in three or four standard sizes. Houses and bungalows built of this material probably look well enough on their own and in other places, but in Cotswold villages beside houses of genuine stone, they stick out like sore thumbs. They are a compromise between unrestricted building in any material which, one has to admit, would be infinitely worse, and the insistence on natural stone, which might be unrealistic. There may be no alternative, but these buildings, like the Council Houses before them, hardly enhance the beauty of the Cotswolds.

Any chapter headed: "Stone" would be sadly deficient if it did not mention dry-stone walls. They are part of the landscape; they are the first unmistakable signs that you have entered the Cotswolds when you come up from the Oxford Plain. There are countless miles of them, surrounding the fields and running beside the lanes. If the trend towards bigger farms and larger fields continues and the walls are removed, as they already have been in some areas, then the hills will look barer and lonelier; they will assume different dimensions altogether. We are so used to these grey lines criss-crossing slopes and valleys, emphazising the contours of the hills and imposing a human scale on the sweeping wolds, that we cannot imagine what the country looked like before they were built. The Cotswolds before the Enclosures must have been bleak indeed without the walls and bare of trees.

A Cotswold dry-stone wall, complete with combers.

For it was only at the time of the Enclosures that this gigantic network of fencing was put up; the duty to fence newly allocated fields went with the allocation. This presented a problem which could only be solved by walling. Timber was scarce, hedging slow to grow and expensive, barbed wire had not been invented, but stone was available in abundance, labour was cheap, and so walls went up by the mile.

Dry-stone walling is even older than slate making. Thousands of years ago the men of the New Stone Age built the mounds round the Burial Chambers of the Long Barrows in the same way as dry-stone walls are built even today. The flat slabs of stone, which are found in such quantities and in manageable sizes, lead, almost naturally, to the technique called dry-stone walling,. The art of building in this way has often been reported as dead or dying, but not so; the reason for the many delapidated walls which can unfortunately be seen all over the Cotswolds is not lack of know-how, it is expense and shortage of manpower. While in 1788 a furlong of wall cost £8 10s, or about 10d a yard, which was the price of labour, for the stone cost nothing, a yard of wall in 1970 cost £7 10s, the price of the stone being 50s ex quarry (one cubic yard of stone equalling one yard of wall without "combers" or toppers),. Transport from the quarry and labour cost bring the price up to £6 10s:-. "A penny a yard is the common price for walling, the raising and wheeling (of the stone) 8d-10d", this is what the men earned who built the miles of field walls at the time of the Enclosures.

You pay more today for your walls and get slightly less than in 1788, for the dimensions are now 22" at the base and 16" at the top against 24" and 18" then for the same height of 4 $1/2$ ft. below the combers or toppers, the row of stones set edge on upon the last course of horizontal stones. You will have to buy the material at the quarry instead of having the stone dug along the line of the wall by the men who did "the raising and wheeling". But your wall will be built in much the same way as Marshall describes in 1788. A shallow foundation trench is dug along the line of the future wall, and the waller begins his work. Stone on stone, but never joint over joint, the two outer walls are raised simultaneously and the space between them is filled up carefully as the wall rises. To ensure that the wall goes up neatly and evenly, a wooden frame defining the profile of the wall is set at the end of the stretch of wall being built and kept strictly vertical by means of a plumb line, and strings are stretched from it along the wall to guide the eye of the waller. It sounds fairly simple - on paper. But there are pitfalls, and a good waller is spoken of with reverence. In the opinion of people of experience walls are superior to any other kind of fencing, for a well-built and maintained wall will last longer than wire or post and rails. Even to maintain the walls and to repair the damage, which the frosts of each winter cause, is nowadays nearly impossible for most of the walls are old, and it is much easier and cheaper to string barbed wire across the gaps. The time may come when the field walls crumble into stony banks and disappear, and with them we shall lose the heritage the men left us who ,"raising and wheeling" and building the walls, slowly moved across the Common land from which they had been alienated for ever.

Before they were tarred, all roads on the Cotswolds were "White Ways", paved with local stone. Even after the main roads were metalled with blue stone, which was unpopular because the horses suffered - bits of the hard stone lodging themselves between hoof and shoe, - the lanes and side roads stayed white until shortly before the war. Tarring was not welcomed by everybody. Protesting voices muttered that the Cotswolds just were not the same any more, the roads being not white but black. That may be so, the new roads, however, are certainly less dusty in summer or muddy in winter than the limestone roads were.

The original function of these Staddle stones was as bases of ricks and barns to prevent vermin and damp getting into the corn. They are now highly valued as garden ornaments,

Stones for the roads came from the quarries, the Compton quarries, too, providing some of the metalling. The stones were broken up into fist-size pieces, damped with water and firmed by steamroller. As Marshall says; "Roads are made across these hills with singular facility....The materials, however, are more plentiful than durable, presently grinding down under heavy carriage. But the repairs are equally easy as

the forming." The Rev. Thomas Nutt paints a harrowing picture of Compton's roads in 1837: "The village of Compton Abdale is very retired and..(illegible) parish deeply overshadowed with surrounding rocky hills. All the roads to it are craggy and very steep, abounding with an adhesive soil, so that persons cannot pass to it but with great difficulty; if, indeed, I were not accustomed to the country having resided in it three years, I could not continue in it." So much for the efforts of the road men, one of whom, Thomas Eden, with his broom and shovel, is still affectionately remembered by the older generation. He died in 1920, aged 83, and he was born 5 days after Rev. Nutt wrote his complaining letter in February 1837.

Obviously, these roads needed constant repair and the roadmen were always in want of stones. When talking to Mr. Ernest Jones about the four or five cottages in the Square which were pulled down, I wondered what had happened to the stones from them. With walls at least 2ft. thick, not to mention the monumental chimneystacks and baking ovens, they must have provided enormous quantities of stone. "Some of it we used to repair field walls, I remember", he answered, "and the rest - well, the roadmen were always glad of stone." Another supply "grew" unfailingly on the fields. Mrs. Kibble told me, and Mr. Stanley Mace later confirmed it, that people from the village went into the fields to pick stones to earn some extra money, and hard earned it was, for they got only 1s. for one cartload of stones. They carried the stones to pre-arranged places, from where they were taken by cart to the roadmen.

William Marshall wrote: "Lime is excessively dear, and sand not to be had, I believe, at any price; nevertheless an excellent mortar is here prepared at a moderate expense."

"Invention is seldom more successful than when necessity prompts it. The scrapings of the public roads, namely levigated limestone, impregnated with the dung and urine of the animals travelling upon them; are found to be an excellent basis for cement. For ordinary walls the scrapings alone, are frequently used. And from what I can learn, the proportion for the best building is not more that one part lime to three of scrapings.

66   Nevertheless, I found mortar, which had not lain in the wall more than ten years, of a stonelike tenacity: much firmer that the ordinary stone of this country ,probably much harder than either of the stones from which the basis or the lime was made."

This was the practice in 1788, and there was no reason to abandon it until the internal combustion engine and the tarring of the roads put an end to the supply of suitable road scrapings, which is just another example that the country has changed more in the last 35 years than in the previous 150.

It is a strange and melancholy fact, that to write of stone is to write in the past historic tense. Not that stone has disappeared - the Cotswold hills are there to prove it, - but we seem unable to make use of it. In times much poorer than the present, stone was used lavishly, the smallest cottage had walls two feet thick, miles of walls were built, and even the roads were paved with it, yet in our affluent age, blessed with every mechanical aid, we cannot afford to keep the walls in repair or to build houses of stone. For us in the midst of abundance, it is barbed wire and ersatz-stone. Sad.

ÁRUM MACULÁTUM
(*Cuckoo-pint*, *Wake-Robin*, *Lords-and-Ladies*)

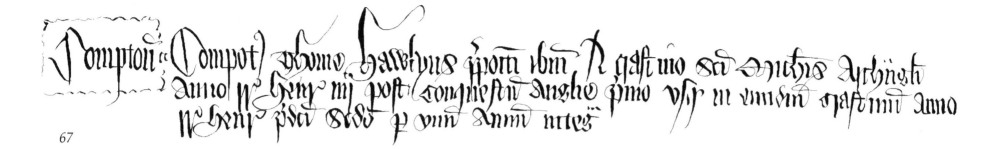

15th Century

Most of what we have been able to find out about Compton's history so far could also have been applied to the other manors of the Barony of Churchdown. It was as a member of the Barony that Compton belonged first to the Priory of St. Oswald and then to the Archbishops of York, and whatever rights and powers the lord had over Compton, he had over Churchdown and the rest. There is nothing that concerns Compton alone, except the Archbishop's visit in 1290, and even on that occasion we did not hear much about Compton and its people remained in the shadow. It is only in 1400 that we come to know some of them by name and learn a little about the village. Not that we are told what we want to know directly and in detail, we have to deduce what we can from the reeve's account of the manor's finances for the year. Any information in the compotus about the number of people and their

circumstances, their wealth or poverty, is incidental and of necessity fragmentary. But it is all we have and we have to make do with it.

During the preceding fifty years, events had taken place which shook the feudal world, though it did not succumb to them entirely. In 1348 the plague had come to England and had spread quickly throughout the country. After the first fierce onslaught it recurred at intervals during the next 40 years and carried off - it is often said - a third of the population, though this estimate of casualties is in the process of being

drastically revised. The Priory, at any rate, suffered heavily and never quite recovered. How did it affect Compton? Was its population reduced by a third? Does the compotus of 1400 give any indication of it, perhaps in the number of vacant holdings?

The Black Death was not the only calamity of a turbulent century. Unrest and ferment among the rural population culminated in the Peasants Revolt of 1381. This had various and complex reasons, but was triggered off by the heavy poll - or head-tax of 1380, which rich and poor alike had to pay and which hit the poor the hardest. To appease the rebels who had occupied London, the king promised abolition of villeinage, of servile tenure and trade restrictions, but, when the tide turned, he went back on his word and told the deputation of peasants: "Villeins ye are still, and villeins ye shall remain" - and the hope for a speedy end to serfdom was crushed.

In the end, neither the Black Death nor the Peasants' Revolt was the most effective factor in the decline of villeinage, but the fact that the lords of the manor were more in need of money than of free labour. For this reason, labour service was commuted into payments and even the demesne lands were rented out, and thereafter labour service was of little importance. If any such changes were made on the Archbishops' manors, the reeve's account should reflect them.

As usual, the compotus begins with the account of rents, first the rents of "free" land, that is, rent for land without obligation in service, then the rents of terra nativa, of land held in villeinage. In 1400, there is one tenant who holds free land only, and eleven who pay for extra terra nativa as manorial tenants. So at first sight it might appear that the Black Death has reaped a rich harvest and that Compton had been reduced to less than half of its Domesday population of 22 villeins and five bordars. But a closer scrutiny of the compotus shows that there are more people in the village than pay rent to the lord. For though there are only eleven names on the rent roll, there are nineteen cottages, and so presumably there are nineteen families. To these we must add Rectory Farm and its inhabitants and perhaps the miller and the miller's family who are not mentioned in any account.

Another apparent sign of shrinkage is the difference in the numbers of previous and present holders: there are fifteen previous occupiers and only eleven who pay rent in 1400, and one could assume that four families had died out. If we had no other and later information this would be the conclusion, however some of the names of the "lost" families appear in later compoti, so they did not die out after all, but merely disappeared from the rent list for some other reason.

So, we can find little evidence of extraordinary mortality in the compotus of 1400, though it is unlikely that Compton escaped the plague altogether. How many died it is impossible to say, but it is certain that the village was not wiped out or even lost an appreciable percentage of its population.

The next item of the compotus shows that labour service had indeed been commuted into payment of money. The reeve collects 57s.6d. in lieu of ploughing 10 virgates of demesne land, at the rate of 6s.4d. for one virgate in tenure. The 5 lb. of wheat for Churchscot are worth 3s.4d. per lb., 20 hens and 150 eggs, once to be delivered at Easter, are now paid for in cash: 2s.6d. for the hens, 5d. for the eggs.

The demesne is let for £9, but the woods remain the lord's and William Rade, the woodward, whose name incidentally does not appear in the rent roll, accounts for the sale of 8 acres of underwood, at 4s. the acre, which is the equivalent of the annual rent for one cottage and one virgate of land. The reeve remarks that there was no sale of either maple or oak that year.

Altogether, the reeve delivers £18 17s- as the income of the manor of Compton for the year from the feast of St, Michael in the first year of Henry IV, till the feast of St. Michael in the second.

Lower Farm House. The original and true Manor House of Compton Abdale, even if this claim has been forgotten for centuries.

A compotus is only a financial account and was never meant to be a report about the village, as in a sense, the protocol of the manor court would be. If we had the Court Rolls of the same year we would know Compton much better, but they have not survived. The compotus, however, gives enough incidental information to turn the amorphous mass of villeins into people whom we come to know by name and whose fortunes we can follow to a certain extent.

The reeve for the year 1400 was Thomas Hawkyns, about whose circumstances and family we shall hear more later. Although the reeve at that time was no longer as powerful as in the days when he ran the whole manor, allocated labour service and was responsible for the demesne, he was still the foremost villein. It was he who had to deal with the Steward of the Barony, he who had to face the auditors with his account; the responsibility of his office might now well outweigh its powers, but the man who holds it may be trusted to look after his own affairs at least as well as after the lord's.

Of the tenants, six, Richard Taylor, Joh.Verne, William Curtais, Walter Hancock, John Grokke and Galfrid Smyth, pay for one tenement and one virgate of land in the common fields, at 4s per annum. John Hancock has only his cottage and one acre of land, but he pays the comparatively high rent of 2s 4d, so he must have had another source of income, apart from his one acre. Perhaps he was the blacksmith. William Curtais and Thomas Hawkyns, however, though villeins, can afford to rent an additional tenement and virgate of free land. The rent for free land is higher just because it is free of obligations and the resulting commutation payments, and so Thomas Pole pays 8s 7d for one messuage and only 16 acres. But the richest man in the village is undoubtedly Thomas Rogers, for he pays rent for 2 virgates, 4 mondaylands and 22 acres with altogether 8

70

cottages He pays the rent for these 8 cottages to the lord and their occupiers pay him or work for him, for he would hardly pay their rent for charity's sake. They are his subtenants and so do not appear on the manorial rent roll. This subtenancy accounts for the "lost" families and the few names mentioned by the reeve.

Thomas Rogers seems a wealthy man, nevertheless he remains a villein, subject to the restrictions of his stand, to the laws of the manor and the Manor Court. Yet the uniform poverty and dejection of the villeins is a thing of the past, if it ever existed, for a village or a manor was probably never composed of strictly equal parts. Since the relations with the lord were put on a monetary basis, there was more scope for ambitious and enterprising families. Their time was now their own and could be spent to their own best advantage, to rise to positions of wealth, providing employment for others not so fortunate.

The tendency towards subtenancy shows even stronger in the compotus of 1441/2. There are only four names on the rent list: John Verne, a virgater, who had the same holding in 1400 (or it might have been his father of the same name), William Curtais, who now pays only for his free messuage and land, and Rogers and Hawkyns. Thomas Rogers and Thomas Hawkyns are gone, the next generation has taken over: William Sen., William Jun.,J ohn and Galfrid Hawkyns, and John, Walter, William and Robert Rogers. The Hawkyns have forged slightly ahead of the Rogers, for only John Rogers holds 3 messuages and Walter, William and Robert are virgaters, while William Hawkyns Sen. has taken over Thomas Rogers' remaining land. He and William Jun. now hold eight cottages, among them William Curtais' holding of terra nativa. Perhaps William Curtais succeeded in becoming a free man, for he

keeps his freeholding and a century later one Thomas Curtais is listed among the free tenants in a court roll of Henry VIII.

Alicia, wife of John Pole the freeholder, had died childless and the Poles' messuage and the sixteen acres which his father had held before must revert to the lord at John's death. Sad for the Poles, but another opportunity for William Hawkyns Jun. who takes over even during John Pole's lifetime.

William Hawkyns Jun. is a great man now and, no longer content to live in a cottage, builds himself a house. Others probably improve their dwellings also, as we can deduce from the fact that the quarry is let to the tenants of the manor, although we hear nothing about it. As long as the buildings went up in their rightful places, they would not be recorded. Had William Hawkyns kept within his bounds and built on his toft, we should not know anything about his house. Fortunately, he did not; he built on the lord's waste and so became involved in a dispute with the Archbishop's steward, as reported in the reeve's compotus. He built this house - domus - called "Barkar" on the waste without permission, or so the steward alleges. William, however, maintains that he can prove licence by copy of Court Roll given during the previous Archbishop's lifetime. As John Kemp, the present Archbishop and incidentally one of the great archbishop-statesmen and several times Chancellor of England, had held the see of York since 1426, this was a conveniently long time ago. When this dispute started, we do not know, because not all compoti survived, but it was resolved in the following year before the Manor Court when William Hawkyns was ordered to pay 26s 8d fine and heriot and 12d p.a., rent henceforth.

The last compotus adds a sad little footnote to this family success story: William Hawkyns Sen. gives back his holdings into the lord's hands because of want and poverty.

We hope Junior found room for him in his house "Barkar". But in 1441, there is no sign of William Sen.'s distress. He buys oak and maple at the timber sale in "Comptones Wood", and so does the Prior of St. Oswald and Robert Olyffe of Shipton, who was a free tenant of Compton Manor, but does not appear on the rent roll. He probably held the demesne or part of it.

If we consider the rise of the Rogers and the Hawkyns, and perhaps William Curtais, the house Barkar, the quarry and the timber sale, and remember the rebuilding of the church, we can, I think, assume that Compton was a thriving place in the 15th century. Unfortunately, the compoti tell us nothing of how this happened, nothing about husbandry and farming; we do not even know how many acres made one virgate. If the reeve had had to give account of the demesne farm, we might

71

have learnt something about land use and the relation between arable and pasture. As it is, he just enters the rent for it and nothing else. We are left to guess and deduce. Was the reason for acquiring subtenants and additional acres really interest in and profit from the extra land? We may doubt it if we remember that the common field system hampered the development of arable severely. Or is it not so much the work the subtenants do, nor their strips in the open fields, but the grazing rights on the common that go with the land which is important? More sheep meant more wool, and it was wool more than virgates that made a man rich. The compoti do not help us with these questions and we have to try other ways to find an answer.

72

Sheep

It is common knowledge that wool played a dominant part in the economy and politics of the Middle Ages, that wars were financed by tax on wool and a king (Richard I) was ransomed by it. Everybody knows of the woolsack on which the Lord Chancellor sat - and still sits - to remind him of the importance of wool. Everybody knows, too, about wool churches and the riches of the wool merchants who built them. So one might think that in the heart of one of the principal wool producing districts, sheep simply could not be avoided. But, as far as Compton is concerned, they are as invisible in the 15th century as they were in Domesday Book, and it is not until the 16th century that some information is forthcoming, when the Rector's farmer had to sue for tithes on wool and, fortunately for us, the record of this law suit survived among the diocesan documents in Gloucester.

But it is the preceding century which is regarded as the time of greatest wealth in the Cotswolds, the century of the wool merchants, when churches like "the Cathedral of the Cotswolds", the parish church of Northleach, were built. This lofty and beautiful church is famed for its graceful south porch and the brasses of the woolmen who built it.

Northleach, only 3 miles from Compton, besides being the market town for the many villages around, was an important place as one of the principal markets for wool. Here came the merchants of the Staple from London to view and buy the wool which was then taken by packhorse either to London or the Medway ports to be shipped to Calais. Among them were the Celys, whose letters, written between 1474 and 1483,

"I praise God and ever shall. It is the sheep hath paid for all"
Thus inscribed an East Anglian woolmerchant on his new house.

give valuable information about the trade methods of their time, about the quantity of wool, shipping and its hazards, traffic and the Staple at Calais. But, far from being dry business accounts, these letters mix domestic and personal news and requests with the business matters in hand and so bring the Cely family, their friends and relations to life.

Unfortunately, we have no time to dwell on Mother and her request for loaves of sugar and spices from the Continent, or listen to Robert, the black sheep of the family and his cries for help, and to Richard Junior's constant preoccupation with horses. Yet we can accompany Richard Senior, the head of family and firm, on his journeys to "Cottyswolde". One or the other of the Celys goes to Northleach several times a year, sometimes taking their hawks to while away the long hours of the ride. A hundred miles on horseback must have been tedious at times, but the Celys do not complain and speak of their journeys quite casually: "Our father rides into Cotswold within 8 days", or " I have been in Cottyswolde and packed 29 sarplers of wool for our father". But for all that they will have been glad to see the tower of John Fortey's new church and the huddle of grey houses in the valley, knowing that then there was only a mile or so between them and their destination.

Wool was bought by sacks and sarplers. I have not been able to find out how much wool makes one sarpler; this is probably so well known that nobody bothers to say. One sack of wool weighed 26 stone; their shape is familiar from the woolmerchants' brasses, they are often pictured there as footrests. Pelts, or fells are counted by number, 400 fells are one pack. The fells are provided by the autumn slaughter when the flocks were drastically reduced because there was no winter feed for them. In 1481, Richard Cely buys 11,464 fells, of which 10,265 are Cotswold fells. This, however, seems to be an exceptionally high figure, for a letter (No.44) of the previous November states that "there is a great death of sheep in England" and "there is like to be many fells, for sheep begin to die fast in divers country" (No.46). But these figures give a better estimate of the numbers of sheep than ordinary amounts would, for not as many sheep would be slaughtered as would die in an epidemic. The year before, Richard Cely bought, for instance, only 2500 pelts (at £3 and £4 per hundred fells), and 2 previous lots of 1500.

The Celys bought most of their wool from William Midwinter, and Midwinter bought it in the villages of the Mid Cotswolds from Coln Denis to Temple Guiting, including Compton Abdale, and this is where the 10,000 fells came from. Of course, the Celys were not the only Staplers, and Midwinter not the only, or even the most prominent woolman in Northleach, so these fells are only a fraction of the total.

William Midwinter, like John Fortey and the other Northleach woolmen, was the middleman between the Staplers and the farmers. He bought the wool and collected it in warehouses in Northleach, where the merchants from London could see it and arrange for packing and transport. Payment was made through a chain of letters of credit which stretched from Northleach to as far afield as Bruges. Such a complicated system was bound to produce difficulties occasionally and poor William Midwinter acquired a quite undeserved bad reputation with posterity through it, for, what is best known about him, is Richard Cely's moan: "God ryd us of him!". Richard Cely need not have invoked the help of the Almighty if he had paid the £200 which he owed Midwinter, who in turn was pressed for payment by the farmers and had no choice but to pester his debtors. "Good debtors are slow payers", Richard remarks cynically to his brother, which was poor comfort to the

Rubbing of
Wm. Midwinter's
grave plate in
Northleach Church.

people at the end of the chain.

Though William Midwinter has our sympathy, caught as he is between the clamour of the farmers, plus rising prices and the "good debtors", the Celys; on the whole the woolmen were nowhere near the breadline, middlemen rarely are. Their houses in Northleach and their church bear witness to their wealth to the present day. But it is good to know that some of the riches made from wool trickled down to the producers, hence William Hawkyns' new house and the wealth of the Rogers. Though the Hawkyns and the Rogers disappeared from the village long ago and we cannot say where Barkar stood, there is one memorial of them that endured for 500 years: the church.

The woolmen of Northleach used a good deal of their money to re-build and beautify the parish church and the people of Compton - and many other villages - did the same. Perhaps the magnificence of Northleach fired their ambition and when the north wall of the church had to be repaired, they enlarged the small, random built church and added a handsome tower whose grace and proportions are still admired today, and in acknowledging that it was "the sheep that paid for all", the builders placed the figure of a crouching ram on each of the tower buttresses.

The Cotswold sheep themselves - "long necked and
74   square of bulk and bone" - have disappeared from the hills. They were bred out of existence in the course of the 18th century improvement of stock and farming methods, except for one flock which was kept by Mr. W. Garne at Aldsworth, until 1968 when on Mr. Garne's death the farm was sold and the famous
75   flock came under the hammer. 43 ewes, 27 ewe lambs, 28 wether lambs and one ram lamb were sold for about £800. They were bought by breeders, so they will not disappear altogether.

Mr. O. Coburn, chairman of the Cotswolds Sheep Society has built up a flock of 100 in Eastington near Northleach, where he farms, and there is a small flock of 17 on Stowell Park Estate. The ancient breed is now kept for breeding interest, or to preserve a historical relic, not for economic reasons. For the emphasis in sheep economy has shifted to meat production. Wool is only of secondary importance, if that, for sheep now play a subsidiary role in husbandry to corn growing. Their main role is to graze and fertilize the ground when it is grassed down after three years of corn, to rest the soil and to break the cycle of plant disease. Comparatively few sheep are required at

76   five sheep per acre of grass, so that Compton Farm and Manor Farm have no more than 100 sheep each: Cluns and Clun Crosses on Compton Farm, Leicesters on Manor Farm.

The yield of wool is about 6 lb. per sheep from the Cluns and 7-8 lb. from the Leicesters, while an average of 10 $\frac{1}{2}$ lb. was

77   recorded in 1905 from a Cotswold sheep, and this is the yield the 15th century wool producers would count on. The numbers of sheep they kept is difficult to estimate; we have only a few scattered hints to go on. John Rogers died in 1498 and leaves in his will 64 sheep to various people, that is, he can afford to give away this number without impairing the interest of Agnes, his wife, to whom he leaves "all the rest of my goods". But neither John Rogers nor anybody else was free to keep more sheep than he was entitled to, for pasturage was "stinted", or related to the share in the common field. So when the Rogers took over and paid the rent for somebody else's messuage and virgate, they acquired the grazing right of that virgate, and could keep more sheep on the waste. Overstocking of the Common was a constant danger, and to prevent it was one of the functions of the Manor Court and the one that survived as long as the Commons. Nearly every one of the few Court Rolls which

Ram couchant. One of four on the tower buttresses of Compton's church. A tribute to the "sheep that paid for all".

have survived imposes a fine on one or the other of the manor's tenants for having too many animals on the common pasture.

78   The most detailed information about sheep comes from the law suit for tithes of the year 1551. We learn from it that it was the custom to "receive stranger's sheep", if a farmer did not take up his grazing rights for his own sheep. It was these visiting sheep which caused the Rector's farmer to sue the owners because they had taken the flocks of 200 and 40 back to Matson, where they came from, had them shorn and brought back to Compton without tithes having been paid. They ought to have paid $\frac{1}{2}$d. per sheep for 6 months grazing in the parish.

The witnesses give name, age and their qualification as witness and it appears from these statements, that 9 score sheep were the average of grazing rights. Three of the six witnesses have so much, one may keep 6 score and two do not specify their number, but give the price and yield of wool. Unfortunately, there is no compotus and no rent roll for 1551, so we do not know how many tenants there were, but in the Court Roll for May 1544 twelve names are mentioned, including Thomas Lane, the tenant of the demesne farm. Calculated very roughly, there must have been at least 1,000 sheep on Compton's Common, even as late as the middle of the sixteenth century, and William Midwinter would have had no difficulty in collecting 10,000 fells from the villages of the Mid Cotwolds.

Thomas Garne, one of the witnesses, reckons that 9 score sheep give 13 tods of wool, and the price of every tod is 22s Thomas Young thinks 200 sheep give 16 tods, each tod at 24s. The Cely papers give the price in 1480 as 13s 4d per tod and William Midwinter bemoaned the rising prices. Fortunately for him - dying in 1501 -he did not live to see the worst of Henry VIII's inflation. But Cotswolds wool had always been dearer than average because of its fineness and high quality. Only the famous "Lemster ore" surpassed it in quality and price.

As it was difficult to find sheep at the time when they were the prime factor in Cotswold economy, we shall not be surprised that they fade from view entirely when wool recedes from the first place in the national economy and the wool industry declines. They show up in wills during the 16th century, when friends and relations are left from one to six sheep, but later we hear nothing more about them. The misery of the decline of wool production and the transition to mixed farming either by-passed Compton or went unrecorded. Compton farmers were probably never exclusively dependent on sheep, for, from Domesday Book on, every kind of farm animal is mentioned at some time or other - except the supposed Cotswolds speciality, the sheep. There are the 11 teams of oxen in 1086; in 1283 Compton and Cerney together had 27 oxen, 3 ploughs, 2 carthorses and one cart. The compoti mention hens and eggs as Easter Offering and the Court Rolls list the number of pigs for the payment of pannage. Most people had 3 or 4 pigs, only one had a solitary pig, and one had five. Straying animals are invariably horses, and though animals in fields and pastures are often subjects for orders and fines in the Court Rolls, sheep are mentioned only once, which is strange, considering that there were more sheep than any other animals.

William Midwinter's woolmark.

The Reformation

Though the connection between the manor of Compton and the Priory had been broken so long ago that it must have been forgotten, strong links remained between the parish and the canons until the Priory ceased to exist in 1536, for the Priory as Rector of the parish appointed the priest and also owned the glebe (Rectory Farm). True, the farm had been let for many, many years, but as we know, the Prior and Chapter had a room, a cellar and stables there. Remembering their fondness of country life, we can be sure, that they made use of this pied-à-terre to the last.

John Rogers' will (1498) confirms the good relations between the village and the Canons, or at least between John Rogers and the Canons. He leaves 4d to each of them, 6s 8d to one particular Canon, Sir Philipp Herford; to the mother-church in Gloucester 20s, "which John Cassy owes me", and 2s. to the three orders of friars, which is a tribute to their popularity as preachers. Canon Herford seems to have been a personal friend, for he witnesses the will and receives more than anybody else outside the family.

Then all this friendly intercourse suddenly came to an end. The Priory was dissolved, the canons dispersed. They would not come riding up from the vale any more and their room in the farmhouse - and their cellar! - would not be needed any longer. Rectory Farm had no more business in Gloucester and the traffic between village and town dwindled. St. Oswald's no longer had a mother-church and the priest was on his own, though nominally the Archbishop of York had spiritual jurisdiction until the new bishopric of Gloucester was created in 1542.

The Dissolution of the Monasteries was, of course, not the first of the profound changes and upheavals which we now call the Reformation and which would continue for a century and more. The king's divorce and the break with Rome had preceded the Dissolution, but how much these events which reverberated throughout Europe shook the small village in the Cotswolds, we have no means of knowing. The disappearance of the Priory would, we imagine, have affected Compton more than the royal Supremacy. But the king's private life, which was not so very private after all, would certainly have been irresistible to comment on unless people in 1535 were very different from people in 1935, although in hushed voices - for it was dangerous to take sides or to express sympathy for the wronged queen. Whatever happened in those fateful days happened in London, and few country people would go there and have firsthand knowledge. Hearsay and rumour must have been the main vehicles by which news travelled into the villages. Then, in 1535, the king and Ann Boleyn came to Gloucestershire. They stayed in Fairford with John Tame and, passing through Cirencester, rode on to Prinknash. Was anybody in Compton curious enough to travel to Cirencester to get a glimpse of the woman who apparently had caused all the turmoil? Who was the reason that the king had put himself in the place of the Holy Father as Head of the Church in England?

But though the King defied the Pope, he did nothing to disturb the faith of his people. He had been given the title Defender of the Faith for his polemic against Martin Luther and he remained as averse to the radical Reformers as he had been before his break with Rome. His Six Articles upheld the tenets of Catholic religion and were enforced with severity. Churches, as well as the Service, kept their reassuring familiarity. Mass was said in Latin, as it always had been, and

Confession and Absolution eased the sinners' consciences. Joan Rogers bequeathes "to ye hye alter a draper bord cloth to make alterclothes and also to ye sacrament a kercheve to be upon ye pyx", and making her will in the 37ᵗʰ year of "our sovereign lorde king Henry ye 8ᵗʰ supreme head immediately under god of the church of England", (1546) she bequeaths "my sowle to Almyghty God, to our Lady Saint Mary and to all the wholy company in Heven" with all the trust of her forebears.

When, however, the young king followed his father on the throne, the Reformers were given free rein, and Protector Somerset constantly asked Calvin, the most radical of them, for advice, Calvin, though, complained that the Reformation in England was not thorough and quick enough. It was, in fact, too fast for the people to assimilate and absorb. Already in Edward's second year as king, Latin in the Service was abolished and the Liturgy had to be in English. Images, tapers, holy water and side altars were removed, the celibacy of the priests done away with, and many made use of the freedom to marry. The saints and - worst of all - the Virgin Mary were banished from Heaven. Belief in Purgatory was disapproved of and prayers for the dead forbidden. Confession was not prohibited outright, but gradually died out through discouragement.

All this went to the very heart of popular faith and religious life, and evasion and resistance were the natural response to such shattering deprivations. But King Edward in his turn was as severe as his father had been. Roman worship was prohibited and offenders were punished with prison for hearing Mass. The king would not even make an exception for Princess Mary, his half-sister, who had petitioned to have Roman Services privately in her residence. All these reforms could not be enforced everywhere at once. The diocese of

Gloucester, however, was not allowed to ignore the new spirit, for its bishop was one of the most ardent Reformers.

Bishop Hooper had early on come under the influence of the Continental Reformers, Zwingli and Bucer, and had had to leave England when the Six Articles came into force in about 1540. He stayed in Switzerland for some years and when he returned to his own country he was, more than ever, convinced of the rightness of the new teaching and more zealous for implementing it. His dedication was soon noticed and he was made Bishop of Gloucester in 1551. But his radical attitude nearly wrecked his episcopal career before it began because he chose to be imprisoned rather than consent to wear the traditional vestments at his consecration. A compromise was eventually reached, he was released from prison, consecrated, and went to Gloucester to redeem his province.

He found much to do. The backwardness of the diocese, the apathy and the conservatism of the higher clergy, the corruptness and ignorance of the parish priests might have discouraged any but the most dedicated and zealous reformer. Nevertheless, Bishop Hooper attacked these evils with untiring energy and devotion, "going about his towns and villages in teaching and preaching to the people there", acting as judge in the diocesan court to defeat the cumbersome medieval procedure, "he left no pains untaken nor ways unsought how to train up the flock of Christ in the true word of salvation." This was always his ultimate aim, but to save the flock, he had to reform the shepherds first.

One of his first acts was to examine the clergy in the fundamental and most important Christian subjects: the Ten Commandments, the Creed and the Lord's Prayer, and only 79 out of 311 examined clergy were wholly satisfactory. Nine did not know how many commandments there were, 33 did not know where to find them, the gospel of St. Matthew being the favourite place to look for them; 168 could not recite them. Only 10 could not recite the Creed, but most of them, - 216 - could not prove it from Scripture; 39 could not find the Lord's Prayer, 34 did not know its author and 10 could not recite it.

83   Judged against this background, Compton's minister, Johannes Roodes, appears quite satisfactory; he could answer all questions, bar one, the scriptural proof of the Creed, but 215 others failed in this point too.

Ignorance was not the only failing of the clergy which Hooper's unceasing vigilance brought to light. The low standard of morals and behaviour is reflected in the cases before the Diocesan Court. Violence, incontinence and keeping a woman in the house, sortilege or sorcery, and forging a will - all these occur. The hawking and hunting for which the vicar of Toddington is taken to task may not become the "sober, modest, keeping hospitality, honest, religious, chaste" parson who was the bishop's ideal, but it was one of the more innocent shortcomings.

A frequently recurring charge is "superstition", that is Roman practice. While the royal Supremacy was fairly easily accepted - the vicar of South Cerney, among others, even thought that the Lord's Prayer was so called because the Lord King had given it in his Book of Common Prayers - the spirit of the Edwardian reform penetrated the depth of the country but slowly. What had been believed and practised since time out of mind could not be eradicated overnight. The incumbents of Hazleton, Hampnett and Turkdean were found guilty of superstition, and the rector of Hawling was ordered to preach more often. John Roodes, Compton's priest, is not mentioned in any of the Court records. He apparently led a quiet and blameless life and conformed, at least enough to keep him out of court. Had he been a gross sinner, he certainly would not have escaped the bishop's attention.

84   The bishop seems to have been satisfied with Compton Abdale, church, priest and parish alike, for it is mentioned but only once in the extensive records of his episcopate and then only in respect of the church yard wall. This was found in need of attention and Compton was given a fortnight to repair it. Strangely enough, four men are recorded to have objected to this request and stranger still, one of them was John Roodes.

There is no record of the Protestantation of Compton church, but no admonition to carry it out either. The reform of the parish churches had begun in piecemeal fashion before Hooper came to Gloucestershire, under his zealous eye, however, it gathered momentum. Of all the changes the Reformation brought, the spoilation of their church certainly was the hardest to accept for the village people. The church then was not aloof from the village, to be visited for Sunday Service and not again until the next Sunday, but part of everyday life; church, village hall and even market place, all in one, the churchyard was a playground and meeting place. The old table-tomb just asked to be used as a seat, and the young men did not hesitate to chip holes into the slab for playing Nine Men's Morris. It was their church, familiar yet mysterious at Service time, when the priest celebrated Mass at the High Altar for which Joan Rogers had left the altar cloth only a few years before. There was the eternal lamp, which her kinsman, John Rogers, had provided by a bequest of 20 sheep to the church, there was the flicker of the candles on the side altars, given and lit in supplication to a saint or the Virgin or as thanks for help received. The paintings on the walls had been studied from childhood and Christ crucified, His Mother and St. John had looked down on them from the Rood Screen all their lives.

By royal command the church was stripped of all these sacred and familiar things. The rood-screen had to be dismantled, the lamp and the candles extinguished, the walls were whitewashed, the "idols" of the saints and Virgin Mary disappeared, the holy water stoop was removed - the church was bare and empty.

We can only try to imagine the pain and bewilderment of the people in Compton, and countless other parishes up and down the country, when they found themselves in this austere place of worship, deprived of the intercession of the "company in heaven" and the comfort of the Mother of Our Lord, venerated and dear, and nearer to the hearts and minds of the worshippers than the remote Godhead. Yet, they had responded loyally, but when the bishop was still not satisfied and ordered the repair of the church yard wall, reasonable though the request appears, they protested. They protested against perhaps more than the churchyard wall.

Bishop Hooper worked unceasingly and never sparing himself, not only in one diocese but two, for he had to look after Worcester as well. His wife worried because of his overworking and feared he might break down. He probably would have ruined his health, given time, but, after two and a half years of his episcopate, King Edward died and with the accession of Queen Mary the Reformation came to a halt. Hooper was ordered to London and deprived of his office because of his marriage and his denial of transsubstantiation. After a stay in Fleetwood prison, where he was treated harshly, he was sent back to Gloucester. People lined the street and wept when he passed, though he had been such a severe task master. He was burned at the stake near the church of St. Mary Lode, half-way between St. Oswald's and the Cathedral, where

85

Bishop Hooper's monument. It was erected on the exact spot where he was burnt at the stake in 1554.

his monument stands now, on February the 9th, 1554. His diocese settled back into Catholicism easily; there were no martyrs in Gloucestershire. His successor, Bishop Brooke, was a mild man, a state of apathy returned and Gloucestershire "enjoyed much quiet". (Fuller)

Rectory Farm since the Reformation

However upsetting the disappearance of the Priory may have been on personal or emotional grounds, to the management of the Rectory Farm the change of ownership made little or no difference. After the Dissolution rent and tithes were paid first to the king, then, in 1542, to Edmund Tame and his wife, Katharine, and soon after to the Dean and Chapter of the newly created Cathedral of Bristol. The tenant in 1536 was one Thomas Jenyns to whom the last prior had let the parsonage farm, a messuage in the occupation of William Graynger and a cottage called the Priest House in 1533.

Thomas Jenyns was one of three men of the same name who were connected with the Priory in its last days; the other two were Sir William Jenyns who surveyed the Priory for the king, and John Jenyns, a member of the king's household who was granted the site of the Priory in 1540. They probably were related, and if so, does the family connection perhaps explain why Compton church was given one of the bells of the mother church? Bells were sought after, and Compton had no special claim on one of the Priory church, but personal and family relations may have secured the "excellent tenor" which rang in lonely splendour for more than two centuries from Compton church tower, until it was joined by the churchwarden's bells in the 18th century.

The next rent agreement is made more than 30 years later, in 1565, between the Dean and Chapter and Thomas Mace, but it refers back to an earlier indenture of the Rogers which Thomas Mace had handed over to the Dean and Chapter, and also to the reversion of Thomas Jenyns' tenancy. Thomas Mace had been the Rector's farmer already in 1551, when he sued for tithes on wool.

The new feature of this agreement is, that Thomas Mace has to find " a good and sufficient Curate to minister all sacraments and sacramentals and to serve and discharge the Cure there at his or their proper expense and charges." As he only pays £2 in rent to the Dean and Chapter, he presumably pays £7 to the curate. This at any rate is the arrangement in all following rent agreements of which a great number is preserved in Bristol City Archives.

From various documents and later correspondence one gets the impression that the Dean and Chapter did not take much interest in their property in Compton. The Trustee for the Maintenance of Ministers whom Cromwell had appointed in 1654, found for instance in 1659, that the lease of the Rectory Farm had expired "some years since" and proposed to dispose of it on January 11th next, "when Mr. Brawn (of Saintbury) present-possessed of ye said tithes has liberty to shew what cause he can, why the same should not be disposed of, when he is to answer the measne profits incurred since the expiration of ye last Lese and to shew cause wherefore he should not allow a competent maintenance to ye Minister of Compton Abdale aforesaid." Evidently he was able to show cause why the lease should not be disposed of, for it was held by Brawns till 1742. Then Mrs Archers was the tenant till 1750, the four Misses Archers till 1764, William Snook in 1766 and Thomas Young in 1785. Then Lord Chedworth rented Parsonage Farm, and two cottages, namely the Priest House and the Churchyard House, which had been let separately. The pay to the curate had been raised to £10 by this time.

In 1791 the Dean and Chapter sent an agent to Compton Abdale to evaluate the tithes and to report on the state of the glebeland. The agent's letter indicates the same lack of interest and care for the Dean and Chapter's land and the tithes as was revealed in 1659. To ascertain the quantity of tithable land he had to consult "the oldest man in the parish and another person who had measured all the land for the several Farmers, Mowers and Reapers," as he had not been given any advance information. He found that the common field system was still in use, but that the few owners of land in the parish had reduced the former three fields to two and had laid their strips together into blocks and "everyone manages his land to their advantage", but that nobody had cared about the glebelands and they still "are very much dispersed in small pieces", and the agent fears that the meres will be lost and the boundaries forgotten once the old man, who alone knows all the lands, is gone. "The Glebeland I have set rather low (in valuation) on account of the Measure being short, as they do not measure so much as they call them, and being so much dispersed about the parish." The extent of the glebeland in 1791 was 167 acres which the agent values at £75 9s 9d, the two tenements with garden, orchard and common field lands, that is the former Priest House - and Churchyard House and the malthouse are worth £10 5s:-

The Rectory Farm was at that time let to Lord Chedworth who sublet it to his tenant, Thomas Walker. Thomas Walker presumably farmed the glebelands together with Lord Chedworth's farm of 838 acres, and one consequence of combining the two farms in one hand was, that the Rectory Farmhouse was now redundant. It is, therefore, not surprising that the next visit of an agent of the Dean and Chapter produces a dismal report. Mr. Hall, land surveyor of Cirencester, reports that the Parsonage Homestead "Consists of a large Mansion, stone built and tiled, in good repair. The House wants a new roof and doors and the Staircase wants repairing; but the principal Timbers are good. The lower part of the House is not occupied, part of the Bedchambers are. The House is considerably too large for the property". This was in 1810, and even after neglect had reduced the house to this melancholy state, the report manages to convey a memory of the Rectory of 1530, when the Prior and Chapter reserved their room, buttery and cellar. Canon Chapman, to whom the report had been sent, remarks that "this epistle of Mr. Hall presents to my mind the mansion in a most ruinous state, the lower part probably converted into Pigsties or Calfhouses and some of the Chambers occupied by Parish Paupers, this is the impression it makes on me. As to the House we have the means in a great measure of retarding the evil." Unfortunately, the canons made no use of their means, though another letter from Mr. Hall points out that an estimate of the repairs amounts to £100 "but I am sure it will cost double the money. It would be right for the lease to have notice to put all the buildings in complete repair without delay as the longer it is postponed the more will be the expense." The lease he mentions refers to a new tenant, Capel Cure, Esq. of London, who held the tenancy from 1811 until 1857. Mr. Hall had made another valuation at the change of tenants, "in the best way I was able as I could learn nothing of the Lessee. I understand he is a man of property, but a very drunken random sort of fellow. This you will keep to yourself." In the following year, 1812, he again urges the Dean and Chapter to insist on repair of the buildings, but it is doubtful that anything worthwhile was ever done to the old house, for in a somewhat confused letter of April 12th, 1819, Mr. Capel Cure alleges that in 1815 it was in a very dilapidated condition,

The Manor House, once the Rectory Farmhouse.
The lean-to of "Lord Howell's Farm House" is clearly visible on the left.

that in 1818 it was a heap of ruins and was taken down in June of that year. The old materials and the rough timber were carefully stored away to be used in the new farmhouse which he proposed to build. He, fortunately, writes this letter round a rough sketch of the old house and a drawing of the new, and this is the only description we have of it. We recognise the new house as the nucleus of what is now called Manor House. A gabled wing and an extension on the opposite side have been added since 1818, but its Georgian character still prevails. It embodies some walls of the old house, so Mr. Capel Cure was not quite correct in his report of total demolition to the owners. The cost of the new farmhouse was estimated at not short of £700, of which the Dean and Chapter should bear £300. They presumably agreed, for the new farmhouse was built in 1819.

Mr. Capel Cure gave all this information about the old

house in his own hand on April 12th 1818, yet in a letter of May 13th, putting the case for a low valuation to Mr. Hall, he writes: "I request you to represent to them (the Dean and Chapter) there is no Farm House on the premises, nor has been from time immemorial; and for want of one their Tenant must always be at the mercy of the Farmer who occupies the adjoining farm and Farm House, this I have severely felt since I have been Tenant to the Dean and Chapter. When the last Fine was fixed, no consideration was made to this circumstance." The curious fact must be added here that there is no sign of the old farmhouse on the Enclosure map of 1805.

Mr. Tucker, the conscientious valuer of 1826 notes "the Tenant of the Parsonage has built a lean to on the parsonage land against Lord Howells (sic) farm House and inclosed a small Court out of the Parsonage yard and opened a Door out of his Lordships Farm House, making a way across the Parsonage Yard. These encroachments are occupied by Lord Howells tenant, and some acknowledgement should be paid for them, to prevent the establishment of a right." This lean-to was probably built when Lord Howell's tenant also held the Parsonage farm and did not scruple to keep his two tenancies apart. The lean-to still exists, and a corresponding one on the other side of what is now called Manor Farmhouse, alias Lord Howell's The farmyard, however, has been turned into gardens, and it is nearly impossible for the imagination to eliminate the curved wall, the lawns, the flowers, the bushes and rockeries and see the open farmyard stretch from the Square right up to the Manor House and from the Manor Farmhouse across to the barn, and to recreate the life of the farm in this space: laden waggons rumbling towards the massive porch of the barn, pigs squealing in their sty, hens scratching about, dairy pails clanking - a long time ago.

Most of the farming now takes place outside the village, the farmhouses are no longer the centre of agricultural life, and even the barn has become a residence.

The Rectory barn was an important building when tithes were paid in kind and one tenth of the village's harvest in corn hay and wool had to be collected and stored. It retained its usefulness even when the tithes were commuted into money and it was well looked after. When it was converted in 1967, it was found that it had been very well built and that the walls and timbers were in excellent condition. Houses and barns on ecclesiastical property were usually very well built, and had the farmhouse received the same care as the barn, it might still be inhabited. That the stones and the timber were not discarded and would be used again in the new house shows the quality of the original building.

The walls of the barn are $2\,^1/_2$ ft. thick, not thicker than a cottage wall, but built solidly of stone, not filled with rubble as cottage walls are. When the modern concrete floor was taken up, the remnants of four walls came to light; they ran across the barn, dividing it into four bays. The builders dug down to 6 ft. but did not reach their foundation. These walls, too, had been built of high quality stone which was re-used in the conversion and some of it can be seen as end pieces of the wall between the barn ground and the Manor garden. The walls of the barn had been raised and possibly the timbers renewed in the 18th century (builder's estimate). Was the little Gothic window perhaps inserted into the south porch wall at the same time? Its origin is unknown, but it still graces the porch which is now the entrance hall of the house.

The barn was used as a barn and a calf sty until Mr. Maddy sold the farm and the Manor House - he was the first to call the old Rectory Farmhouse by that name - in 1935. But "in

Mr. Maddy's time" the old barn saw some gay times. Dinners and Teas in celebration of King George V's Jubilee and similar national occasions, or concerts were organised by Mr. Maddy. It is still remembered how the men cleared out the hay and straw, brought green boughs and decorated the barn while the women saw to the food. After the meal, the trestle tables were removed, the melodion tuned up, and the dancers went into action. Everybody contributed to the entertainment and Mr. Alec Mace remembers standing on a table and reciting:-

The way was long and narrow
He did not know it well,
The wheels came off the donkey cart
And tipped him into hell..

He was 8 years old at the time, and the occasion was the celebration of VE-Day.

The Tithe Barn. The best preserved building of the ancient Rectory Farm. Used as a barn until converted in 1967.

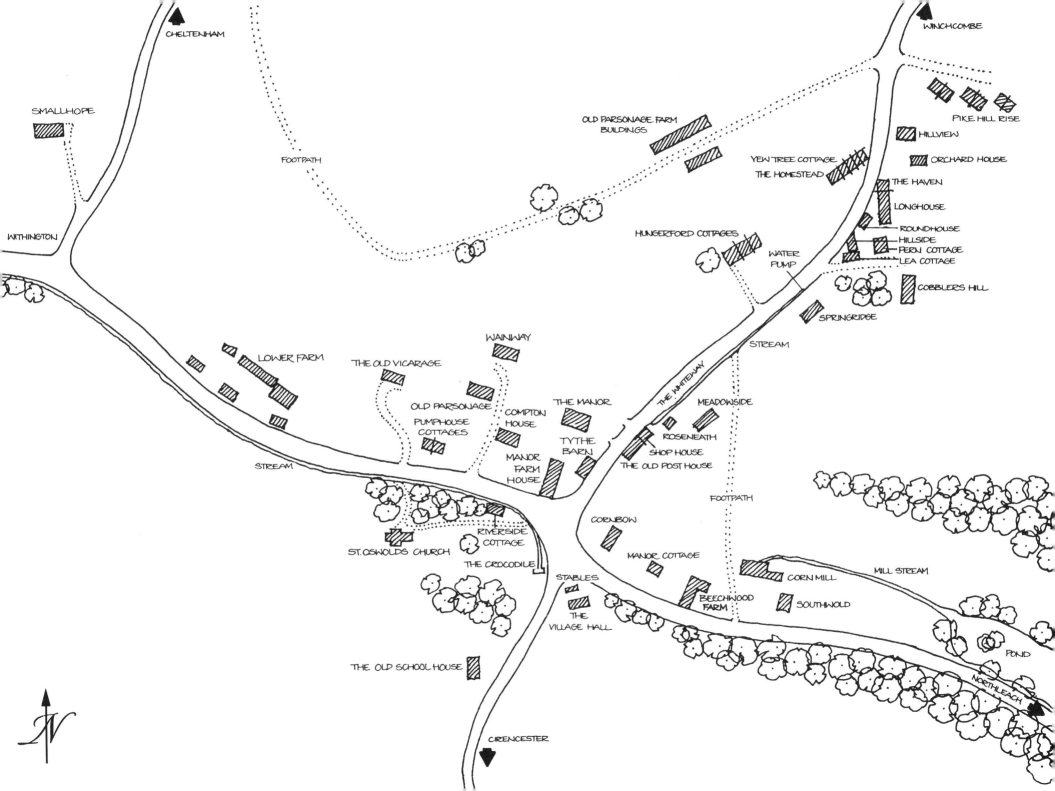

As mentioned elsewhere, there is nothing left in the village to remind people of the many centuries of working the fields without tractors, of milking the cows by hand, of the blacksmith and his forge, of the 22 working horses. Only a few small things were overlooked when the sheds were cleared and the old-fashioned tools and machines were disposed of, and, usually, taken to the quarry. What later could be salvaged from Compton and other villages can now be seen in the Cotswold Countryside Collection in Northleach, and I would like to thank the curator for allowing us to use the scythe and the cat for our illustration.

A device to hold gateposts steady when they were driven into the ground. This was found abandoned and forgotten in a field wall.

The cat scared the birds. He is one of the blacksmith's artifacts and was quite effective when the wind turned it and moved its dangly legs.

A scythe, for cutting grass or corn, which in its turn replaced the reaping hooks.

A wooden yoke helped to carry pails of milk or water.

The Priest House

"All that their Rectory... together with one cottage there callyd the priste house and all Lands medowes leasues and pastures to the same belonging with th'appertunance in as ample and large manner form and condition as William Rogers or any other for hym or under hym the same now holdith or occupieth for terme of yeres yet enduring" and "all that messuage and all land etc...in Compton wherein William Graynger now Dwellith" - all this is let to Thomas Jenyns in 1533, and this is the first time that the Priest House is mentioned. The other messuage is later called Churchyard House and both belonged to the Priory of St. Oswald in the same way as the glebeland did. Both are also let in the same way, and since at least 1530, when William Rogers' lease started, they were held and occupied by all manner of men, some from outside Compton who then sub-let them, but never by the priest, and it is a mystery where the poor curates lived. Sometimes these cottages go together with Rectory Farm, sometimes they are let separately, but they keep their identity to the last, and numerous leases for them are kept in Bristol.

The leases of 1695/6 give a detailed description of the cottages and we can place them in the village with accuracy; they stood on the east side of the lane leading up to Old Parsonage Farm. There is only one house on this site at present, and it has nothing to do with the cottages of the leases. Compton House is, in fact, of such recent origin that its former name, the New Cottages, is not yet forgotten. The lane itself now has the character of a private drive to Old Parsonage Farm, and yet it was once a busy, village street, for there was a smithy between the Priest House and the Churchyard House, and the two cottages which stood on the site of the paddock below Old Parsonage, also made the lane more a part of the village than it is now.

Four acres of land in the common fields went with each of the cottages and the Priest House had grazing rights for six sheep and one beast. These are very small holdings; in Domesday Book their occupiers would have been called bordarii, and they reflect the low economic standing of Compton's priests in the Middle Ages, when the priests actually held the Priest's House. Six sheep are a very modest portion of the thousand or more which thronged the pastures, when the men who were called as witnesses by the Rector's

Compton House, once the New Cottages.

89

farmer in the tithe suit of 1551, had grazing rights for 180 and 120 sheep.

From the beginning of the 19th century the cottages were held together with Rectory Farm by Mr. Capel Cure until the Church commissioners sold both to Lord Eldon of Stowell Park in 1860. The smithy had been turned into a tenement early in the 18th century, and a malthouse joined the three cottages sometime later. By the early years of this century the cottages were dilapidated, the malthouse no longer in use and they were all pulled down and made room for the New Cottages. Fragments of the perforated bricks of the hop drying floor of the malthouse are still found here and there, and they are a puzzle to most people, as there is nobody left who could identify and explain them, though Mrs. Purvey remembers that her father, Reuben Smith, who died in 1958, aged 89, had to clear the holes of the bricks as a boy, when there was no other work to do in rainy weather, and that he mentioned the boys did not like this chore and tried to avoid it if they could.

It is ironical that the best documented houses have vanished while the evidently old farmhouses, Manor Farmhouse and the Old Parsonage "have no history" and it is difficult to provide any without a good deal of speculation. As far as I can see, Old Parsonage never had anything to do with the parsonage or Rectory Farm. Perhaps it inherited its name from the Churchyard - and Priest House across the lane. An old and substantial house might have seemed more likely to have been the parsonage in the dim past than the small cottage called

When Compton was taken out of the Barony of Churchdown (in 1580) it needed its own bailiff, and he needed a house, which is probably the origin of this stately building, its gable end facing the road in the fashion of the time. The bay is a much later addition.

Priest House. William Dyer owned it in 1805, but rightly or wrongly, Dyers' farm has now been known as Old Parsonage Farm for a good many years and, it is hoped, will keep this name. Changing the names of farms and houses should be discouraged, the ensuing confusion makes it difficult for anybody who wants to trace the descent of properties or their owners. Compton Farm, in 1970, for instance, is not the same farm as Compton Farm in the 18th century. The East and West Farms of 1811 may or may not be Manor Farm and Lower Farm of later date; the Manor House is not Compton's manor house, but Old Rectory Farmhouse. The Manor Farmhouse, however, has a right to its name, because it did belong to the lord of the manor (as far as ascertainable) and was the house of the lord's tenant farmer and/or bailiff.

If Old Parsonage Farmhouse is not the former parsonage and the Priest House had not seen a priest since the Middle Ages, where did the curates live? We cannot answer for all of them, but we know that in the last century several clergymen applied to the bishop to be allowed to live outside the parish "because there is no glebehouse"; The Rev. Daniel Dobrée resided in Withington, Rev. Thos. Hill in Notgrove, Rev. Mellersh in Shipton, Rev. Garrow in Sevenhampton.

It was not until 1884 that Compton had its own parsonage. The Church Commissioners then bought 3 acres of land and gave £1500 to build a house, and the Rev. Henry Morgan was no doubt delighted to move into a modern house after eleven years of ministry without a vicarage. He contributed about £400 of his own money for "the erection of suitable outbuildings to harmonize with the house and the Architect's fees and Expenses of laying out the grounds, and excavation" - "but the benefit to the Living and the ornament to the Parish allow no room to regret the outlay."

The parish has been "ornamented" by the vicarage and Rev. Morgan's grounds ever since and its distinctive Victorian period flavour is an important part of Compton and its history. But it is The Old Vicarage now; Compton is held together with Withington, and the minister lives in Withington. The vicarage was sold in 1965 and is now a private residence.

The Old Vicarage, Compton's first vicarage, built in 1885.

Trees and Woods

"In leaving Cirencester…., I came up hill into a country, apparently formerly a down or common, but now divided into large fields by stone walls. Anything so ugly I have never seen before. The stone, which, on the other side of Cirencester, lay a good way under ground, here lies very near to the surface. The plough is continually bringing it up, and thus, in general, come the means of making the walls that serve as fences. Anything quite so cheerless as this I do not recollect to have seen; for the Bagshot country, and the common between Farmham and Haslemere, have heath at any rate; but these stones are quite abominable. With the exception of a little dell about eight miles from Ciciter, this miserable country continued to the distance of ten miles, when, all of a sudden, I looked down from the top of a high hill into the vale of Gloucester! Never was there, surely such a contrast in this world!" Cobbett does not mince his words; the Cotswolds clearly are not his kind of country. A ride along Ermine Street on a November day is perhaps not the best introduction to this country, but the return journey on the Oxford Road does nothing to make him change his mind:…"We proceeded on, between stone walls, over a country little better than that from Cirencester to Burlip-hill. A very poor, dull, and uninteresting country all the way to Oxford."

Five years later, Cobbett has to cross the Cotswolds again and decides to avoid the turnpike road through Cirencester. So "we came through Dodeswell, Withington, Chedworth, Winston and the two Colnes. At Dodeswell we came up a long and steep hill which brought us out of the great vale of Gloucester and up upon the Cotswold hills…This wold is, in itself, an ugly country.

The soil is what is called a stone brash below, with a reddish earth mixed with little bits of this brash at top, and for the greater part of the wold, even this soil is very shallow; and as fields are divided by walls made of this brash, and as there are for a mile or two together, no trees to be seen, and as the surface is not smooth and green like the down, this is a sort of country having less to please the eye than any other that I have ever seen, always save except the heaths like those of Bagshot and Hindhead." "Yet even this wold", he writes, and he seems surprised at the discovery, "has many fertile dells in it, and sends out, from its highest parts, several streams, each of which has its pretty valley and its meadows." But this is all he can bring himself to say in praise of the Cotswold valleys, and particularly the Coln valley about which, in our day, more lyrical and loving books have been written than about any other part of the Cotswolds. The bleakness of the wold has soured his soul.

Before we become indignant at his lack of appreciation, however, we have to remember that the Cotswolds he saw are not the same landscape we know and love, for it is more than just a change in taste which turned Cobbett's "ugly country" into an Area of Outstanding Natural and Architectural Beauty. He saw a country where there were no trees to be seen for a mile or two together, and whose unmitigated dominant element was stone, and this could only mean desolation to this tree lover who never missed an opportunity to point out the beauties of a wooded landscape. This land finds no grace before his eyes; he is less than fair to it and mentions neither Dowdeswell Wood, which Marshall praised in 1789, nor Chedworth Woods, nor Lord Chedworth's plantation, which Rudder thought the outstanding feature of Compton parish, and which Cobbett must have seen on his way from Withington to Chedworth.

Seeing the wolds through Cobbett's eyes, we can now

understand why a tree like the Puesdown Ash was regarded as a landmark and named on Isaac Taylor's map (County of Gloucester, 1777-86-1800).

Cobbett's antipathy to the Cotswolds may have been due to his preference for more sylvan landscapes, but he was not alone in complaining about the treelessness of the country. William Marshall who wrote 30 years before him, laments the bareness of the hills, too: "There are some patches of woodland scattered among these hills, one of them (in Chedworth) large - a thousand acres. But in general, the country is bare, much too bare of wood. A circumstance which those who have no property in it, can only regret. But utility and ornament call equally loud on those who have, to cover its present nakedness. What a lovely passage of hill country lies above Dodeswell. Almost every other part of these hills is capable of being rendered equally beautiful." "The Cotswolds are, or might be made, a delightful land to reside in." "As subject of RURAL 92 ORNAMENT, they are of course, susceptible of great beauty", he remarks in another place.

If Cobbett could ride across the Cotswolds now, he might be surprised at the change; he might perhaps even find a few words of mild praise for the tree planters who have made the hills "a delightful land to reside in". There is now not one mile of his route where he would be out of sight of trees, of woods, plantations, windbreaks or at least single trees in pastures. Even the high wold, grim as it still can be in winter, is not the treeless, cheerless country he knew. There are now more trees on the Cotswolds than there have ever been. But we are so used to seeing them everywhere that we cannot visualise the former vast stretches of bare fields and pastures, and we must be grateful to Cobbett for bringing to

grateful to Cobbett for bringing to mind how much we take for granted.

The Great Oolite, which is the main formation of the Mid Cotswolds, is not tree-bearing and forests, like those of the lowland, do not grow naturally on it. Once the scrub of thorn and hazel which covered the hill tracts had been cleared - a process which started with the first farmers, the Neolithic Barrow builders - the land was bare and trees had to be tended and encouraged, and few of those who lived by tilling the hard won acres would have been inclined to tend trees.

Domesday Book does not mention woodland for Compton. If the Grove existed then, it would have been only insignificant scrub which grew up, on and around the shunned site of the Roman Villa, and not worth mentioning. For the Middle Ages our knowledge of the manor, including its woodland, if any, is scanty. By 1400, however, the first year for which a compotus has survived and gives some details, Compton had some woodland and the reeve accounts for 34s. for 8 acres of under wood at 4s. the acre (sic), he also mentions the woodward who is responsible for the sale. The wood is not named in this account, but subsequent sales take place in a wood "called Comptones Wood", where not only underwood, for fuel and fences, but also oak and maple are sold. The buyers are mostly, but not only, men from Compton; there is also Robert Olyffe from Shipton, buying oak, the Prior of St. Oswald who also buys oak, and three men from Turkdean, which shows that people sometimes had to go to places miles away to buy wood.

The woodland, at present known as Compton Wood, lies in the south of the parish and is one part of a larger wood of

Sir Richard Grubham, name or specify the woodland which belonged to the manor. The Grove comes to our notice only late, when in 1791 it is listed in a tithe valuation as 161 acres of Common.

How fortunate Compton was in having such an extensive wooded Common, is brought home by W. Marshall's reflections on the lack of wood which he observed when, in 1788, he stayed in Northleach to make his survey of the agricultural state of the Cotswolds: "Unfortunately for the Cotswold Hills, a spirit of planting has never been generally diffused among them. Something has been done about Guiting and Dowdeswell...Sherborne and Cirencester...but all these with a view to ornament merely....There are no woods for the use of estates. Only a few ash coppices for hurdles in the valleys. Farms in general may be said to be totally destitute of wood. Coals are fetched 20 to 30 miles by land carriage, and faggot wood perhaps 8 or 10 miles. Not a pole upon the farm to assist in making a temporary fence, nor perhaps even a handful of brush wood to kindle the fire. Straw, I am afraid, is here considered an article of fuel: a circumstance which reflects no credit on the owners of landed estates. Odd corners ought to be filled up with coppice wood, and the more central farms ought each of them to have its screen coppice; sufficiently extensive to admit of a plot being filled every year, for the use of the farm and the cottagers of the township it lies in.

In winter, the poor on these shelterless hills, must be in a wretched state as to fuel. There are few hill countries which do not afford either wood, coals, peat, or at least turf; but here straw may be said to be the only fuel the country at present produces. Fortunately for the farmers, stone walls will not readily burn."

In 1805, Compton was enclosed and the Commons were abolished. The lord of the manor "claimed to be entitled to the soil of the wastes within the said manors (Chedworth and Compton Abdale)" and the Grove, together with the Common on the Downs, became private property. In Chedworth, provision for the poor was made by allotting them twelve acres of Furzey Commons, yet no such consideration was shown for Compton. Perhaps the villagers were still allowed to gather firewood in the Grove, but now they could do so only by grace and favour of Lord Chedworth, not by right, as before the Enclosure.

Nobody can remember when the last timber in the Grove was cut. Now some parts of it have almost reverted to scrub. Here and there a tree still rises above the level of the ancient stooled ash and the elder, but there is nothing that could be called timber. The stooled ash which had been grown to supply poles for sheep hurdles are so overgrown that they could not be reclaimed any more; the stools will not regenerate themselves if the shoots are left to grow beyond a certain size. Not that it matters, for sheep are not folded any more on turnips and swedes and hurdles are no longer wanted; the village carpenter who made them shut his shop long ago.

When the hurdles were still used, the poles for them were auctioned in the Grove. The wood would be marked out in strips of 5 to 7 acres and the poles cut and laid out in so-called drifts so that the buyers could view them before the auction. The strips were rotated, so that each strip was cut at regular intervals. The last cutting and selling took place sometime in the First World War and since then the Grove has led a non-utilitarian existence. When Mr. E. Turner's estate came up for sale in 1930, the catalogue pointed out that "the Estate is very compact and famed for its shooting, and the woods and plantations, including the wellknown Compton Grove are admirably placed for holding a large number of pheasants". It still is, and, in fact, this is now its main function.

auctioned in the Grove. The wood would be marked out in strips of 5 to 7 acres and the poles cut and laid out in so-called drifts so that the buyers could view them before the auction. The strips were rotated, so that each strip was cut at regular intervals. The last cutting and selling took place sometime in the First World War and since then the Grove has led a non-utilitarian existence. When Mr. E. Turner's estate came up for sale in 1930, the catalogue pointed out that "the Estate is very compact and famed for its shooting, and the woods and plantations, including the wellknown Compton Grove are admirably placed for holding a large number of pheasants". It still is, and, in fact, this is now its main function.

Besides the lord's wood and the Common, there is one other place which needs to be considered for its trees - the churchyard. The right to herbage and trees of the churchyard usually belongs to the parish priest. But the Priory of St. Oswald retained this right with the glebelands and the tithes from its chapels and churches; and the Injunctions of the Archbishops of York to the Priory deal, besides many other topics, also with trees. As usual, malpractice had occasioned the Archbishop's intervention. Apparently, members of some parishes had helped themselves to timber from the churchyard and so Archbishop Romeyn decreed, in 1289, that the parishioners of Churchdown, Compton Abdale, Norton, Twigworth and Hucclecote must not dispose of or meddle with the trees and herbage of the churchyard, "seeing that the administration therein belongs not to them, but to the Prior of St. Oswald's who is the rector of the same place." But the rector cannot do as he likes either, he is forbidden to uproot or fell trees in growth, though he can remove barren and useless trees, and trees blown down by the wind. However, timber was always in demand, and trees, any trees, were a tempting source of quick profit for the short-sighted and thoughtless, and these rules were likely to be broken or circumvented whenever a loophole presented itself. So, a few years later, the Prior was found to have felled no fewer than 200 trees, when a certain meadow with its trees and herbage was included in the chapelyard at Norton which had been given to the Priory. He was then forbidden to do anything connected with timber trees without the view and consent of the Warden of the Jurisdiction who would determine how much timber was needed in any particular case. Though this mandate mentions only churchyards, the misuse of churchyard trees being the original reason for making the rule, it is addressed to the Prior as Rector and would apply to all rectorial land. Therefore, when the Compton glebeland, that is, the Rectory Farm is let, the Prior reserves for himself all trees, except dead ones and the loppings, he being, in this matter, under the authority of the Warden, was, in fact, not at liberty to dispose of them.

In 1542, the Dean and Chapter of the Cathedral of Bristol replaced the Priory of St. Oswald as rectors of Compton Abdale. They let the Rectory Farm and took little further interest in their property which, after the Enclosure, included 11 acres of the Grove. The lessee, who usually was an absentee, sublet the farm to a Compton farmer. At the beginning of last century the Dean and Chapter sent agents to inspect their property and to value the tithes, and their reports show that the farmer was as indifferent to the preservation of the Dean and Chapter's woodland as he was to the upkeep of the farmhouse. "I then went to Compton Grove," Mr. Hall

One of the several venerable churchyard yews.

provide timber for the re-building of Rectory Farmhouse, for in 1818 the agent applies for permission to fell 10 to 15 oaks, which is granted and the Dean and Chapter "requests you (the agent) will cut down on the Compton Abdale Estate such Oak Trees as you think are ripe for felling and will not improve by standing. Take care of the Bark and the Timber on their account."....When cut down inform us as near as you can of what will be the weight of the Bark and Quantity of the Timber. You will be so good as to inform us what are the present current prices of Bark and Timber in your neighbourhood." Unfortunately, this information has not survived.

This correspondence shows how heavily timbered the Grove once was and by what process it shrank from 161 acres in 1791 to 43 acres at present - the plough encroached on the woodlands until only its steepest slopes remained. It is also a reminder of the importance of oak bark for the tanning of leather before the chemical industry provided substitutes. Indeed, the bark seems almost as valuable as the timber, even if, or particularly if, the timber is of inferior quality, as the agent alleges.

93 The "barking season", Mr. Hall mentions, is April to June, which is the only time in the year when the bark can be removed from the oak tree in clean sheets. Spring is, therefore, the felling season for oak.

In 1860, the Church Commissioners sold the 11 acres of the Grove together with the Rectory Farm, to Lord Chedworth, and the long association between Compton and the successors of the Priory came to an end. But before leaving the woods and trees, ecclesiastical and otherwise, we have to take a look at the churchyard.

The most conspicuous vegetation in the churchyard is a number of old yew trees. This is nothing extraordinary or in any way peculiar to Compton. Yews in churchyards are so common that one expects to see them there. A churchyard without yews is the exception. Yet it is not easy to explain why this should be so. Yews are native trees of chalk and limestone and they seed freely and should be widespread, but outside churchyards and parks, they are rare. They may have been exterminated because their leaves are said to be poisonous to animals, and so their last refuge is the churchyard. But, there must be another reason for their presence, as they are found in churchyards outside the range of their natural habitat. It has been suggested that yews were sacred trees in pre-Christian times and that they still grow

on hallowed ground, their pagan origin forgotten; ancient yews in a churchyard indicate that it was a sacred place long before the church replaced the heathen temple. The yew is reputed to be the longest lived native tree and there are specimens that are known to be several centuries old, so it would not take many generations of yews to span the Christian era.

Again, it was - and still is - widely believed that churchyard yews were grown to provide wood for bows. This wood is hard, compact, yet elastic and, therefore, highly valued.

94 However, native yew is now thought to have been unsuitable for bows. Wood for bows was imported by the ships engaged in the wine trade. This may have been true for bows used in warfare, but surely not every bow carried for hunting throughout the land can have been made from imported, and therefore expensive wood, though it seems unlikely that yews were planted in the churchyard for bow making only.

There are the theories, and no doubt other explanations will be attempted, and there are the yews. May they flourish whatever the reason for their existence.

The Manor after the departure of the Archbishop of York

"My friend Richard Pates...could shortly spy something meet to purchase from the king)", so wrote Sir Thomas Chamberlayne to a friend in 1545. Richard Pates was in a good position to spy "something meet", for he had been appointed to deal with diverse ecclesiastical property in Gloucestershire, his home county. He was certainly familiar with the Barony of Churchdown, for he had married Maud Lane, whose late husband, Thomas, had been the lessee or "chief steward", as one Compton Court Roll calls him, when Archbishop Holgate of York, through an exchange of property, handed the Barony to the Crown in 1544. But whether Richard Pates gave Sir Thomas a hint or not, the latter acquired the Barony in 1552.

In the tradition of his ancient family, Sir Thomas Chamberlayne was a diplomat and politician who served Henry VIII and his successors, and the king granted the Barony "without fee or fine in consideration of good and faithful service to us by our dear servant, Thomas Chamberlayne, knight", as the confirmatory grant of Edward VI expresses it. The Dissolution of the Monasteries and the Reformation had made vast lands available, and Sir Thomas, like other men in a position to take advantage of this opportunity, had seen to it that he had his share. Besides the Barony of Churchdown, he owned Upton St. Leonards and Prestbury "which I lately bought from the Earl of Leicester", as he says in his will, and

where he resided if and when his service to the government allowed. He died in 1580 and left the manor of Compton Abdale to his second son, Edmund. Compton Abdale, however, had been mortgaged to William Pierson, Sir Thomas' son-in-law, and the will requests that it be redeemed with the "overplus" after the various bequests had been settled. Edmund Chamberlayne lived at the manor of Maugersbury, which he also owned, and which remained in the possession of his descendents until the beginning of this century.

Edmund Chamberlayne sold Compton in 1608 to Sir Richard Grubham of Wishford in Wiltshire, who already owned large estates in this and other counties. Sir Richard, dying childless, Compton together with Wishford, Chedworth and Yanworth, went to his sister's son, John Howe in 1629. Once more Compton became part of a larger complex, a small manor among many others in the same ownership, and in its 1000 years as a manor it has never had a resident lord.

It is sometimes said that Cassey Compton was the Manor House of Compton Abdale, and it is tempting to think that the beautiful but now empty and neglected house that bears the name of Compton and lies only a mile and a half behind the steep hill to the south, belongs to Compton Abdale as its "Big House". In fact, Cassey Compton belongs to the parish of Withington and has been part of it ever since Saxon times, though this is true only of the house, for most of its grounds lie in Compton parish. It takes its surname from the family of Cassey who owned it till Elizabethan times. One of them figures in John Rogers' will of 1498 as owing him 20s. The Howes bought Cassey Compton in about 1700, and Sir Richard Howe, the son of the first Howe to own Compton Abdale, is always referred to as "of Compton", but as Compton is not specified, it may be either, Abdale or Cassey. He owned both, and this common ownership is the only connection betwen them, but he resided at Cassey Compton, and "of Compton" more likely refers to his place of residence.

One of the plates in Atkyns' *"the Present and Ancient State of Gloucestershire"* shows Little Compton (alias Cassey Compton), the Seat of Sir Richard Howe, Bart. as a three winged house with a centre court yard and a large stable block, with many small formal gardens, a deer park and, in the background, a plantation divided by drives radiating like the spokes of a wheel. All this splendour is gone. An old orchard fills the space of the formal beds, cows graze where gentlemen once played bowls, and the deer have disappeard. A row of ancient limes along the White Way is the only relic of the Park which lives on only as the name of the pasture on its site. Faint traces of the pattern of the radiating drives are still discernible in the plantation which is now called Star Wood because of them. The stables and the gate pillars still survive, but the house itself lost one wing in a fire long ago. Still and lifeless, yet beautiful, it is a melancholy sight and it is not surprising that it is firmly believed to be haunted.

While Sir Richard Howe lived at Cassey Compton, his nephew, John, bought Stowell Park. This John's son, John Howe, inherited his great-uncle Richard's estate in 1730 and from then Compton Abdale was part of the Stowell Park estate, until in 1911 Lord Eldon sold the last of his land in Compton proper under its ancient and rightful name of Parsonage Farm. Large tracts in the east and, particularly, the south of the parish, namely, Compton Wood and Star Wood still belong to Stowell Park Estate.

When Edmund Chamberlayne sold the manor of Compton Abdale to Sir Richard Grubham, he had to exempt two properties from the deal: the Rectory Farm which belonged to the Dean and Chapter of Bristol, and "that farm...which is part of the inheritance of Susan Lovett and now in occupation of the said Edmund Chamberlayne or his assigne or assignees by lease and under the right of the said Susan Lovett."

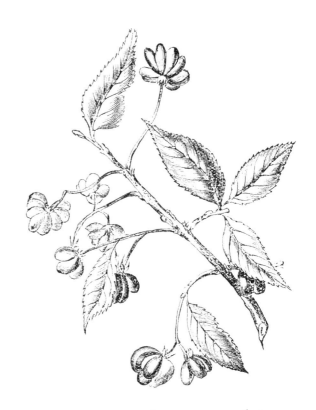

FRUIT OF EUÓNYMUS EUROPÆUS
(*Common Spindle-tree*)

Reformation to Restoration

We left Gloucestershire in 1554 quietly settling back into Catholicism after Bishop Hooper's death at the stake. There were no martyrs in the county during Mary Tudor's reign, but elsewhere the re-establishment of the Catholic faith met with much resistance and caused heavy persecution. When Elizabeth followed her half-sister on the throne in 1559, the Protestants who had fled to the Continent on Mary's accession returned eager to complete the Reformation which had been interrupted by the Catholic queen. But Elizabeth had no intention to replace one orthodoxy by another and so to perpetuate the persecutions, the hatred and the strife. Her Church may have appeared to the disappointed Reformers who had become imbued with the rigid faith of Calvin as "cloaked papistry and a mingle mangle," but its establishment prevented the religious civil wars which rent many countries on the Continent.

As Supreme Governor of a hierarchical church, the queen could not but be hostile to the Calvinists and their idea of Presbyterian government. In their enmity towards the bishops, she sensed a threat to the monarch who stood behind the bishops, a threat possibly not only to the monarch as head of the Church, but of the State also. She thought it necessary to warn King James of Scotland against "this sect of perilous consequence such as would have no kings but presbytery and take our place while they enjoyed our privileges... Yea, look we well unto them. When they have made in our people's heart a doubt of our religion and that we err if they say so, what perilous issues this may make I rather think than write..."

Acting accordingly, the queen suppressed the Puritans ruthlessly. But the spirit of the Reformation could not be extinguished. Convinced of their rightness, fortified by their faith in being the chosen ones after their dogma of predestination, the Puritans survived long years of persecution.

King James lost no time in making his attitude to the Puritans clear. Soon after he became King of England in 1603, he said in his famous closing speech at the Conference at Hampton Court: "...once you (the bishops) are out and they in, I know what would become of my supremacy, for no bishop, no king." He dismissed the Puritans' plea for moderate reforms and latitude in minor matters as "snivelling about imaginary evils" and said, in conclusion: "If that be all your party has to say, I will make them conform themselves, or else harry them out of the land or do worse."

In the course of his reign, King James had to learn that there was no such easy way of getting rid of the problem; that it was not a question of silencing a few non-conforming ministers; even that his conflict with the Puritans was not confined to the Church. Clergy and laity alike had been affected by the new spirit. Religion and politics could not be separated and the king found himself opposed by a strong Puritan party in Parliament. He was so exasperated by them that, as he wrote to Lord Howard, he "had rather live (as God judge me) like an Hermite in this Forrest than be king over such a People as the pack of Puritans are that overrules the lower-house". Though he did in the end prefer his throne, his court and his favourites to a hermitage, he remained implacably hostile to reforms and concessions. By his attitude of fear and resistance, he created the situation he was so afraid of: Puritanism and Parliament were more and more thrown together and confronted King, Court and Court Clergy.

This confrontation hardened into increasing bitterness and at last became irreversible under his son, Charles I, who, if anything, was even more obstinate and unbending. Before the opponents took to the field in 1642, their battles - not so bloody, but no less deadly - were fought in and out of Parliament by means of royal prerogative and parliamentary sanctions. The king depended for the greater part of his income on subsidies and taxes which Parliament had to sanction, and Parliament would grant money only on condition that the king would hear and rectify their grievances. Conciliation and concession were never Charles' characteristics, and after the dissolution of his third recalcitrant Parliament in 1629, he ruled for eleven years without it.

To raise money during this time, the king and his advisers revived ancient and obsolete customs and claims which he could impose without parliamentary consent. While some of these, like the enforced knighthoods and the Forest Laws, hit only certain sections of the population, Ship-money had to be paid by everybody and spread the unpopularity of the king throughout the land.

Ship-money had, of old , been imposed on coastal towns in times of danger from enemies or pirates to provide ships for the protection of the ports, but now was extended beyond the time of emergency. Gradually, the king extended its application in time as well as in space and it developed into a permanent tax on everybody. Resistance against it never ceased and collection became more and more difficult so that by 1639, five years after its introduction, only 20% could be brought in. The king had lost far more than he gained, for no amount of money would have been worth the ill-will and resistance Ship-money caused.

But, despite the general mood of smouldering resentment, it was most unwise for anybody, high or low, to show enmity or discontent; the king's judges and the Star Chamber saw to that. In this atmosphere of repression and latent revolt, personal quarrels and animosities could easily be given a political tinge. Denunciation flourishes under such circumstances, as anybody knows who has or has had the misfortune to live in a police state. A careless word, a personal grudge - and the consequences can be disastrous.

"To Richard Barkley, Esq. Justice of Peace of the County of Gloucester. We have received ye Examinacons by you taken touching some treasonable words uttered by Tho: Mace of Compton Abdale in that County of Gloucester, and do find cause to approve & recommend your care, and dilligence in this Business, and to give you thanks for the same. As touching the said Mace, we think fitt that he remayne in the Prison where he now stands committed to be proceeded with by the Justices of Assize, in their next Circuit for that County."

103

Poor Thomas Mace. The 'Examinacons' which earned the Justice of Peace such praise are, fortunately, also preserved among the State Papers and tell us what treasonable words brought Thomas Mace to these straits. "The Examination of Thomas Welsh alias Wood of Compton Abdale in ye said County Laborer taken before me upon othe at Rendcomb ye 11th day of Aprill 1638.

Who saith -

that about Shrovetide last, threshing at the house of Elisabeth Mace of Compton aforesaid widdow, the said Elisabeth, talking with him of Shipping mony, she saying that mony for that, & the many other payments that came daily on, one upon another, she thought she should not be able to live; he, that Examinee, answered, that however payments went, & her ability was, the King must be served; upon which her son Thomas Mace, then present, Made this reply: If it be so, that the King must have all, I would the King were dead."

Thomas Mace was examined on the following day, and, needless to say, his statement did not agree with the accusation at all: "Who examined concerning the words he hath bene accused to speake, & wish he should make, that his Majesty were dead, denieth that ever he used any such speach at all. Confesseth, that about a month or five weekes since (the Plaine time he remembreth not) Thomas Wood, working at his, this Examinee's mother's house, the said Wood told his mother that he must go to the justices for some more reliefe, to which his mother answered, that then she saw more trouble & mony must be, & he, this Examinee, added, that God's will must be done: other than these, or ought of Shipping mony, or any word at all concerning the King, he denieth to have used then, or at any other time Whatsoever."

Naturally, this denial did Thomas no good and he was committed to prison. The accusation was a grave one, and had the accused held a higher station in life than labourer in an obscure small village, committal to prison would have been only the first step towards the block. To utter such words, even in a village and in one's mother's house, in anybody's presence, seems unbelievably foolish. But even if the words were spoken, Thomas Wood could have kept silent - unless he was bent on making trouble. We know nothing more about him than that he had lived in Compton since at least 1608 when he was listed in *"Men and Armour in Gloucestershire"* as about 20 years old and of tall stature. The Maces were among the prominent and well-to do families of Compton and had been in the village for more than a century. Perhaps Thomas Welsh, alias Wood, had a score to settle with them or a personal grievance - we do not know.

Unfortunately, the documents of the Assizes are lost and with them the conclusion of this sordid story. We hope that the worst that happened was, that Thomas Mace was kept in Gloucester prison and released in 1641, when the Long Parliament declared Ship-money illegal and procured the release of all prisoners committed on account of it. He was, at any rate alive in 1649, when he is named in his mother's will as executor.

In one respect Compton still suffers from Thomas' misfortune, for according to village tradition, it is the cause of the loss of the inn. It is true that one Thomas Mace is mentioned as the rector's farmer and innkeeper, and another in 1608 just as innkeeper, and there is no mention of the disappearance of the inn in any document to gainsay the tradition, so it may well be that Thomas Mace's collision with the authorities, followed as it was by years of civil war - and the prevalence of the Puritan spirit - led to the closure of the inn.

Nobody knows where Compton's inn stood, though it is said that the barn at Lower Farm now occupies the site. But the Maces had nothing to do with this farm. As long as they were the rector's farmers they lived at Rectory Farm, now known as the Manor House, and the inn, which might have developed from the church ale house, would have been on or near this farm. There used to be an open shed, attached to the Manor House garden and now demolished, which was known as the Swan. Was this otherwise inexplicable name the last echo of the long-vanished inn?

They are all gone: the inn, the shed and even its name, and the nearest place to get a pint of beer today is the Puesdown Inn on the A 40, one and a half long miles away.

Thursday night is club night, however, and the Village Hall bar is open - though for members of the Compton Abdale Social Club and their guests only.

When Thomas Mace was taken to prison, many a man may have remembered with unease a word or two he should not have spoken and would hope were forgotten. What happened to Thomas could happen to anybody, for who did not grumble unless he were an ardent royalist? But why should the villagers support the king? He was remote from their lives; his tax collectors, however, were not, and payments "that came daily on one upon the other" and the hated Ship-money were their lot. The lord of the manor usually decided on whose side his tenants had to be, but in Compton he was non-resident and his influence hardly counted. What of the minister, next to the lord, the most influential man in the village? Do we know anything about him? Very little, but enough to learn where he stood.

Henry Galpen was curate of Compton from at least 1616 to about 1638, during the years of tension and conflict between the king, the higher clergy and the Puritans, when nobody could avoid taking one side or the other. When Archbishop Laud imposed his High Church regime in 1633, every minister had to conform to strict rules or lose his living. He had to wear vestments, he was not to preach against any particular person and no longer than one hour, and only in his own cure; he had to use the cross in baptism and the ring in marriage, move the Communion table to the upper end of the Chancel and provide rails. He had to remove muckhills, sinks and sawpits from the churchyard and exhort his audience to obedience. Also he had to read the Book of Sports at every service. To be quite certain that it had been read, the churchwardens had to certify the reading and send their certificates to the Archdeacon.

This Book of Sports had its origin in the Declaration of Sports of 1618. King James had been presented with a petition complaining about Puritan magistrates and ministers who tried to suppress the people's Sunday sport. The Puritans took a stern view of amusements, particularly on the Lord's Day. They endeavoured to make it a day of worship and rest and nothing else. Sunday had never before been treated with such solemnity. Attendance at church in the morning had, of course, been compulsory, but the rest of the day was spent in games or social gatherings.

King James decided to rescue the traditional Sunday and, incidentally, to restrict preaching, which was the Puritans' strong point, to one service in the morning, and so he issued the Declaration of Sports: no person should be "disturbed, letted or discouraged from any lawful recreation, such as dancing, either of men or women, archery for men, leaping, vaulting, or any such harmless recreations, nor having May games, Whitsun-ales, or morrisdances, or setting up of May poles, or other sports therewith used...and that women should have leave to carry rushes to the church, for the decorating of it according to old custom". All this, however, is allowed only if a service had been attended in the morning.

The effect of this moderate, unrevolutionary and perhaps even well-meaning admonition was totally unexpected, at least by the king. There was no relief and no rejoicing. On the contrary, the Declaration of Sports was so much resented and the king became so unpopular, that for once he bowed to the spirit of the time, quietly withdrew and left the people to the "excessive gloom" of their Sunday.

Undeterred by King James' failure, Archbishop Laud revived the "Dancing Book" and forced it on the clergy.

104

Many ministers who had borne with the many restrictions and harrassments could not agree to read the Book of Sports and so to recommend the desecration of the Lord's Day. They resigned their livings for their conscience' sake and condemned themselves and - what must have been worse for them - their families to a life of poverty and misery, leaving behind their shepherdless flocks.

Only a deeply committed and dedicated Puritan would take such a step, and the "sabbatical" ministers who did so are to be admired for the strength of their conviction. But not everybody is called to be a martyr and we cannot blame the Rev. Galpen for not making such a sacrifice. He stayed in his parish. Yet the Archdeacon's Visitations reveal that he was far from being an ardent High Churchman. He is regularly presented - and once severely reprimanded - for not saying prayers on Wednesday, Friday and Saturday, and for not catechising on Sunday afternoon, as had been ordered by Laud.

105 As for the Book of Sports, we have no evidence that he may or may not have read it, at any rate, the churchwardens - one of them being William Mace, Thomas' brother - were so lax in sending in their certificates that they were presented as regularly as their minister. Moreover, in 1636, three years after the Laudian rules came into force, they were censured for not "placeing the Communion table north and south at ye Upper end of ye chancel" and were ordered "to raile it in before

106 Candlemas". This was no small matter. Great bitterness was caused by this removal of the Communion table and many communicants refused to come up to the rails to receive the Sacrament. Several hundred were fined or excommunicated for this refusal, and it is surprising that nothing worse than being presented to the Diocesan Court happened to the minister and churchwardens of Compton Abdale. Their safety

lay in numbers; they were not alone in their lack of enthusiasm for the new regime. Nearly every parish in the Deanery of Cirencester was presented for failing to deliver certificates, though Henry Galpen was by far the most recalcitrant of ministers.

So Compton was not exactly a citadel of Archbishop Laud's High Church or its political equivalent, royalism, and Thomas Mace was not a lonely rebel. But because his alleged words were treasonable and not just grumblings about Ship-money, Compton acquired the distinction of being enshrined in the State Papers.

The victory of the Puritans in the Civil War brought another upheaval. Archbishop Laud was executed, the bishops were impeached and the episcopalian clergy were now in the position the Puritans had been in before the Revolution. Nevertheless, Cromwell was as tolerant as political circumstances allowed and there was no persecution on religious grounds alone. Soon after he became Lord Protector in 1654, he instituted Commissions to examine candidates for ordination. These Triers, as they were called, were resented by the remnants of the episcopalians, but even Cromwell's enemies had to admit that these examinations did much to

107 raise the standard of the parish clergy. Their principles were of course strictly Puritan and William Beckett was admittted to the vicarage of Compton Abdale in 1658 "approved, for the grace of God in him, his holy and unblamable conversation, as also for his knowledge and utterance, able and fit to preach the gospel".

He may have been appointed in answer to a petition signed by ten parishioners of Compton Abdale to the

108 Committee of Compounding "asking grant to pay a faithful minister, their then minister had but £7 per annum, had never

preached in twenty years, often absent, months together". The stipend of the curate had not been increased since 1565, when Thomas Mace undertook to find a good curate and to pay him £7 as part of the rent of Rectory Farm. The curate depended on the good will of the Dean and Chapter of Bristol's tenant farmer and could suffer if he was not on amiable terms with him, as in 1605, when Elisabeth Mace was presented for

109 "detayning the clerk's wages". These financial circumstances were not likely to attract good men, and so there is no curate in 1584, and in 1599 it is noted that William Brown, curate, "serveth the Communion, not being ordained nor licenced". Henry Galpen's was an exceptionally long ministry; perhaps he had means of his own to supplement his poor stipend; he could not have suppported himself on the £7 per annum. John Brown is mentioned as curate in 1642, but in 1650 the Parliamentary Survey of Church livings finds "that there is no minister there, the maintenance being but a stipend of seven pounds per annum. There are about 12 families in it".

When William Beckett was admitted, it was "ordered by His Highness the Lord Protector and the Councell that it be recommended to the Trustees for maintenance of Ministers to settle upon the Minister of Compton in the County of Gloucester an Augmentacion of £40 per annum for the better

110 maintenance and encouragement". The Committee for plundered ministers specified in detail how £30 should be made up of various tithes, the remaining £10 being a charge on Rectory Farm. It came to light then, that the lease of the farm had expired "some years since" and that the owners, the Dean and Chapter of Bristol, were apparently not even aware of it.

"Any publishing of disaffection to the present government by conversation, preaching, writing, or otherwise; frequent playing of cards, profaning the sabbath, the encouragement of Whitsum-ales, wakes, morris-dances, may poles, and stage plays; the frequent use of the Common Prayer,

111 and all reviling of the strict profession of godliness" - these things were declared as scandalous in a minister soon after Mr. Beckett was appointed. He would surely have passed this stricter test as well, for he was a convinced Puritan, as he proved in 1662 when Charles II consented to the Act of Uniformity. He then resigned his living as one of two thousand Puritan ministers who once more went into the wilderness. Calamy says of him that "he was originally a tradesman, and no scholar; but it was not on that account he was ejected. He was a good man, and

112 useful to many of the meaner sort of people". We hope that he could go back to his trade and so escape the destitution which was the lot of most of the expelled ministers. He fled to Winchcombe when he was ejected and was licensed to teach

113 "Congregationals" there in his own house.

We know nothing about Compton's fate during the Civil War, but this does not mean that the village escaped unscathed. There were clashes of the opposing parties not far away, at Sudeley Castle and in Cirencester, and Compton cannot have been overlooked entirely by the armies and their foraging parties who moved about the Cotswolds. Yet there are no traditions or stories connected with the Civil War. The skeletons which were found at Spring Hill and promptly proclaimed to be the result of a skirmish between Roundheads and Cavaliers, were not examined by archaeological experts, and the Civil War, like the Black Death, comes all too readily to mind to explain bones and burials.

"Whole in mind and sycke in body. . . ."

We have met with quite a number of Compton people from 1400 onward and learnt something of their rising prosperity and their changing fortunes, but it is still difficult to picture them in their daily life and to relate them to our village. It is good to know that William Hawkyns could afford a new house; it would be even better if we knew what "mod. cons.", Mistress Hawkyns enjoyed in "Barkar" and without doubt, showed off to her friends, who would do the same in their turn. It is the details of domestic life which would give substance to the shadowy figures of whom we know nothing but their names, and perhaps even to the nameless cottagers who are in danger of being overlooked and forgotten.

The most prolific source for such information are the Inventories: the lists of a deceased person's possessions, room by room, of his or her house. Unfortunately, few of them survive for Compton, and none before 1685. There are, however, a number of wills which, though nothing like as detailed as inventories would be, still provide some glimpses of domestic life, at least of people who possessed enough to make a last will worthwhile. There were others to whom Walter Palmer's will of 1543 would apply too: " My Solle to God my Saver and Hys Blessyd and Glorys Mother and to all the Company of Hewn. To be buried yn Church yerd of Comton Abdall." and nothing else.

John Rogers' will of 1498 is the earliest one and we have quoted it before. As a man's will - as the majority of wills are -

it gives few domestic details. Besides, he leaves a wife, though no children, who would need "all the rest of my goods". There would be a bed to spare from now on, and so he can leave his sister Joan"a bed, 20 sheep and a cow".

But this was not a matter of just a spare bed; beds were a luxury, and if proof were needed that the Rogers could afford the rising standard of living and comfort which by now had reached the villages, sister Joan's bed would provide it. As late as 1577, William Harrison, a country parson, comments on the changing bed, of which he does not altogether approve and describes the customs of our fathers of sleeping on a pallett of straw, covered only with a sheet, under coverlets made of dogswain or hop harlots, a good round log under their heads instead of a bolster. If the good man of the house had a flock mattress he thought himself as well lodged as the lord of the village. Pillows, they said, were meet only for women in childbed. Unfortunately, John Rogers does not elaborate and we do not know if Joan enjoyed the comfort of a lordly flock mattress. One would have thought that the ingenuity and thrift of the housewife of those days must have contrived some sort of blanket or quilt from the left-over and substandard wool which must have been available, even if most of the shearing went to the wool market.

The pair of sheets which another Joan Rogers leaves nearly 50 years later conforms so much to our notion of a bed that it is hard to realise that this pair of sheets represents another stage of sleeping luxury. Robert Rocke leaves to his third son, Robert, in 1597 "one beadstead, standing in John Colett's house in Stow with a featherbed, a feather bolster and all other furniture belonging to the same (and one little brass pot)". "All other furniture belonging to the same" perhaps means curtains, and the whole seems to have been a four-poster, well fortified against draughts and cold. William Harrison would have frowned on so much softness and decadence. But the last word in bedding is left to Elisabeth Mace who in 1649 bequeaths to her daughter Elinor "the best bed and beadstead, such bolsters, pillows, sheets, blankets and coverlets as is thereto belonging", and Elinor is so much better off than poor Ann Hathaway who was only left Shakespeare's second best bed, surely the most famous bed in history.

The Joan Rogers who died in 1545 was the widow of William Rogers who rented Rectory Farm from the last Prior of St. Oswald in 1530. Hers was rather an unusual position, for the rent agreement names her as equal partner with her husband and contains a clause that the surviving partner can dispose of the remaining years of the lease by last will and testament. So, Joan Rogers "gives and resigns the years of my parsonage to Thomas Townsend and Thomas Mace and the years of the court land" "and my goods movable", and she makes them her full executors "to have and occupy my goods as they think best". To Lawrence Mace goes the tithe on his house "for the years of my taking", and the tithe on a yardland in the court field.

Joan Rogers died childless too, and so she leaves to her friends personal belongings which otherwise her family would have inherited: to Elisabeth Hall a pair of sheets and "my gowne and my red peticote", to Katharin Ardwey "my best kyrtyll and my whyte peticote, and my black cowe", to Agnes Wade "my harness gyrdyll and a red kyrtyll", to Elene Cappar a "kercheve and an apurne". Thomas Townsend, Thomas Mace and Lawrence Mace each get three spoons. Lawrence Mace has also "ye elder potte and six pewter vessel". John Mace is left 2 sheep and a calf, Richard Ardwey 6 acres of barley, William Ardwey a sheep and Richard Wright a heifer.

It is strange that the will does not name a single Rogers; one could think that Joan is the last one of this family which had been in the village since 1400 and probably longer, but in fact Rogers appear in the village records until 1742. The main beneficiaries are the Maces. Thomas Townsend is not mentioned any more in connection with Rectory Farm and Thomas Mace is the Rector's farmer for the remaining 15 years of the lease and then in 1565, makes his own rent agreement with the Dean and Chapter of Bristol who had succeeded the Prior as landlords, against the surrender of the previous indenture and a great sum of money.

Judging from this and other wills, the Maces must have been very popular in the village. No other name recurs so frequently, either as executor or beneficiary. James Midwinter, for instance, leaves the residue of his goods to Lawrence Mace, after numerous bequests to the children of his friends. He mentions neither wife nor children of his own, so he was a bachelor or a widower. Bequests to friends and their children are frequent; Compton was a friendly village, even in those days.

The Maces seem to have come to the village comparatively late. They are not mentioned before 1543, when Lawrence Mace signs the collection against the Turks as churchwarden. There is an abundance of Thomases and several Lawrences and it is impossible to unravel their relationship. The earliest Thomas is the Rector's farmer, another died in 1603, one is the innkeeper and is aged about 50 in 1608, one dies in 1625, making his father Thomas, who presumably is then among the living, overseer of his will, and finally there is the Thomas who gets into difficulties over Ship Money in 1638. One is grateful for the occasional George, Edmund, William and John, not to mention Epaphroditus.

Thomas, who died in 1625, had progressed towards the state of yeoman. He had bought free land, the rent of which his wife is to enjoy "towards the breeding up of his children" until the eldest, William, comes of age. The heir of the free land is to pay his two brothers and his sister £20, presumably as compensation.

We have met Thomas' widow, Elisabeth, and his son, Thomas, in a previous chapter in connection with Ship-money. Elisabeth then, in 1638, thought that "with that, and the many other payments that came daily on, one upon another, she should not be able to live". But despite all her worries and troubles, she lived another eleven years and she did not die destitute either, as her will shows. Her and Thomas' four children, all having survived the hazards of childhood, were grown up when their mother died in 1649. William had taken over his father's free land and receives only a token sum of 10s. His little son, Epaphroditus, his grandmother's godson, is given a ewe and a lamb, worth 10s. Edmund had £10, one little brass pot, one little kettle and one pair of Hempen sheets. It is Elinor, the only daughter, who receives the lion's share of the named bequests. In addition to the aforementioned best bed "Also I give unto my said daughter the biggest kettle and the skillet with the skimmer. And also 2 great pewter platters, one can, one salt cellar. One pair of Holland sheets, 2 pairs of Hempen sheets. To be given within one year of my decease. Should she die within this yeare, the executor keeps half her share. Also I give more to my daughter Elinor: one chest, one chair, the biggest drink barrel and churn, one broad cloth." All this is additional to "three score pounds of good and lawful money of England". So Elinor is well provided for. We do not know whether she was just her mother's favourite, or whether there was a special reason for this provision. Thomas is the

executor and all other goods and chattels, unnamed and undisposed, are given into his power to dispose of.

There are a few more bequests at the end of Elisabeth Mace's will: "10s to the church to buy some table cloth or any other needful or necessary therein wanting. 6s 8d to the minister that shall pronounce my funeral sermon, one mark (13s 4d) to the poor", and last but truly not least: "£5 to be bestowed upon a terment at my funerall", a terment being a funeral service of some pomp. We may wonder what her heirs thought of her wishes, but, no doubt, she was buried in style, the poor were duly grateful for their 13s 4d and enjoyed the £5 worth of terment.

Joan Rogers wished to be buried in the Chancel, the most sacred and honoured part of the church; Elisabeth Mace provides for her terment; Ann Cassould in 1685 requests her executor to "provide me with a coffin and to bury me in decent manner", a modest enough request to our minds, but burial in a coffin was only just becoming established for all, not merely the rich, at this time, the end of the 17th century, and Ann Cassould may have thought it prudent to remind her executor and mention her coffin specially; however, she wants only 40s. to be spent on her funeral. She is yet another childless woman, or her children died in infancy, and her bequests go to her nephew, Henry Young, her sisters and Mary and Elisabeth Wright. It is now customary to dispose of the remaining years of a lease by will, instead of handing them back into the hands of the lord, and so Henry Young has his aunt's house for the term remaining. Her sister, Margaret, is left 50s. with the proviso: "for her only use and not that her husband shall have any right or propriety to it". This, or a similar condition, is made whenever a married sister or daughter is left money, for without it, the legacy would automatically become the husband's property. Only since the Married Woman's Property Act of 1870, has a married woman had a right to her own money. Conversely, Mary Greenway will receive £60 in the will of her Father, Josiah Dyer, only "at the time her husband pays my executor the money due to me on bond." and some wills stipulate that the children's share should be paid out if and when their mother remarries, that is, before her property becomes that of her second husband.

Ann Cassould's will continues: Sister Margaret shall also have the white "peticote" "with a green ribbon at the tayle" two...(illegible) coats and an apron, Sister Elisabeth a "peticote" with an apron, another apron and "my box of small linen at Harvill at John Rogers' house." Another relation is even left her old "peticote". Edmund Cassould receives her gold ring - and this is the only time in a long series of wills that any precious metal or jewellery is mentioned. Brass pots and kettles, great and small, occur frequently, also pewter platters, and one iron pot (in 1795), but no silver or gold.

In this same year, 1685, an account of the will of Thomas Mace Sen. was given by his wife, Mary, because of a dispute over it. The will itself has not survived. The sum total of Thomas' goods, money etc., was £123 2s 6d. After paying expenses and a few debts, Mary Mace was left with £68 1s 0d. One item of the expenses is £3 15s 0d, heriot to the Lord of the Manor; it is surprising to find the manor still in working order to this extent at this late stage. Thomas Mace's will might have given us a few more details about his family and the disposal of his goods, but its loss is compensated by the inventory of his house. This is the oldest inventory we have, also the most detailed, and gives a good picture of one of the wealthier and bigger houses in the village. We can take this, and Lawrence Wright's inventory of the same year, which is nearly identical,

as characteristic of the houses of farmers who, in the next century, like to call themselves yeomen.

Inventory of Thomas Mace Senior, who died March 2nd 1684.

The writing and spelling of this inventory are atrocious, and despite the kind and patient help by the librarian in deciphering it, some question marks remain.

Wearing Apparel

In his bedchamber:
2 beds, 1 old coffer and all that belongs to them

In the chamber over the Hall:
2 old beadsteads, 2 old coffers, one linen (?) wheel, one (fire) dowser (?), one bushel and other lumber.

In the Hall:
One table board and frame, 1 joyne stool, one old form, one old cupboard, 3 old chairs.
One old bacon Park, two flitches and $1/2$ of bacon.
2 Store piggs
One pair of ondirons, one Spit, one Ironbar, one fireshovel and tongues, 1 pair of bellows, 1 stool, one frying pan.
One little brasspot, 3 old kettles (?) and Candlesticks, one old flagon, 2 little plattes, And some pewter spoons, one simer (similar?)

In the Buttery:

> 2 barrels, 3 shelves, 2 benches, 1 Churn, 1 Cream pot, 2 bottles,
> 2 cheese fats (?) and other lumber.

In the kitchen:

> 1 hoare (?), 1 Cheese press, 1 fate (?), 2 cowls, 1 pail, 2 buckets, 3 old sieves, 4 logers (?), 4 lockes, one woollen wheel and other lumber.

In the Barn and about the House:

> One quarter of wheat, six bushels of barley, six bushels of malt.

In the stable:

> 2 old horses - at 10s. a piece, 2 young ones - at £4 a piece, with ploughs, carts, harness, and all implements for husbandry.

Corn growing in the fields: 27 acres barley
                                8 acres of wheat
                                12 acres of Oats and pease

One hundred and one sheep for store
Fine Pudder (Fodder) Cow and 3 yearling calves
One Pood (?) Saddle, one pod, 4 old bags, one male.

Lawrence Wright's inventory is much like Thomas Mace's, his house similarly has a hall, 2 chambers, kitchen and buttery. If the Wright inventory has no spinning wheels, it lists

a spice mortar. There are 4 "puder" cows, of which he leaves one "which Cow is named by the name of Sprunt" to his loving wife, Kattron, as well as a house, sublet to Robert Hathaway, and half of what is known as Brassington's yardland, and "what household goods is needful and convenient for her for and during her natural life", not to mention "the bed and bedstead whereon I lie with all things thereunto belonging." The rest of his wordly belongings goes to his six children.

The furnishing of these houses is certainly not what we would consider luxurious or even adequate, but it is quite up to the standard of home comfort in the 17th century. Bedsteads are evidently the main and most important furniture and so we understand why they play such a prominent part in wills, for there are few in the nearly 50 Compton wills in the Gloucester Diocesan Records in which beds are not mentioned. Tables consist of board and frame, that is, they are trestle tables which have the great advantage that they can be dismantled and stacked, so that they are out of the way when not required. Rooms were small and there were few of them, and space was precious.

The coffers and chests take the place of wardrobes, and mirrors are not mentioned. Chairs are becoming more numerous at the end of the 17th century, while previously, stools and settles had been the usual seating furniture. Mary Corbett's will of the same date (1685) first mentions a rug, but in the context of: "my best bed and bolster, one blanket and the best rug", and likewise from Thos. Jaynes' inventory (1727), where it says: "one bed, 2 blankets, one rug, one pair of sheets", it seems that these rugs were bedspreads rather than floor coverings.

The makers of the inventories who valued the contents of the houses had - for us - the unfortunate habit of listing only the main furniture and then adding: "...and all other things belonging to this room" or "...and the rest of the lumber" and "Firewood and Other Trumpery about the House". We wish we could visualise the trumpery; it might dispel the impression the inventories give that those houses were sparsely furnished and bare of comfort, for it is the "lumber" of small things that make a house into a home.

BRÍZA MÉDIA
(*Common Quaking-grass*)

Parish Registers

The keeping of registers of baptisms, marriages and burials with the names of the parties, was made compulsory in 1538. It was then also ordered that the parish provide a "sure coffer" with two locks, one for the parson and one for a churchwarden, to keep the registers safe. Compton's early registers are lost and of the copies which since 1597 had to be sent to the bishop, only a few survive. The "sure coffer" too, if it ever existed, has vanished and at present the registers are kept in a locked metal box, donated by Col. Mead. The registers start in 1722, several pages having been cut out, and the entries in the earliest foolscap parchment book are higgledy-piggledy, baptisms, marriages and burials all mixed up, just as they occurred one after another. Even after they have been separated, burials appear among the baptisms and vice versa. It happens repeatedly, too, that someone is buried years before he is born. Still, they can be arranged according to families and so give a fair, though nothing more than fair, picture of life and death in the village from 1722 on. How cautiously the registers have to be treated becomes apparent in the next century, when they can be checked against the official census. Families which - according to the parish registers - consist of parents and two children are shown by the census to be much larger; there may be four or even six children, and only the two that were born in Compton are registered. Nevertheless, there is still enough interesting information, though the registers are useless as statistics.

It is regrettable that the keepers of the records restricted themselves to the barest necessities. There is not one word of comment in the whole 250 years since 1722. When we find an entry like the following: John and Mary, children of Thomas and Mary Mustoe, buried the 3rd November 1785, we should like to know the story behind this double burial. John was 24 and Mary 20 when they died - of what? Was it an accident, a fire perhaps? We shall never know.

Fortunately, the series of wills in the Gloucester Diocesan records continue to the end of the century and bring the names of the registers to life and into relation with each other, and relation for once is the right word, for the village seems to be one big family. Within three generations, intermarriage makes nearly everybody into a son-in-law, a grandchild, uncle or cousin of somebody else. This, however, may not be a new feature of Compton life; in the absence of registers we have no means of checking. But on the few occasions when last wills mention a relationship, they confirm that there was a network of Maces and Wrights, of Wrights and Youngs and Corbetts and Cassoulds, already before 1722.

To judge by the burial register, the years 1727-29 must have been years of sorrow and anxiety for Compton. John Rogers was buried on 4th October 1727, a fortnight later John Wright was carried up the hill and laid to rest in the church. The funeral of his wife, Mary, took place exactly a month later, and Elisabeth Mace had died a few days before her. One funeral followed another throughout this winter, the following summer and into 1729. Four members of the Wright family died, and Mary Wilson's little girl, Beana, as well as two travelling men who came to the village at different times. What caused these deaths, 14 altogether in 18 months? We do not know, for as usual, the registers offer no explanation. The burials are recorded without comment. Had one or the other of the travellers, who probably were itinerant tradesmen, died first, he could be suspected of having carried an infectious disease. But they are both innocent, victims themselves, for one died in February 1728, the other in 1729.

John and Mary Wright had time to make a will, but Edmund Faulkes apparently did not. He and his wife, Mary, had died in May 1728 and the inventory of their goods and chattels reveals that they were the shopkeeper and his wife. Indeed, without the calamity of that epidemic, we should not know that there was a shop at all in Compton. It is surprising that there was one, for with Northleach so near, one might have thought shopping was done there on market days.

"This true and perfect inventory" is dated 25.10.1731, that is, 3 years after Edmund Faulkes died. What happened to and in the shop in these years is idle to speculate. Here it is:

Wearing apparel and money in purse:	£1	0s	0d
Salt		1s	0d
Ginger and Clover		1s	0d
Money in the box		8s	0d
Sugar and Currants			10d
Honey and Treackle		1s	10d
Starch and Blew		10s	0d
Seven Dozen of Laces and Thread		2s	0d
Ineles (?)		2s	0d
Cadoses (?)		3s	6d
Four papers of Buckles		4s	0d
2 pieces of Dutch Cadoes			6d
Rubbers		2s	0d
Stone Brimstone			6d
Rassom and Allom			6d
2 pair of Scales and the Weights		2s	0d
Boxes and the rest of the lumber in the shop		2s	0d

In the Kitchen:			
8 pewter dishes and a cup		3s	6d
One kettle and warming pan		3s	0d
One Table Board and Form, one Coffer		3s	6d
One Hanging Cupboard and Trencher Rack		1s	0d
In the Buttery: 2 Barrels		2s	0d
In the Inner Chamber: 3 Coffers and one Trunk		5s	0d
In the Outer Chamber:			
One bedstead, 1 pair of Hampen and the rest of the lumber	£1	0s	0d
2 sheep and 2 lambs	£1	0s	0d
Pitch and Tarr		5s	0d
One Horse Bridle, one Saddle, on male pillion		15s	0d
Four Stocks of Bees	£1	0s	0d
One pig		9s	0d
A Mortar and Pestle		6s	0d
	£5	5s	6d

If the stock of the shop does not seem very impressive to our spoiled twentieth century eyes, we have to keep in mind how much the value of money has changed and that many things which we are used to buying were made at home. As to money, Rudder gives the price of labour for 1779 as 10d a day in the winter, 1s. in the spring, 1s 6d in grass mowing, 1s 8d or 2s. for about 5 weeks at corn harvest. The churchwardens' account has an item for 1783 for the repair of the churchyard wall: George Hall - 10s. for 10 days digging stones. The 2s. worth of luxury goods like laces and thread do not appear so insignificant any more.

For the labouring man, £1 represents 3 weeks of work, and this scale of values has to be applied to the sums which are left in wills. They show how rich the wealthy were, and how great the gulf between "the poor" and the people who made the wills. The greatest sum given to a single person was the £60 which Elisabeth Mace left to her daughter, Elinor, while Edmund inherited a mere £10. (William, we may remember, had the free land and Thomas the residue). To quote some other random examples, Lawrence Wright in 1684 left altogether £60 to his children, Thomas Young £52 in 1620, (another) Lawrence Wright in 1710, £152. He was Edmund Faulkes' maternal grandfather and left £31 to his daughter, Hanna Faulkes, in addition to the inevitable "one new bed and bedstead, 1 bolster, two blankets, 1 Red Rug, the bedstead that was Isaac Joullins' and one Coffer which she shall choose." James Faulkes, her husband, however, "shall have no power to receive legacy"; he gets 1s.

What did Hanna Faulkes, or for that matter, the other women who were left money "for their own use", do with it? Did they really spend it on themselves? It must at any rate have given them some freedom and independence while it lasted. Did their husbands resent it? It is annoying that silence is the only answer to these questions, and it is a great temptation to leave the confines of documentation and to supply colour and background from imagination. These wills and registers give just glimpses of personal relations, of family complications, and sometimes of tragedy; they provide characters, some as colourful as the Panter family, and all this information could be woven into stories which might be

imaginary, but need not be untruthful. This, fortunately, is not our business and the temptation has been resisted, besides, the 18th century is only one of quite a few since Compton's beginning and must be kept in proportion.

Another epidemic must have occurred in 1742, when there are 12 burials in one year, the highest figure ever. Two families were particularly hard hit: the Wheelers and the Freemans. Only Mary Wheeler, aged eight and her baby sister, Ann, survive, we do not know who cared for them, the registers do not mention any Wheelers after this catastrophic year. Mary Freeman was buried on Christmas Day, John Freeman, a relation, the following day, Little Betty died in January, and the father is left with baby Richard. Sarah Dean lost her husband just before Christmas and is left with 3 children. Elinor Mustoe, too, was widowed and was to lose both her daughters within the next few years, one aged 17 and the other 18. Two Elisabeth Rogers died in the same year. They may have been mother and daughter, and Elisabeth's three base-born children, as they were so meanly called, are alone. We can only guess at the fate of these fatherless orphans. Sara, at eleven would have been considered old enough to be taken into some household as servant. The other two, William Cook, seven, and Betty Cook, five, may have been absorbed into the Cook family otherwise they would have been a charge on the parish. Though a Cook is not mentioned until 1761, this is no proof that they did not exist in 1742, and in the next century the family is so numerous that its members defy any attempt to put them in order or to bring them into relation with each other.

The incidence of illegitimate births in Compton corresponds to the national pattern. They were rare in the 16th and 17th centuries, increased sharply in the second half of the

118

18th and were most numerous in the 19th, a pattern for which a satisfactory explanation has not been found. Enclosure, the demolition of cottages and the resulting poverty and overcrowding have been blamed, but, in Compton at any rate, Enclosure did not take place until 1805 and nothing is known of demolition of cottages by the landowners.

One of the supposedly rare cases occurred in 1603 when at every Archdeacon's Visitation, the churchwardens presented Elinor Jefferies for having a bastard. Yet she is not the only one in the deanery of Cirencester to have committed this "Offence against God and Man"; there are three in Eastleach Turville, and in Chedworth, Elisabeth Holland is presented for "harbouring Ann Dunhill being delivered of a bastard child and suffering her to depart.." Poor Elinor Jefferies, however, has to do public penance, and though the father of the child is known, he is "one John Rogers", it is only the mother who has to suffer the full brunt of Church discipline which bears down on this, and the other carnal sin of fornication, with Old Testament wrath - St. John, Chapter 8, might never have been written.

Significantly, it is Bishop Hooper's strict regime which provides the example of how the Consistory Court dealt with these offenders. Margaret Haynes, Elisabeth Freeman, Robert Young and William Bustede of Compton Abdale with Richard Redwood of Northleach, appear before the Court in February 1552/3, confess and are enjoined not to consort and to do public penance - the men in their parish church only, Elisabeth Freeman has also to stand in the market place of Northleach on 3 market days, in a white sheet with a piece of paper pinned to her front and back pronouncing her sin. As penance in church, the sinners have to come up to the minister at the end of the service, bareheaded and barefoot, wearing a white sheet and confess: "I..do in the Presence of God and this Congregation confess and acknowledge with shame and confusion of Face that, not having the Fear of God before mine eyes and being seduced by the Temptation of the Devil and mine own filthy lusts, I have greatly offended Almighty God and endangered my own Soul and given an evil Example and Scandal to all good Christians for which I am heartily sorry and do humbly beg pardon of God and this Congregation for the same and I do herewith promise (God Almighty assisting me with his Grace) never to offend in like manner again but to live chastly hereafter, beseeching this Congregation to pray with me and for me saying: Our Father..."

This is what, eighty years later, Elinor Jefferies had to do; penance in the market place is not mentioned. The other methods of dealing with the illegitimate mother - prison and public flogging - are not recorded for Compton. By the second half of the 18th century, the moral indignation had worn off and the economic aspect of the problem was the most important - the maintenance of mother and child fell on the parish of her settlement unless the father could be made responsible. Maintenance seems not to have been a great difficulty in Compton. There were 15 illegitimate births between 1730 and 1800, Elisabeth Rogers accounts for three of them between 1731 and 1737, the others came with increasing frequency from 1764 onwards. Of these 15 children, 9 bear a surname as their second name, and this must surely imply admitted paternity, for a family would hardly consent to give its name to a base-born child without compelling reason. Once paternity was admitted, the churchwardens had power to make the father pay for the upkeep of his child. Also, to prevent the charge on the parish, the woman should be married before the birth of the child and the overseers or churchwardens often used considerable pressure or even bribes to achieve this aim. There were five belated weddings in Compton between 1768 and 1800, but as we have only the figures in the registers to go on, we do not know if the churchwardens had to apply pressure or not.

It is obvious from the names of some of the mothers, and more often from that of the children, that it was not only the poor who created the problem of illegitimacy. Young, Goodrich and Dyer are prominent names in 18th century Compton and they all appear as second names. Edmund Goodrich was tenant of Compton Farm and churchwarden and, according to Rev. H. Morgan, he gave a bell to the church. His successor on the farm was John Cook, hardly a poor man; his family name appears no fewer than three times as second name.

What was the fate of these fifteen children? Three died in infancy, one at 10 years, four grow up, marry and stay in Compton, the other seven disappear from the records as soon as they are born. The one best provided for certainly was Thomas Young Dyer, Susanna Dyer's son. His father was Thomas Young, the son of Thomas Young "of this parish yeoman", whose beautifully lettered tombstone of grey slate lies between the pulpit and the organ. Thomas Young Junior married Elisabeth Dyer in 1774, and two years later, Susanna Dyer's son was born. Thomas Young had no other children, only three stepchildren, for his wife, Elisabeth, had been Samuel Dyer's widow. Thomas Young died in 1782 when his son was six years old. In his will, he leaves him all his wordly goods, "all my Freehold and Leasehold Messuages, Lands etc. and all other my personal estate of whatever nature or kind". He wants an inventory made and his belongings sold, the money to be invested for Thomas Young Dyer's benefit. "To

Elisabeth, my wife = £5, to be paid within one year of my decease.". This is all Elisabeth Young is left by her second husband. A curious and most single-minded last will and testament.

It is generally agreed that "in the old days", families were enormous, infant mortality fearsome, women died in childbed and hardly anybody grew older than 40 or so. Do the parish registers confirm this popular belief? It has been pointed out before, that the usefulness of the registers is limited, that errors and omissions are frequent and therefore no cast iron statistics can be produced, only a few observations supported by the most reliable figures obtainable.

Approximately 297 children were baptised between 1722 and 1800, in families of varying size. There are 25 families with 3 or fewer children, however, for 11 of them the registers record the early death of either father, mother or both parents. How many of the remaining 14 families were, in fact, of small size or moved from Compton, is impossible to say. At the other end of the scale are the Dyers, Lawrence with 13 children and later, Josiah with 15. However, they are exceptional.

There are: 5 families of 9 children
2	"	"	8	"	
5	"	"	7	"	
9	"	"	6	"	
4	"	"	5	"	
7	"	"	4	"	

For what these numbers are worth - they show that families were larger than now, but perhaps not so large as commonly thought.

Josiah Dyer's first wife died with her fifth child, his

second wife, Hester, had a baby every two years, ten in all, and all but one survived (according to the registers); their mother lived to be 90 and died in 1832. Only one of the fifteen is registered as dying in childhood, but Josiah's will of 1795 mentions only eleven surviving children, three disappeared without record - so much for our statistics.

Josiah died when his eldest child was 30 and his youngest six, and his will shows how well he provided for his big family, and that he had the means to do so. Hester, his wife, has "the westernmost cottage at a place called Small Hope with appertunances for life and those 2 cottages and tenements with the blacksmith shop and quit rent from Anthony Harris situate at place called Rudgeway for life", also the furniture of the room "where I sleep at the time of my decease", another bed with its furniture, one large brass kettle, one brass pot, one iron pot, 2 barrels, 4 chairs and 2 cowls or tubs.

His son, Josiah, had all the rest of the real estate in Compton Abdale called Hill Hay, and the rest of the goods and chattels. The family is to go on living in the house and not be turned out by the executors; 2 tons of coal yearly are to be delivered to them, carriage free, by the executors during Hester's natural life. Each of the seven daughters have £60, William and Thomas have £40, and John £30.

Smallhope is one of the few places which can be identified in present day Compton though it was re-named Landamere a few years ago; Rudgeway is dimly remembered but cannot be located and Hill Hay is completely forgotten.

119   Elisabeth Dyer, Josiah's first wife, was one of only three women who died in childbed, another one is Mary Eden, so Robert Eden's experience of losing first his infant son and then his wife, together with the new baby, all within 15 months, is a

Smallhope. First mentioned in Josiah Dyer's will of 1795.

hard one, even by 18th century standards. Many more women die in early middle age than in childbed; about fifteen families out of forty lose their mothers when their youngest children are between one and ten years old. The registers are too defective to say whether the mortality of the men corresponded to that of the women. Of only three can it be said with certainty that they died in their thirties.

Out of the 297 children baptised, 24 died as infants, and 10 in childhood - even if these figures are not absolutely correct, they are correct enough to be relevant. There is no pattern in the occurrence of infant mortality; Harry and Phyllis Wright lose three of their seven children before they are five, John and Mary Taylor lose two out of four; on the other hand, families of four, six or even eight, are raised without loss. Some large families may, and do lose one or two babies, but it is not the large families only who suffer.

Did anybody survive the hazards of infancy, childhood and early middle age? Some did, indeed, and the record of longevity for the 18th century is as good as for the 19th. Eleven people born before 1775 reached the age of 86 and over, of these, two were 90, one 91, two 93, and James Casswell, at 95, was only one year short of being the oldest ever - as far as records go - in Compton. Only four of those born after 1775, including the 19th century, were over 90 when they died, one of them, Margaret Lockey, who died in 1953 at the age of 96, was the longest lived Comptonian on record.

That iron pot and the 2 tons of coal in Josiah Dyer's will bring a new note into the world of brass and pewter. They signify the change, imperceptible perhaps at first, to the age which we are pleased to call modern. Another few years and the open fields will disappear, the lord of the manor becomes the landowner, the Common private property, and the end of the old order will be made manifest.

Now, before the manor is extinguished officially by Private Act of Parliament, is perhaps the right moment to look back, if not over the whole nine hundred years of the manor, then over the four hundred in which we have accompanied some of the people of Compton, since that first compotus allowed us a glimpse of them. It is a period of time long enough to observe the mobility of population or/and the durability of families.

The compotus of 1400 mentions nine names, of which five re-appear in 1441 while five new ones are added. In 1543, all but one of these have been replaced by new names. We have no means of knowing whether the families which are not mentioned anymore have died out or moved away, or have just sunk in the social scale and merged with the anonymous sub-

tenants and cottagers whom the records ignored. If they lived quietly and did not come to the attention of one court or the other, they might be overlooked for generations. It is the conflict with authority, the law suits and other irregularities which provide a great deal of the records and knowledge of the past. We cannot conclude, therefore, that whoever is not mentioned, did not exist.

Theoretically, the population of the manor was strictly controlled and could neither leave nor enter the manor without the lord's permission and the acknowledgement of the Manor Court, and any change should be reflected in the compoti or the Court Rolls. But there is no reference to leaving or entering in any manor document of the 15th century. The late Court Rolls of Henry VIII's time, however, could make one think that the manor still had control over the movement of people, for there John and Richard Hale, who then live in Hawling, acknowledge they are *nativeis* of the manor of Compton and pay chevage, and John Smythe and John Brushe are presented for harbouring strangers. Yet a few years later, in 1551, when Thomas Mace sues for tithes, only one of his six witnesses is described as "of Compton" without any qualification, the other five had lived in the village for only a number of years: John Fyfield, aged sixty, for thirty years; Edmund Adams, aged forty, for seventeen years; Richard Rogers, aged sixty, for forty years; Thomas Garne, aged thirty, for twenty years, and Thomas Young, aged thirty, for sixteen years. As they moved into the village, people presumably moved out as well, and why only the Hale brothers had to pay chevage is difficult to see.

The Hawkyns, the Garnes and the Fyfields are mentioned in wills till the 1570s, then they disappear. The two names that appear consistently in compoti, court rolls and wills are Rogers and Young. The Rogers family is already prominent in 1400 and though they lose their prominence after 1550, they remain in the village until 1742, when the last of them, Elisabeth Rogers, dies. The Youngs are mentioned from 1583 till the end of the 18th century. Thomas Young Dyer is the last of them. We have followed the Maces from 1543 to 1685, when the last Thomas we hear of is a tenant farmer whose heriot is the last to be mentioned in Compton's manorial history. Nothing further is heard of the family until the parish registers record the burials of the last two generations between 1722 and 1763. Epaphroditus Mace, labourer, who died last, is mentioned as tenant of one of the three cottages which belonged to the Dean and Chapter of Bristol. We may wonder if he knew, or cared, that 200 years before, a Mace was tenant of the other church property, the Rector's Farm.

Richard Wright is mentioned in John Young's will of 1560, and again in 1588, when he is called R. Wright alias Glover, Lawrence is listed in *"Men and Armour in Gloustershire"* in 1608, as aged about 40, of tall stature, fit to make a pikeman. Later, we know them best when they have risen to will-making status in the first half of the 18th century.   The last of them died in 1769. The first Thomas Dyer is mentioned in 1583. In the 18th century they were "yeomen of this parish" and Thomas Dyer's tombstone is still witness to their position in the village. The last one, Lawrence Dyer, labourer, appears in the registers as father of four daughters, baptised between 1836 and 1842, but his burial is not recorded, so he may have moved away.

These five families are known to be the longest-lived in the village, known because they played a leading part in their time and left records of their existence in the compoti, in rent agreements and in their wills. But they are only a handful, spread over four centuries. There are many, many more who came and went and left no mark of their passing. Some may have stayed for generations, but many did not, and even in the 18th century only 15 families out of 38 stay for another generation, only two achieve three generations and none go any further. So, perhaps we should not take too gloomy a view of the present quick change of population, when we still have families in the village whose young generation are the fourth and fifth in Compton, and one young brother and sister who are the seventh generation from Robert Eden who came to the village in 1795.

BRYÓNIA DIÓICA
(*White Bryony*)

The Church

"The church is very small, dedicated to St. Oswald, and has nothing in it worth notice", says Rudder in his County history. He might have mentioned the 15th century timber roof, or the fact that the pillars are far from upright, but he was probably looking for tombs and monuments, and looking in vain. For Compton never had a resident lord whose family might have provided a knight in armour and his lady, or some brasses. This is a true village church and the villagers of old rest in anonymity.

There are no medieval monuments or other relics of the past, and it is indeed difficult to imagine that generations of Compton people down the centuries worshipped here and were at home in their church, and that the church existed before the Reformation. Bishop Hooper's severe hand swept away all traces of Catholic faith and worship, and if we want to know what our church looked like, we have to go to North Cerney, where the Rood Screen has been restored, and to Hayles' tiny parish church with its wall paintings.

Neither Rudder nor the other County historians refer to its situation which modern observers, if they trouble with the village at all, find remarkable. If one had the task of finding a place for the church in the village, one would certainly not choose the site high up on a steep slope. Convenience and accessibility were evidently not the guiding principles of choice. What then were they?

Ulric Daubeny in his book about "*Ancient Cotswold Churches*" , draws attention to "the continued association of one particular spot with religious observance throughout the

The Church from the Square. St. Oswald's on its hill.

120 successive ages", and to the fact that not only Normans and Saxons, but Romans and even people of the Stone Age worshipped in the same place. He gives Lower Swell churchyard and its Round Barrows as an example of pre-historic sites and Notgrove, Bisley and Daglingworth as Roman. So Compton would not be exceptional if it had retained the same sacred place that the Roman-Christians used, and perhaps pre-historic people before them. Though we have no material evidence that it was so, we do know that people have lived here continuously since the New Stone Age, and we have no reason to believe that they were less conservative in Compton than in Lower Swell. If it is too fanciful to think of Stonehenge when the early morning sun

lights up the church tower, it is at any rate, easy to believe that the sanctuary existed before the village was built, for why should the worshippers deliberately punish themselves by that stiff climb up the hillside, not to mention the men who have to carry the dead to their last resting place? They could surely have found room for the church in the valley or on one of the lesser hills, if the choice had been theirs.

Also, churches dedicated to St. Oswald are often built near a spring because of and in memory of the miracle-working spring on the battlefield of Maserfield where King Oswald was killed. One of the springs in the valley might have attracted the churchbuilders if there had not been a site whose sanctity had a greater claim.

The present church is mainly perpendicular, built in the 15th century. But it was not built entirely from new at that time. An existing church was repaired and enlarged. The tower and part of the north wall are "new", the chancel, the south wall and a short length of the north wall belong to the previous church. Yet even the older part is Gothic and there is nothing left of a Norman church, if ever there was one. This is strange, for Cotswold churches with Norman features are no rarity, and Compton, as chapel of a Saxon minster, could be expected to have had a church at a very early time. Even, if at first, it was only a modest timber structure, it would have been replaced in due course with a stone building. If anywhere, this would be the place for a Norman church, or at least some Norman features incorporated into a later church. But there is no trace of it.

The reason for the last large-scale repair and rebuilding, when the church was given the shape we know now, was subsidence of the soil, a hazard inherent in the site, an artificial platform cut into the face of a steep hill. Subsidence may have

occurred before and more than once, and may be another reason, besides the periodic restyling of churches, why there is nothing left of an early church.

After ascending steeply across the slope of the hill, the church path levels out and passes under the branches of the old yews which hide the view of the valley. It leads to the Early English porch on the north side of the church. The porch was rebuilt, too, and only the lower parts of the walls and the stone benches are original. A small crowned head, probably representing St. Oswald, is set into the porch gable. It looks

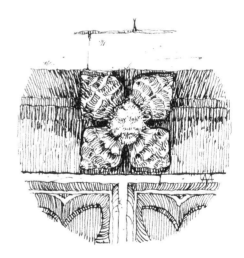

A "Green Man", on the outside, above a window in the south wall. Not uncommon but still mysterious. Pagan? Then why in, or about churches?

older than the surrounding masonry and may have been saved from the previous building. The perpendicular doorway of the church proper has a hoodmould ending in corbel heads, a woman's head wearing an almost Norman type of head gear, and a man in the "sugar bag" cap which was the fashion in Henry V's time.

So let us open the heavy door and look around the "very small church" and see if there really is "nothing worth notice". The first impression of the church is not that of smallness, but of light and airiness. But then we do not see the church as Rudder saw it, for in its present form it is essentially the Reverend Henry Morgan's church and he made it his own, a century after Rudder. Though he did not add anything to the structure - there is still only the chancel, the nave and one aisle - the changes he made make the church look larger.

The Rev. H. Morgan held the perpetual curacy of Compton Abdale from 1873 to 1893. He evidently had great affection for his church and some private means, for he spent a great deal of money on improvements. Fortunately, he realised that "the particulars inserted in the Parish Book respecting the Parish, may be interesting and valuable in future years, as the inevitable changes occasioned by death and removal blurred and finally obliterated the memory of things done within a generation. To have been permitted to see improvements made, and to have assisted in making them, must always be a satisfaction to the Incumbent of a Parish, and an encouragement to his successors, to whom and the churchwardens and the Parishioners, he dedicates his brief account of the Parish of Compton Abdale." And very grateful we are for everything he saved from oblivion, for he recorded not only what he had done, but what he knew of the history of the organ and the bells.

The late 19th century was a great time for restoring churches and there are very few in the land that escaped. This enthusiasm has often been deplored, because of the recklessness with which the restorers imposed their ideas of what ought to be on the old churches, and doubtlessly, they destroyed much that we should preserve and cherish. The Rev. Morgan acted in the spirit of his time when he "replaced two very unsightly windows in the Nave by two appropriate windows of squareheaded perpendicular type, of which the tracery was borrowed from the pattern of the small window in the Nave which the Vicar filled with stained glass in 1883." He also filled the church with light, but we might have preferred the original windows, of which unfortunately, no record exists, other than the Vicar's description. He removed them solely because he did not like them, as he does not mention that they were dilapidated.

This was only the beginning. After the south wall had been dried out by removing soil which was 18" higher than the foundations, and a stone drain was laid, "the Vicar and Parishioners repaired and refitted the Church, with new open seats, standard bracket lamps to make provision for Evening Service; and the Ecclesiastical Commissioners, as Lay Rectors restored the Chancel. The Funds for the restoration of the Nave and North Aisle were chiefly supplied by the moneys accruing at interest from a Church Bazaar organised by the previous Vicar in 1871, and the accommodation provided amounts to about 140 sittings."

Once more, the parishioners must have been dazed by the changed appearance of their church, but unlike their forebears in 1551, they probably felt nothing but pride in the change, in achieving, under the Vicar's leadership, an improved and modern church. Or were there some old-fashioned souls who hankered after the dimmer light and the homelier box pews they had been used to all their lives? If there were any, they kept their feelings to themselves. The oil lamps and the brackets were in use until 1939 when electricity was introduced. They were then removed and stored in the belfry and eventually sold at a Jumble Sale in 1966, together with the cast-iron oil-stoves which central heating had made 123   redundant in 1939.

In 1904/5 the work of restoration and improvement was completed by the Earl of Eldon, the lord of the manor. The Chancel which had cost the Church Commission £200 in 1881 was enlarged, together with the Choir, and provided with new seats. A new pulpit of carved oak, and altar table and the Vestry were added. Mr. F. W. Waller, architect of Gloucester, 124   supervised the work."

"A Bassoon for the Singers: £1 11s 5d" is one item of the churchwardens' account for 1784, and this intriguing entry makes one wonder about church music in organless days. No other instruments are ever mentioned and the choir was evidently the musical mainstay of the Service. Compton church now has only a small harmonium, but it once had an organ and the Rev. Morgan records its history. It came from the church of SS. Philip and James at Leckhampton and was bought during the incumbency of the Rev. E.S. Garrow (1847-67) by subscription of his friends. A new keyboard and a new range of pipes were added in 1886 and the pedal keyboard was restored by Mr. Morgan. A new platform was erected and the organ replaced on it in 1890 at the expense of the Vicar and parishioners. "It is hoped that the Organ, thus restored, and protected from decay and damp may be serviceable in leading the devotion of the venerable Sanctuary for many years to come." It was indeed serviceable and led the devotions until

125   1925 when an unfortunate dispute between the Vicar and the congregation kept the church locked and unused for a considerable time and the organ perished in the damp.

The Rev. Morgan and Lord Eldon certainly left their mark upon the church, and yet - what did they achieve? Certainly light and airiness and an atmosphere of ageless "modernity". There is no sense of continuity with the past. It takes an effort of the imagination to recall even a few past generations of worshippers; it is impossible to visualise the Rogers, the Hawkyns and their contemporaries coming up the hill path to their new church. But essentially it is still their church, their pillars and arches, their timber. However, much that was familiar to them has been lost in the course of progress.

126   Compton Abdale obtained one of the bells of the Priory. This tenor bell was, according to the Rev. Morgan's notes, the only bell until 1680. It was one of twenty-six in Gloucestershire which had been dedicated to the Virgin Mary and bore the Lombardic inscription: "Protege Virgo Maria quos convoco S. Maria". Or, according to another authority: "Vocor Compana Marie - Virginis Egregie". Not that it matters very much any more which is the correct text for the Rev. Morgan had the old bell recast in 1880. The original bell was cast in the foundry of Robert Hendrey, whose name appears first in the period of 1450-1500. Old bells are rare, for their precious metal attracted robbers, from even the kings, who sold and exported them as gun metal, down to the profiteers at the Dissolution who made fortunes out of church property.

"The bell mentioned was the only one till 1680", writes the Rev. Morgan, "when Mr. Gines whose name is still commemorated in the Parish by Gines Hill (now no longer known) being churchwarden, added two bells, and

Mr. Goodrich, churchwarden in 1760, gave a fourth". The four bells of unequal weight and disproportionate size, the Tenor, the old bell transferred from the Priory about 1540, being the only excellent one, continued to occupy the Belfry till 1880 when the Vicar had them taken down, and recast with new additional metal, into the present peal of six bells, by the wellknown firm of Warner & Sons, London, and rehung on a new oak frame, the Timber being valued at £40 and given by the Earl of Eldon, the Lord of the Manor". On the flyleaf of the Burial Register the Vicar records on 14th January 1881 that: "This day by the Providence of God, we had divine service and opened a new peal of bells which were then rung for the first time", that 3.0.18 of new metal was added to the metal of the old bells, and that the frame was made and the bells rehung by Messrs. Savoury of Gloucester. "The particulars are recorded on a frame of wood, standing in the ringing loft, and the present Vicar records his thanks to Allmighty God that the erection of these bells, and of the new windows in the nave which also he was privileged to present to the Church about the same time, was effected without injury or accident. The Churchwardens of the Parish, Messrs. Hewer and Sydney Thomas Tayler paid the Carriage of the Bells to Cheltenham and back and of the Timber for the frame." He adds that the third window in the nave was filled with stained glass in memory of his wife and son, 10th October 1883.

The frame eventually weakened and the bells could not be rung any more, but only chimed. In 1949 an Ellacombe Chime was installed as a thanksgiving for the safe return of all who had gone from the village to the war of 1939-45, as is recorded on a tablet in the north aisle.

How much stained glass the church had originally, is impossible to say. Only a few pieces of old glass survived in the corners of the west window in the tower. Leaded windows are perishable things even without deliberate or careless breakage. It is striking that the glazier appears more often than any other craftsman in the Churchwardens' Disbursement Book. Between 1772 and 1886 there are nineteen payments identifiably made to the glazier against fourteen to the blacksmith, twelve to the slater and only six to the carpenter. There are now two stained glass windows, both modern. The window in the chancel above the altar was given by James Read and Elisa Dorothea, his wife in 1896, and as mentioned before, the small window beside the belfry was filled with stained glass by the Rev. H. Morgan in memory of his wife and son, in 1883.

The cross on the altar was given in 1939 by Lt. Col. Delme Davies-Evans who lived at the Manor at the time. The candlesticks are the gift of Col. R.S. Meade of Lower Farm.

Two things of interest have been discovered in the church since Rudder's time: an early low relief plaque and a mural painting. The relief was found in the wall where it now is, above and just beside the pulpit. It came to light during repairs in 1939. It is 29" high, 28" wide, at the lower edge and the top corners are rounded. It shows a man on a horse which rears above a shape on the ground. The figures are now indistinct, particularly the one lying on the ground, because the protruding parts of the relief had been chiselled flat before the plaque was plastered over. This had probably been done at the Reformation when the church was cleansed of all "idols", but the chisel marks are as fresh as if the deed had been perpetrated only recently and what remains of the figures stands out white against the green and red background.

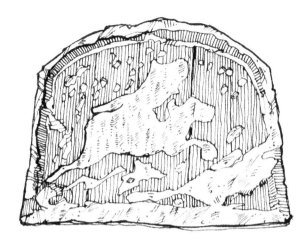

The Plaque. It is a pity that the ancient mutilation makes identification impossible. Unrepentant in the face of expert opinion , the author still favours the interpretation of it as a Roman tombstone.

The plaque has been named St. George and the Dragon and is dated 1366-1410 - on whose authority it does not say - in the notes about the church which were placed on the pillar above the Church Fund box in 1941. St. George, of nebulous provenance and doubtful authenticity, and now demoted as a saint, was not adopted by England until the reign of Edward III (1327-1377). If the dating is correct, this plaque in Compton church would be an early tribute to the new patron saint of the nation. It reminds me of the tombstone of a Thracian cavalry man, now in the City Museum in Gloucester, but expert opinion is against it being Roman. It is perhaps only the family

likeness between the two which makes them seem similar, for the Gloucester tombstone and St. George share the same ancestor: The Rider God of Thracia.

The mural, too, was discovered in the course of repair work. In 1965 the discerning foreman of the building firm which carried out the work, noticed the painting on the west wall and took care not to damage it. It was later inspected by Mrs. Eve Baker who identified it as part of a 17th century cartouche, consisting of a satyrlike head and a large crown above it. "A very charming fragment", Mrs. Baker described it, "and one wishes there were more of it." Unfortunately, the wall below the head is so damaged that it was not worthwhile to uncover more. More and earlier paintings were noticed on the south wall, but because of lack of funds, they were not worked on and were covered up again. There are at least three layers of painting with a very good range of colour, including reds, ochres, greens and blacks. Mrs. Baker thinks that "at some future date when there is interest and money available" "there should be more paintings uncovered in this church".

It is certainly not lack of interest that keeps the wall paintings hidden beneath the layers of whitewash and plaster. It is expensive to uncover and preserve murals, - the cost for the preservation of the fragment was generously borne by Mrs. Brutton and came to £25 - and so far there have been more urgent demands on the funds available. To maintain an old church in good repair, as Compton's church is, taxes the resources of a small village and congregation. But perhaps one day, it will be possible to bring more paintings back to light and link us with the medieval Compton people to whom these pictures meant so much, teaching them, comforting them or threatening them with the terrors of hell.

The outside of the church has suffered less from the

127

The Parish Church of St. Oswald, King and Martyr - There is no trace of Norman architecture to be found, as might be expected in a church that had been a chapel of a mother church in Gloucester since A.D.909.
The disproportionate size of the tower shows clearly.

restorers and cannot have been much different in appearance when it was built in the 15th century, though the enlarged windows naturally show on the south side. But this side, being close to the hill, is out of sight. At the moment it is disfigured by the furnace pit for the central heating, but since the heating was electrified the pit is redundant and will be done away with as soon as means allow. The stairlike structure at the joint of the Chancel with the Nave is the last remnant of the newel staircase which led up to the roodloft. The function of the small walled up window low in the wall is obscure. These small windows occur in many old churches and the explanation for them ranges from lepers to ventilation, the latter being preferred at present. The sundial shows that this side of the church was not always as neglected as it is now.

The tower is beautifully proportioned, with finely carved heads on the string-course and fierce gargoyles. The rams on the buttresses and the head of St. Oswald on the west side have already been mentioned. There remain the pinnacles - the wolves or dogs sitting on their hindlegs holding an upright stave in their front paws. It is difficult - in fact, so far impossible - to explain these strange beasts. If they have a heraldic meaning they could be connected with the Howe coat of arms. But the Howes acquired Compton only in 1608, more than a hundred years after the tower was built.

One of the four "wolves" or "dogs" from the tower.

Unless the pinnacles were put up by the Howe family when they were lords of the manor, this explanation will not hold. Besides, these "dogs" are not exclusively Compton's, they are also found on Highworth (Wilts) church tower where they are so weathered that only one of the four is still recognisable. Their significance is not known in Highworth either. The pinnacles on Compton church and all the outside sculptures are very well preserved, except one of the rams, which has lost its head.

That this handsome tower is too large for the original small church is apparent only when it is seen from a distance across the valley. It dwarfs the Chancel and the Nave, bearing testimony to the pride and wealth of the men who built it.

There is only one medieval tombstone in the churchyard, a 14th century table-tomb. It consists of a large slab of stone supported by four uprights. Only a sculpted head wearing a scroll-like headdress rises above the flat surface of the stone. A pedimented cross which is incised below the head is so weathered that it is nearly invisible. The carvings on the supports, motives of the tree-of-life flanking a cross, are much better preserved. There is no inscription and nobody knows who the person was in whose honour this tomb was erected. Memorials last longer than memory.

This venerable table tomb is also a reminder that centuries ago the churchyard was a place of life, a place for fun and games and social gatherings, not the gloomy assemblage of graves it is for us. They played Nine Men's Morris on the stone slab and chiselled the holes for it into its surface while we should think it gross irreverence to play noughts and crosses on a grave.

Table-tomb. The sole medieval monument. The cross is now scarcely visible, although this was not the case 30 years ago. The tree-of-life motif on the uprights and the holes for Nine Men's Morris are better preserved.

The 17th century gravestones belong mostly to the Mace family. They are modest stones, simply ornamented, and their irregular, untidy lettering shows them to be of local origin. Elisabeth Bateman's headstone was made to a popular pattern of an angel's head, a cornucopia at each side and folds of drapery falling down the sides of the tablet with the name, and date of death, 1708.

These old gravestones have been removed from their original positions and now stand against the north wall of the Chancel. There is nothing remarkable about the later gravestones, except that there are so few of them. Many more people rest in unmarked graves than are commemorated by a tombstone, as are the many generations of Compton people who have been buried on this hillside since the first church was built here.

Seventeenth and eighteenth century gravestones which have become displaced over time and now stand against a wall of the church - one belonging to one of the Thomas Maces whom we seem to know so well.

The Churchwarden's Disbursement Book

"This valuable old book has served 4 generations - 120 years -", wrote the Rev. H. Morgan on the last page in 1892. It was started by Edmund Goodrich in 1772, and he set a standard of handwriting and clear, detailed accounting which, alas, was not kept up by his successors, particularly towards the end. Entries like: Mr. Brown, - £10 12s 2^1/$_2$d are then common, but it would be more interesting if we knew who Mr. Brown was and what he did for his £10 12s 2^1/$_2$d. The last five years are even less enlightening and the account shrinks to: "Expenses as usual", or "£6 15s as last year".

Even at its most explicit, the disbursement book, like the registers, offers nothing but bare statements, and except for a few items, restricts itself entirely to the church and its expenses. The exceptions are: the cost of two Parish coffins in 1781 - 19s; the burial of an Irish child - 1s; and 4 desks, presumably for the school, in 1873 - £5 12s, with a few additional bills. Payment for work on the road is the last extraneous item.

Visitation fees, payment for washing the church linen, writing, winding up the church clock and the oil for it, and the bells, appear in the book, of course, year after year. The oil costs 1s p.a. and from 1786 is payable to Anthony Panter, who seems to have been the verger. He signs as witness at every wedding, bar his own, from 1783 to the end of his days in 1816. At first he signs by "his mark", but within three years he has learned to write his name and his laborious but bold signature

in the register cannot be overlooked. The last of the Panters is still dimly remembered; he was the cobbler after whom Cobbler's Hill is named, the cottage which in old days and before it was enlarged and modernised was known as Cats' Abbey.

Bell ropes have to be replaced from time to time - in 1800 one costs 6s., in 1964 £1 7s 9d. The last reference to the clock is made in 1855. It was then very old and probably beyond repair, for it was in existence when the accounts begin, and when it had expired, it was evidently decided not to have another one. The winding of the clock cost 13s. yearly and since 1795 was the clerk's duty; his salary was £1 6s 6d and in 1787 a new pew was made for him. But from 1820 he has to make do with only the clock winding fee until 1856 when his salary is raised to £3 3s. From 1839 on, the clerk has an additional duty which earns him another 1s 6d - he has to attend to the stove. There is no bill for this stove, so it presumably was a gift, and there are no fuel bills until 1856, when 15 cwt of coal are bought at £1 a ton. This price remains unchanged to the end of the book. A new stove seems to have been bought in 1878, when there is a large payment (£19 11s 2d) to "Mr. Mallory for Stove".

Heating by slow combustion coke-burning stove was in use till 1939, when just before the war central heating was installed. This heating system, electric light and general decoration cost £800, which was found by public subscription and the help of the lord of the manor, Lord Vestey of Stowell Park. The Church Meeting Minutes recall that: "All this we would have been quite unable to attain without everyone's help. Some of you will remember that all the materials for the heating chambers were carried up from the road on one Saturday afternoon by all the population down to the youngest children, giving a helping hand. A Very Fine Effort." In 1965 the heating was electrified at a cost of £500, mainly raised by public subscription. This eliminated the chore of carrying the fuel for the boiler from the road up to the church.

Lighting is mentioned only once, in 1886, when it cost 15s., and this item and the bill for paraffin (12s 6d) in the previous year are for the standard bracket lamps which had been installed in 1883 when the church was extensively modernised. These oil lamps were in use till 1939. At present there is only one outside light at the corner of the church, and the path is so dark that it is negotiable only with a torch. Once there had been two lights, one of their discarded heads stood in the ringing chamber, the other one lay on the rubbish heap. It was suggested to the Church Meeting in 1962 that these antiques should be rescued and restored, but before anything could be done for them, they disappeared. A pity, because these graceful early Victorian lamps could have been an asset to the churchyard, as the identical lamp in Elkstone is.

The guttering and the waterspouts which are still in existence, were installed in 1845, at the cost (including a new Christening Basin) of £2 3s 7d, plus 5s to the blacksmith for putting them up.

A new churchyard gate became necessary in 1798 and cost 7s; this lasted until 1841, when its replacement cost £1. In 1881 the churchwardens had to pay £1 15s 6d for theirs. The present gate was donated in 1967 by Miss E. Crosse in memory of her sister, Dorothy.

Women were paid even less than men; in 1848 two women received 2s. for 2 days' work cleaning the church. At other times the cleaning was apparently done by voluntary unpaid labour, but for the use of mops and brushes the churchwardens had to find 1s 6d. At 3s, an occasional new besom or broom seems surprisingly expensive.

The main bills, naturally, are for repair and upkeep of the church fabric and the churchyard walls. As mentioned before, the glazier's bills are by far the biggest. It is obvious that the church was, and still is, well cared for and the churchyard kept tidy. The walls were repaired when necessary - a waller's wage was 1s. a day in 1781 and 2s 6d in 1835. A major repair which took more than three weeks of digging stone and walling cost £3 4s in 1840.

"Mowing the grass" (25s) appears only late, in 1884; a motorised lawn-mower replaced the scythe in 1968. It is more efficient, of course, and there are not many men in the village who would know how to use a scythe.

Mrs. Beckford made a gift of altarcloth, vestry and bell chamber curtains in 1963, Mr. Lovett-Turner gave another altar cloth the next year, and Mr. and Mrs. J. Cooper, who lived in Grove House, gave a new carpet for the sanctuary in 1965, thus carrying on a tradition which goes back to time immemorial. We remember Joan Rogers who left an altar cloth and a kerchief for the pyx, and John Rogers' twenty sheep for the maintenance of a lamp. There is hardly one of the 16th and early 17th century wills which does not designate some sum to the church, mainly for repairs. But this pious custom, and the related one of leaving something to the poor of the parish died out towards the end of the 17th century.

In 1969 a private donation provided a bench which was put halfway up the path to the church.

It is very nearly 200 years since Mr. Goodrich started the Disbursement Book, and thanks to this account and, later, the Church Meeting Minutes, we were able to see how the practical and mundane side of church administration was carried out during the last 198 years. We shall leave the last word to Canon Noott, who left Compton in 1969, and who - though he spoke in sorrow of the small attendance at service - declared that: "he was glad to say that owing to some generous gifts the church was solvent, the fabric well looked after, the church yard tidy, the voluntary organists faithful, and the flowers and festival decorations beautiful".

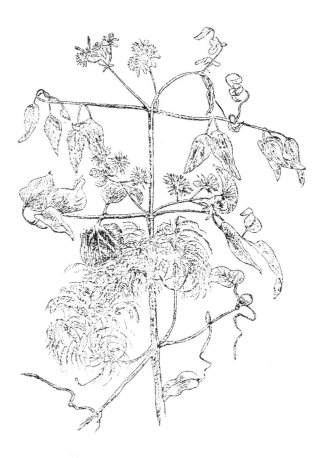

CLÉMATIS VITÁLBA
(*Traveller's Joy*)

Enclosure

The fault is great in man and woman
Who steals a goose from off the Common
But what can plead that man's excuse
Who steals a Common from a goose?

Anon.

"According to Sir Robert Atkyns, there were thirty houses and about 130 inhabitants in this parish, whereof 4 were freeholders; yearly births 4, burials 3. In ten years, beginning with 1760, there were registered 34 baptisms, and 28 burials, and the inhabitants are at present 130 in number" - these are Rudder's statistics for 1712, when Sir Robert Atkyns' History was published, and for 1779, when his own appeared. The population of Compton in these years remained static, at, in fact, nearly the same number as recorded in Domesday Book. This seems to be the level of population which the manor, or the parish, of a little more than 2,000 acres of hill land under the open field system could support. The fact that there were 4 freeholders shows that the process of buying free land - which we saw in Thomas Mace's will of 1625 - had continued and the manorial organisation at last declined, though the lord of the manor, Lord Chedworth, still owned most of the parish. Enclosure had not yet reached Compton and the open fields with the Common were still in existence. Rudder says that most of the parish is arable, but the sheep have not disappeared, for the Dean and Chapter of Bristol's agent reports in 1792 that: "the Land is sound for sheep and with the Common belonging to the Parish enables them to keep up a large stock". He gives the Common on the Downs as eighty acres, which seems hardly sufficient to keep a large stock of sheep and any other beasts, like cows. Indeed, overstocking the Common and the resulting poor quality of livestock was one valid reason for Enclosure, for doing away with the Common altogether. William Dyer's inventory of 1712 tends to support this view; it lists: "Two small lean beasts, Cowes."

The same Tithe Valuation (1792) also indicates that the farmers had remedied the pasturing situation by enclosing small lots of meadow and pasture for their farms. This is the century of agricultural progress and innovation which the strict strip system had hitherto prevented, though some improvement was possible even in the open fields if the strips of one "owner" were laid together in blocks and the restriction of communal sowing, reaping and crop rotation were taken off, as Rudder says "...in such places where envy least prevails and the farmers have discernment enough to see their own interest, they take a hitching out of the common field, by general consent, and plant with turnips or pease, in the year for fallowing". This was done in Compton, as in many other places, and the land improved in value; all, that is, except the glebeland, which was still "very much dispersed about the parish" and therefore set rather low in value.

The indenture of the three cottages, the Priest House, the Churchyard messuage and the former smithy, all part of the glebeland, affords a good example of the intricacies of strip management. Twelve acres went with the cottages, dispersed originally over four fields in the following way:
Two acres in the West field: one in the furlong at Thistle Court, and one at the lower end of the same.
Two acres in the South field: one in the furlong at the West Wales and one in the Moor Slade.

Four acres in the East field: one abutting upon Ditch Acre
Close, one lying further up the same field and abutting
at the South end upon the highway that leadeth to
Northleach, one shooting upon the fieldway that
leadeth to Square Hedge Close and one in the Grass
Furlong.
One parcel of two acres shooting over Squire Hedgeway,
half an acre shooting in the New Ditch, half an acre on
Compton Hill, shooting upon Hawkeswell furlong, and
one lying above Squire Hedgeway.

Some of the field names have disappeared and it is no
longer possible to locate every acre with accuracy; but
Compton Hill, Hawkeswell, alias Hawkeshill or Arkell, and the
East field can be identified. The East field, or part of it, is now
known as Flitgo, Compton Hill and Hawkeswell have kept
their names and lie to the South of the Church. These fields are
about two miles apart. The field which is now called The
Moors, lies between Westfield and Moors Hill, near the north-
west parish boundary, and is at least the same distance from
either of the other two fields.

It does not take much discernment to perceive the
awkwardness and the disadvantages of this fragmentation, it is
more difficult to understand why and how this system lasted
for a thousand years. But however cumbersome open field
farming may appear to us, it had the great advantage that
everybody had some land of right, even if it was only an
allotment or the toft of the cottage; the Common and the fallow
field afforded grazing, if just for a few sheep or a meagre cow.
The Grove - in 1791 classed as Common - provided fuel. Poor
the cottagers may have been, but they were not destitute.

"As there are so few Proprietors, a great improvement
might be made to the advantage of each Proprietor to inclose
the Parish" - this was the opinion of the Dean and Chapter of
Bristol's agent when he surveyed it for Tithes valuation. This
was in 1792, but the farmers had to wait another eleven years
for the recommended improvement.

As we saw before, the strip cultivation had been
gradually eroded by laying the strips together and working
them without restriction. Total Enclosure was the next natural
step. Enclosure, however, was not just a re-shuffling of fields,
it was a fundamental change, as the Enclosure Act expresses it:
"And whereas the said Common Fields, Common Pastures,
Downs and Commonable Woods and Wasteland are in the
present State incapable of any considerable Improvement and
it would be advantageous to the several Proprietors thereof if
the Commonable Rights thereon were extinguished and the
same were divided and specific Parts and Shares thereof
assigned and allotted to and among the several Proprietors,
according to their respective Rights and Interests therein, and
such Allotments enclosed..." In theory, the change-over from
Common and open fields to privately owned and enclosed
plots looked fair and simple, but in practice it worked out in
such a way that Enclosure has been blamed for every evil in the
country, for rural destitution, for high poor rates and low
morals. Controversy about it rivals that about Domesday
Book, ever since Arthur Young wrote: *An Inquiry Into the
Propriety of Applying Wastes to the Better Maintenance and Support
of the Poor*". While nobody denied that Enclosure was
necessary for the improvement of the land and the
development of agriculture, Arthur Young and others deplored
the resulting total dispossession of the poor as inhuman,
shortsighted and uneconomic.

In theory, nearly everybody should have had "rights

and interests" in the Common and so should have had a share when it was distributed. Just as, on the other hand, the lord of the manor claimed a fourteenth of the Waste Land as compensation for relinquishing manorial rights over it, thus asserting his right, however unreal it had become.

In reality, the obstacles in the way of the small landholders were insurmountable. Commonable rights were hard to prove, unless they were put in writing and they very rarely were, and the expense of enclosure was considerable and had to be shared by the several owners in proportion to their lands or rights of Common. Though Lord Chedworth had agreed to pay for obtaining and passing the Act, "the expenses of the Commissioners (there were three, their duty was to examine claims and to supervise the operation; their fee was 2gns a day), the Clerk or Clerks surveying, measuring, planning, dividing and allotting, roads, Copies of Award and all other reasonable expenses" had still to be paid. In addition, each owner had to bear the cost of fencing his land. All this proved prohibitive to anybody who could have claimed but a few acres.

Therefore, no cottager seems to have made a claim, for the Enclosure Award Map is beautifully tidy; there are only four names on it: Lord Chedworth, the lord of the manor; the Dean and Chapter of Bristol, who owned the glebeland (that is, Rectory Farm); William Dyer, who had 84 acres, and Bartley Wilson, who was the tenant of the twelve acres which went with the three cottages: the Priest House, the Churchyard Messuage and the former smithy. Lord Chedworth had held Rectory Farm on lease since 1785 and bought Compton Farm in 1804, so he was in possession of the whole parish, bar 96 acres. On the map, Compton parish in 1805, looked remarkably like the manor in Domesday Book times and after - with the

fundamental difference that the Common land had disappeared. The Downs were shared out between Lord Chedworth and the Dean and Chapter, and the Grove became private property and inaccessible except by trespass.

The Commissioners had considerable power and could have used their influence to compensate "the poor" for the loss of grazing on the Common and fuel from the Waste and the Grove by assigning them allotments. In Chedworth, twelve acres of Furzey Commons had been set aside for them - and poor land it sounds too - but nothing of the kind was done in Compton. For any land to grow food, the labourers depended on the good will of the farmers. Much later in the century we hear something about the war over potato land, a war which certainly did not start in 1872, but had gone on for a long time.

Unfortunately, we know nothing of the immediate effect of the Enclosure in 1805 on the non-landowning majority of Compton's population. William Marshal comments in 1789 that: "labourers are remarkably numerous for the nature of the country, and their wages are as remarkably low. A shilling a day, no beer, in autumn winter and spring. Fourteen pence in haytime except for mowing (when it is 18d), and 2s a day for 5 weeks certain in harvest. Women in autumn and spring 6d, in haytime 7d, in harvest 1s. No beer, except where it is given voluntarily." These figures correspond to the pay mentioned in the Disbursement Book and in Rudder. They had not risen in the intervening years and were not to rise for an incredibly long time. Mr. S. Mace told me that in 1916, when he started work on the farm at the age of eleven (because of wartime), he received 3s a week, the wage of a grown man was 10s. With incomes so low, every halfpenny, that need not be spent, counted; free wood from the Waste and the Grove must have been of immense help, and geese on the Common, a treasure.

Even if we have no evidence, we can imagine what it meant for the landless to be deprived of these resources and thrown back on their wages only.

Another consequence of Enclosure, however, we need not imagine, we can see it all around us, up and down the hills: the walls between the fields, then newly measured. They were boundary walls in the first place, but had a secondary and very important function, they provided shelter and broke the force of the wind which, in a dry spring, was strong and persistent enough to lift the seed and carry it away; "the Quality is in general good Cornland and will produce some fair Crops, but being very much exposed and without Fences it is rather a disadvantage to the Farmers", as the tithes valuer puts it. Hedges of whitethorn would have been better and a combination of hedge and wall best, but hedges were expensive, the bushes had to be raised from seed or bought from a nursery, the young hedge needed two guard fences until established and timber was scarce. Stones for walls were, however, plentiful and on the spot, and once built, walls "are fences immediately. This alone can apologize for their frequency. The country in general is still to the eye as naked and is almost as destitute of shelter, as it was before the enclosure took place", remarks W.Marshall, regretfully. "The wall and the live hedge together will be a much better shelter than either of them alone. The climature of the bleaker swells would by this means be rendered much more genial than it is *131* at present." The climature, however, was not, and perhaps could not, be considered, the walls were raised and provided work and income for their builders and eased the adjustment to the new order.

Lord Chedworth bought Compton Farm in 1804, and it was ironic that he bought it just when he liquidated the manor by Enclosure, for Compton Farm was no ordinary farm, but the demesne, the Manor Farm. For the first time since the Archbishop of York ceased to be the lord of the manor, the chief messuage and the site of the manor were united in the same hand and the Manor House was owned by the lord. It is doubtful if Lord Chedworth was aware of the significance of his purchase, its former status may have been forgotten. Its history, however, is well documented.

The tenant of the manor of Compton at the time of the Dissolution was Thomas Lane of Matson. When Compton was sold by the Crown to Sir Thomas Chamberlayne in 1554, Thomas Lane somehow retained the chief messuage and 8 yardlands of demesne land. This he left to his wife Maud, who later married Richard Pate. Only one of the four Pate children, Margaret, grew up and married. Both she and her husband, Richard Brooks, died when their daughter, Susan, was a small child. Susan was brought up by her Pate grandparents and inherited Richard Pate's estate, including property in Compton Abdale, namely the demesne farm which came to her through her grandmother Maud (Lane) Pate. Though he tried, Richard Pate could not protect his young heiress from an unsuitable marriage; her husband, the Marquess of Willoughby, began to squander his wife's fortune as soon as he had power to do so. Susan separated from him after only three years, and the lordship of Compton (which went with the chief messuage) figures in the separation settlement. After the Marquess' early death, Susan married Robert Lovett.

When Edmund Chamberlayne, who had inherited the manor of Compton from his father, Sir Thomas Chamberlayne, sold it in 1608 to Sir Richard Grubham, he excepted the glebeland and "all that farm in Compton Abdale aforesaid which is parcell of the inheritance of Susan Lovett and now in the occupation of the said Edmund Chamberlayne by lease and under the right of the said Susan Lovett." Susan and Robert Lovett sold their property in Compton, among many other lands, in 1618 to William Guise of Elmore. But Edmund Chamberlayne remains in occupation, for he lets "the Style of the manor of Compton Abdale and the chief messuage" and eight yardlands to Symon Egerton of Hackney in 1622, for 30 years.

It passed through various hands, always intact with its 8 yardlands of free land. In the 18th century it was in the possession of the Heart family and, in a marriage settlement, the 8 yardlands are defined as 320 acres in the Common fields and various closes. The names of the closes are still known today: Mead Bottom and Mead Hill; Land Dew and Land Dew Bottom; Slaters or Slaughters Mead; Croft; Pigeonhouse Close (this name alone shows that the land belonged to the Manor House); Puesdown Closes and Stancombe.

This ancient demesne land - probably unchanged since the manor's beginning - merged with the rest, "the site" of the manor in 1804 when Miss Mary Sophia Heart, the last of the Hearts, sold the farm to Lord Chedworth. In 1821 it had been sold again. A Survey of the estate of Thomas Hope, now called

Lower Farm, shows that it consisted of 662 acres. It remained in the possession of this family until 1911, when Mr. John Hughes bought it. By 1930 it was part of the estate of E.E. Turner and, when it was sold in the same year, the land of 532.534 acres parted company from the house and its 30 acres. The farmhouse was bought by Col. R.S. Meade who sold it in 1971.

If any house in the village can claim to be the Manor House, it is Lower Farmhouse. Though the lords of the manor never lived in it, it is, nevertheless, the lord's house, the "chief messuage", the Manor House. As such, it surely is the oldest house in the village though, of course, not in its present form. In its long history it was changed, re-built and enlarged many times, and no visible trace remains of the Archbishop's house which he wanted crenellated after his visit in 1281. There are no airs of grandeur and no pretence about the old house; it has the dignity of a large and important farmhouse in its spacious courtyard, a little aloof from the road - no more and no less than what it has been for centuries.

Farmers and Labourers

"The village of Compton Abdale is a very retired and small parish deeply overshadowed with surrounding rocky hills. All the roads to it are craggy and very steep, abounding with an adhesive soil, so that persons cannot pass to it but with great difficulty; if indeed, I were not accustomed to the country, having resided in it three years I could not continue in it.

The population, by the last Census, was 168 but I do not...that it has much increased since that period.

The above is a true statement of the situation of this parish; to the best of my knowledge it has frequent floods of water in it, but it has, likewise, many beautiful springs.- There is not a lady or a gentleman residing in it, or near it, consisting almost entirely of Farm labourers, there are 2 small grocery shops and a carpenter's. There are 2 decent farmers in it, Churchwardens and brothers: - they govern the whole parish, being tenants under the Stowell family..."

This is Compton Abdale in 1837 according to the Rev. T. Nutt, who had looked after the parish for three years for the incumbent, the Rev. J. Holmes, who was also Rector of Colesbourne. He makes the village look rather like a settlement in the Rockies, but he had reasons of his own not to advertise its charms. In all essentials he is, however, correct and the Census of 1841 confirms this.

Rudge in 1807 had rejoiced that improved agriculture would provide an increase in foodstuffs and so lead to an increase in population. His hopes - and other men's fears - were certainly fulfilled on the national scale and locally. The total population of England, Wales and Scotland rose from eleven to sixteen and a half million between 1801 and 1831, Compton's from 157 - which was already higher than the "normal" 130 - to 168. Twenty years later, the peak figure of 258 was reached, from then on the numbers fell fairly rapidly to 159 in 1901. William Marshall had found farm labourers remarkably numerous in 1788, and "for the nature of the country", as he said, the numbers may have been high, and they were to rise very much higher, but there was no choice for the villagers than to work on the land. Compton had been a farming village throughout its history and there is no evidence of any other occupation. Weaving and spinning were taken as much for granted as sheep and are as little mentioned. A weaver appears only once in the records, in *"Men and Armour"* (1608) and two spinning wheels are listed in inventories. This is the sum total of the evidence of the wool-based home industries which by the 19th century had withered anyway, and there was nothing left but farming.

The Census of 1841 which gives the occupation of the enumerated allows us to see the social structure of the village and to check the Rev. Nutt's description: there are 2 tenant farmers - the landowners are absent - and 49 agricultural labourers and their families. A number of auxiliary trades complete the statistics: 1 mason, blacksmith, miller and shepherd; 2 carpenters; 2 shoemakers; 2 grocers, one of whom is also a carpenter; 1 cordwainer and 2 governesses. The cordwainer is perhaps the most surprising and the governesses the most significant of the occupations mentioned. But there is no trade or job which is not connected with or dependent on agriculture.

The "Churchwardens and brothers" were Thomas and William Walker, and as nearly everybody in the village depended on them for their livelihood, they were in a good

133

134

position to govern the parish. Thomas Walker was also the tenant of Mr. Capel Cure who held Rectory Farm from the Dean and Chapter of Bristol. Mr. Capel Cure expressed his opinion of Compton and its "decent farmers" forcefully in a letter to the Dean and Chapter in 1826: "The land is bad, the system of farming worse and the tenants most troublesome to manage." But then he lived in London, had nothing to do with the farm than receive the rent and write an occasional letter of complaint to the owners, which he was doing now, in fact, he was protesting against the raising of the price of the lease which the agents had urged on the Dean and Chapter for years. He points out that "the fine in 1819 was only £770 and the then prices of agricultural produce was much higher than they are at present (1826), nor is any rise to be now expected...With the present prospect of the Introduction into the country of foreign corn I shall as a beneficial Tenant hope for favourable consideration of the Dean and Chapter. I cannot accept the present estimate. it appears to me quite impossible that it ought to exceed the fine paid in 1819." His fears were premature, foreign corn was not allowed into the country until 1843, the prices for wheat remained high; farmers, landowners and the receivers of tithes did well. Only the poor suffered, because they could not afford their daily bread.

Though Mr. Capel Cure says in 1826 that the fine was "only" £770 in 1819, he then complained that it was "far beyond what I could let the Glebe and Tithes at, though fixed at the extreme of one year and a half of rack-rent. And although I made an agreement with the Farmers for 7 years at an abated rate, they went from their word when the unfavourable times arrived, and I was compelled to accept of their terms." The farmers were most troublesome to manage. In 1812 they had been so awkward that the agent, Mr. Crouch

"got out of temper with the Compton Abdale Tenants respecting the tithes and wrote to Mr. Cure. He would have nothing more to do with it." It seems they governed more than the parish.

The "unfavourable times" arrived after Waterloo when the price of wheat dropped from its wartime peak of 126s per quarter and the profits with it. Ruin for the corngrowers was held at bay by the Corn Law of 1815, which prohibited the import of foreign corn unless homegrown wheat had reached the price of 80s per quart. This safeguarded the profit of the landowners and tenant farmers, never mind the misery and deprivation which the high price of bread brought to the wage-earners in town and country alike. Agricultural wages had not risen since 1792 when wheat cost 42s, and even in 1856 the average wages in Gloucestershire were still only 9-10s a week. George Curtis who was a skilled craftsman earned 2s 6d a day and William Dean is paid 6s 8s for 5 days work repairing the church road in 1844. Supply and demand determined the price, and abundant manpower kept wages low. Yet the population was still rising. In 1851 Elisabeth Walker, widow (of Thomas), employs 50 labourers on her 800 acre farm, William Walker has 53 men working for him on 774 acres; Josiah Cosins has three men for 78 acres. Surely this must be saturation point even if there were no machines in use on the farms. Only the decrease of population in the 1870s raised the wages slightly; Thomas Curtis earned 2s 2d a day in 1874, against 1s 6d in 1845.

Did the rapid doubling of the population change the appearance and character of the village? Not to the extent the same expansion would change a town. The narrow valley with its brook sets the limit for the development, and new cottages had to be built outside the core of the old village. According to

This is the Tithe map of 1843. Compton 150 years ago looks essentially the same as now - on paper. It may, however, seem strange to find thatched cottages in Cornbow's garden. Bessy Smith lived in one. The doctor respected the opinions of this village "wise woman", and when he rode over from Northleach, he never failed to call on her to get a health survey of the village.

Let us explore further. Mind the water splash! No Crocodile yet. It is a pity the map does not show details, but we can make out the malt house, and some cottages. You had to go down some steps to reach their front door. How do I know? The cottages and the malthouse were demolished long ago? Mr. Ernest Jones told me, he ought to have known, he was born in one.

Besides, their neighbour, Manor Farm House is still below street level even today. There is another cottage we are not familiar with, in the paddock across the lane to the Old Parsonage Farm and two more higher up, they are gone as well.

This is all, some buildings we know so well we look in vain for, there is no Vicarage, no Riverside Cottage, no Old Post house, no school, but surprisingly, there is Shoemaker Panter's little work shop, there is "Freemans", alias Manor Cottage.

We would expect to find the big houses and of course, there they are: The "Manor", the Tithe Barn, Manor Farmhouse, Old Parsonage, Lower Farm and Smallhope, not to forget the cottages of "Upper Compton".

We know enough of Compton's people to be able to picture the life of the place, but this I'll leave to you.

the Census, there were 48 houses in 1841, that is 18 more than Rudder's 30. The Tithes Award Map of 1842 shows the growth since 1805 when the Enclosure Map was drawn. There were no new farmhouses, as the number of farmers had not changed. New cottages were built at Spring Hill, in the Grove and on the Pike road to the north of the village. Here, Hungerford and a row of six Cottages on the west side of the lane are already on the 1805 map. On the opposite side Robert Dyer had a house and one acre of land wedged between the road and a field lane. Into this triangular piece of ground - by no means the whole of Robert Dyer's acre - nine cottages were crammed. Another two rose on the bank beyond the field lane, later called Cats' Abbey. There were no cottages as yet on Rooks Hill, though a large new barn had been built there, but the first and smallest of the present four cottages was to appear soon, in 1843. The development of Rooks Hill illustrates a trend which Rudge had observed in 1807: "The unsheltered state of the Cotswolds exposes them to the full effects of bleak winds, and, therefore throughout the whole extent, a sharp climate is predominant. In the dens and vallies, a milder air is felt; and in consequence of this, in former times, the villages were generally built in these; but since the cultivation of the higher lands, the conveniences resulting from a central situation with regard to the farm, have occasioned the building of houses in very exposed situations. Hence has arisen a hardy race of men; and the hill farmer is easily distinguished, by his complexion, from the 136 husbandman of the Vale." By this token, our Council House dwellers should be the hardiest, for they are most exposed to the full effects of bleak winds.

Once an open spring - until 1960 the only water supply for "Upper Compton". In hot summers when the spring was reduced to a trickle, buckets filled but slowly if left unattended, for poaching somebody else's water was not unknown. Such unneighbourly deeds just called for retaliation.

The water supply for the cluster of 17 cottages on the Pike road - which incidentally, never acquired a name of its own - was a spring beside the road just below the lowest cottage. This spring was probably stronger when the cottages were built than it is now, but even so it can scarcely have been adequate for so many people. The hardships it caused in dry seasons by dwindling to a trickle, and the treks to the icy pump in winter are still recalled with feeling, for the spring was made redundant by mains water only in 1960.

The dire consequences of Enclosure for the poor, the landlessness of the labourers and the lack of fuel occupied the thoughts not only of Arthur Young. Thomas Rudge, and later, of course, Cobbett comment on it, and the former makes his recommendations to the Board of Agriculture in 1807. Though he holds that: "the greatest of evils to agriculture would be to place the labourer in a state of independence, and thus destroy the indispensable gradations of society", he thinks that the labourer should be given the opportunity to rise in the scale of society by his industry and exertion and be supplied with the means of doing more than earn his daily wages, namely, more land than is usually held with cottages, so that he can subsist without parochial relief. Furthermore, he should have the legal right to build a cottage for himself.

These recommendations went largely unheeded, and the labourer remained dependent on the farmer for housing and allotment. The "potato land" was desperately needed and the loss of it was such a calamity for a large family - and most families were large - that a man would go to great lengths to avoid the displeasure of the farmer. The farmers were well aware of this situation and did not hesitate to make use of it to bring recalcitrant employees to heel, as in and after 1872, when the National Agricultural Labourers' Union threatened to endanger the status quo. This is the origin of the Compton Tater Song. I heard a fragment of it from Mr. Juggins of Chedworth, who was born in Compton, and asked Mr. E. Jones about it. "Oh yes, the tater song, that's from Joe Arch's time", he said, "I know it, I often heard John Harris sing it. It goes like that:

It's the 'tater land
It's the 'tater land
There is nothing like the 'tater land
And if you in the Union stand
You get deprived of your 'tater land.

There was one Union man who had some ground
He thought it was all safe and sound
But when the farmer smelled some rat
He said: Oh no me man you shan't have that

The Compton men they do declare
The 'tater land for many a year
The Compton men they won't be done
They goes over the hill to Withington
And soon the news is got to hand
That they had got some 'tater land

You black-legged men you must look out
And in the harvest scout about
And for your master knock about
Or else get deprived of your 'tater land."

Times, fortunately, have changed, but the attachment to the allotment and the garden have remained.

In 1608, 13 messuages, 13 gardens and 13 orchards belonged to the manor, and to complete the village we have to add Susan Lovett's farm and Rectory Farm with the 3 cottages. Sir Robert Atkyns (1712) and Samuel Rudder (1779) record 30 houses and 130 inhabitants. In 1841, there are 48 houses and 238 inhabitants, in 1851, the population had reached its peak of

258, yet the census lists 2 uninhabited houses. "Houses" here probably means cottages, for apart from the four farmhouses, the village consisted entirely of cottages. Cottages of "one up and one down" of 16' by 11', and often smaller. The room downstairs, usually stone-flagged, truly was the living room, the only room for everybody and every activity, from cooking over the open fire and washing, for which the water had to be fetched from the spring, to eating and the thousand and one jobs which filled the day. Some cottages had a scullery, but not many had a larder or store room and a slice of the living room was partitioned off to serve as a store. There was hardly room for furniture except a table and a dresser, or shelves, and perhaps a chest of drawers. Not to mention the people; - families were larger in the 19th century than in the previous one and six children were nothing exceptional. In the 1851 Census, we find for instance, the Hope (Lower Farm?) family. There were six children from 19 to 3 years, all living at home, and there was room for a lodger as well. Children seem to have stayed at home till they married, at least in 1851, for the Census mentioned other families whose elder children are of similar ages as the Hopes'. Mrs. Kibble, however, told me that her elder brothers had to leave home as soon as they moved to Compton (1886), because their cottage was so small that there simply was not room for all of them. This was the little old cottage on Rooks Hill, or rather only half of it, for incredible as it seems today, two families had to share it. "My parents were very disappointed with this small house", Mrs. Kibble said, "they had not seen it before they moved in, because my father took this job (he was a shepherd) at a fair; you know how this used to be done in those days, and so the boys had to leave. Jack went at once and Frank followed him soon. To the coal mines in South Wales." Later the Hooper family moved down to the village into one of the cottages on the Pike road - it was bigger, but still only one up and one down.

There were 7 lodgers in the village in 1851: 1 single woman, a widow; 3 young men and 2 elderly men. One of them was 70 years old, but perhaps he was still able to work and support himself. If he had not been, he would have had to go to the Workhouse, as happened later to the single woman who died in the Northleach Workhouse at the age of 81. Workhouses had existed here and there for a long time, but became a national institution in 1834, another desperate attempt to deal with the problem of the destitute. In the Middle Ages it was the Church and the monasteries who bore the main burden of what we now call social services, but long before the Reformation, the task had become too big for their resources and there were several Acts concerning the genuinely poor and also the beggars and "sturdy vagabonds". Voluntary charity was regarded as the proper means of providing for the poor until, in 1601, the great Elizabethan Poor Law introduced the principle of taxation to raise funds which were to be administered by the churchwardens with several substantial householders as overseers. The Act of 1662 added the law of settlement and removal, authorising the removal of any stranger to his place of birth unless he had rented a tenement of £10 or had security to pay the parish for any expense he might cause. Incorrigible rogues, vagabonds and sturdy beggars could be transported to the plantations. This Act brought untold hardship and misery to many unfortunate people who were shunted back and forth between parishes because none would admit liability for them.

The Act of 1601 had thrown the responsibility for the "impotent poor" on the parish, and this system lasted until 1834, though it had never been able to deal with an

139

overwhelming problem. It was open to abuse and to cruelty, and it was badly administered. The Poor Rate rose to such crippling proportions that it was feared the entire rent of the country would be spent on it without any improvement of the situation. The last, and greatest strain, imposed on the Poor Rate was the Speenhamland System, legalised by the Act of 1796, by which low wages were supplemented by parish relief based on the price of bread. The proposal to tie wages directly to the cost of living was unacceptable to Parliament for political reasons. The result of the Speenhamland System was that the farmers kept the wages at the absolute minimum, the labourers, deprived of incentive and pride of work, were demoralised and the small landowners ruined by the resulting enormous Poor Rate. By 1832 the complaints about the System moved the Government to set up a royal commission of enquiry. As a result, the whole parochial system of poor-relief was abolished in 1834. It was then replaced by the centralised control of the Poor Law Commissioners who delegated the local administration to guardians of groups of parishes, called Unions. Each Union had a workhouse, and as every other relief was abolished, this was, from now on, the place for the "impotent poor".

We do not hear much about the poor in Compton. The early wills all leave some money to the poor, but these donations cease in the 18th century. The Churchwardens' Disbursement Book has no entries connected with poor-relief except the cost of 2 Parish coffins for 1781. In 1768, William Constable of Tetbury, a pauper, is buried; no explanation of how he came to be in Compton is offered. Perhaps he was one of those unfortunates who were sent to their place of birth, and never reached it.

In 1826, the Tithe Valuer wrote to the Dean and Chapter of Bristol that he could not get any information about the amount of Poor Rate: "but as there are but few inhabitants in the Parish, and those employed in Agriculture, I concluded the Rate must be low". By that time the Parish had been enclosed for twenty-one years and the population had already increased considerably, but the poor apparently were still no problem. In 1805, the Poor Rate had been 1s 6d in each £ of tithes paid, a very modest sum, compared to other parishes.

After 1834, Compton belonged to the Northleach Poor Law Union and from then on we find an occasional remark in the Burial Registers: "Died in the Union Workhouse". There are not many of them; seven for the years 1843 to 1906. Four of the seven are old people who apparently had nobody who would, or more likely who could, look after them in their old age. Of the others, we know nothing, but what the figures in the parish registers tell us. The first on that sad list is Elisabeth Holtham. She was the mother of three illegitimate children and died at the age of thirty-five. William Jones lost his wife in March 1895 and died himself in Northleach in December, leaving two children of two and four years. Of Caroline Hicks, who dies at forty one, we know nothing. We can only guess at the distress and unhappiness behind the figures in the Burial Register.

Curates, Methodists and Others

Ever since it was established as a chapel of the mother church of St. Oswald in Gloucester, the church of Compton has retained its lowly status as Perpetual Curacy. The Priory appointed - and presumably paid - the chaplain and retained for itself the glebeland whose original purpose was to maintain church and priest. After the Dissolution, both the appropriation of the living and the glebeland were given to the Dean and Chapter of the Cathedral of Bristol. In 1565, they charged their tenant, Thomas Mace, to find a good curate and to pay him £7 which was counted as part of the rent of Rectory Farm. These £7 remained the only remuneration of the minister until 1658 when Cromwell's Commissioners fixed the pay at £40. In 1715, Joshua Aylworth of Aylworth left a sum of £200 each for the augmentation of the spiritual income of the poor benefices of Charlton Abbots, Cold Saperton, Sevenhampton and Compton Abdale, "in a purchase to be made of Lands in Fee Simple". This sum of £800 was accordingly spent by the Trustees to buy land at Arle "within the manor of Cheltenham." In 1737, the stipend was increased by Queen Ann's Bounty, and again, in 1760, by donations from Alexander Colston, Esq., and the Rev. Charles Page, the then curate, whose generosity is commemorated by a plaque over the church door of which, unfortunately, only a part is preserved.

Despite these augmentations Compton remained a poor living and could not support its minister without him having either means of his own or an additional parish. Ministers who held two parishes did not usually live in Compton, because there was no glebe-house, or vicarage, and some of them appointed a curate who might be non-resident also.

The Rev. James Holmes, who held Compton Abdale together with the rectory of Colesbourne for 27 years (1810-1837), had a succession of curates in Compton, the last of whom, the Rev. Thomas Nutt, we have already met. We know him from the letters he wrote to the Dean and Chapter in 1837, which we have quoted before. When he was appointed by the bishop in 1834 "for special reasons the full amount of salary allowed (£50) or required has not been assigned". What a pity the special reasons were not defined. Despite this cut in salary he is most, indeed desperately anxious to remain in Compton, and one can't help but have compassion on him and his old housekeeper when he has to leave. As soon as he learns of the death of the Rev. Holmes, he writes to the Dean and Chapter:

"Allow me to mention, Gentlemen, that I have served the Established Church nearly thirty years, during which time I have officiated at between 40 and 50 Churches - not in view to emolument but to oblige my Betters, except once or twice on a succession of holiday duties. I have however acted as Curate from Church to Church but thrice on account of the death of my Rector and twice from intervening circumstances; having from the beginning gone through most laborious duties of Country Churches."

A confused letter, and his ecclesiastical career is more a handicap than a recommendation, but he writes again, and makes matters worse. His handwriting is so bad that several words are undecipherable.

"Reverend Gentlemen, Allow me to intreat your pardon of my obtrusion of this second letter; but presuming it my duty & that it may be acceptable to You, I venture to give you all the information in my power concerning the living in Compton Abdale now vacant. (Here follows the description of the village, which we have already quoted.) The late Perpetual Curate, the Rev. J. Holmes, told me a few months past, "that the income of it (Compton) to him did not amount to £70 p.a." out of which I am licensed at £50 p.a." performing Double Duty in it from Lady Day till Michaelmas, as is appointed at some other Church in this Diocese. Permit me, under favour, Rev. Gentlemen, to add that, should the future Incumbent be non-resident, I should be thankful & happy to be continued the humble Sub-Curate of Compton Abdale, not serving nor desiring to serve any other Curacy. Since being resident here, I have occasionally preached at several other Churches & having a strong voice with good health have (if I may believe my friends) generally given satisfaction.

Again..for forgiveness for this intrusion I remain, Rev. Gentlemen, Your most obedient, humble & very faithful Servt...

.... There is a good Church; its windows well adapted to my natural (?) near-sight. My lodging is at one. The Farmers, here which would (I presume) be eligible to <u>very</u> few, were it vacant, but my Amusement being chiefly walking, nearly the whole of the day, penning down the memoranda of my studies, I do not experience the annoyance at Home I otherwise should...from a very noisy Family. Being far advanced in years & having but a small income of my own, no other small Church to serve nor knowing any suitable to me & likely to be; my family being only myself & a very old housekeeper. This little Church therefore would be very acceptable to an <u>old and</u> <u>faithful Servant</u> of the Establishment.

I have resided first & last 9 years...in this Diocese &...16 years in the Diocese of Oxford.

Perhaps, Very Rev. Sir and Rev. Gentlemen, You will favour me with an Answer when the succeeding Perpetual Curate shall have been appointed.

N.B. The late Incumbent of Compton Abdale repeatedly recommended me since first I undertook the Curacy to write to you. He died at the age of 79 yrs. He had known me for Twenty years past. The present Bishop also has seen me & knows something of me.

N.B Pray forgive the illegibility of this writing as I could not delay (?) & it is very difficult to obtain...good paper & pens in this sequestered place when required".

While the Rev. Nutt waited for their answer, the Dean and Chapter received an anonymous letter from Cheltenham:

"Gentlemen, I understand that Mr. Nutt the present curate of Compton Abdale in your gift has applied for the perpetual curacy. I wish you to know that Dissent has so increased in the Parish during his Ministry that they want a person qualified to bring back the sheep to their proper flock. Mr. Nutt is nearly blind and his moral conduct will not bear inquiry".- Cheltenham, March 9th 1837.

The weeks passed without any sign that the patrons were concerned about the vacancy and the churchwardens became alarmed at the prospect of the Rev. Nutt's indefinite stay. So, Mr. William Walker wrote to the Dean:

"Rev. Sir -

In Consequence of the death of Mr. Holmes, the late incumbent, the living of Compton Abdale has been vacant about 3 months. His curate who still officiates is in every respect incapacitated from discharging his duties properly which has no doubt been one cause of the increase of dissenters in our village. The living is very small and there is no house for a resident Clergyman but a gentleman in this neighbourhood about 2 miles distant is desirous to hold it in conjunction with his own and there is no doubt of his fulfilling the duties very differently to what they have been for some time past. It is the Rev. Mr. Mellish of Shipton.

I am Rev. Sir Yours respectfully
William Walker, Churchwarden.

The Rev. W. P. Mellersh (the inconsistency of spelling (see Mellish above) is nothing unusual for the period) was appointed curate of Compton Abdale and nothing more is heard of the Rev. T. Nutt and his very old housekeeper. We hope that they found a modest home somewhere and that their last years were not too distressed.

The Dissenters registered James Harris' house as a place of religious worship in 1834, the same year the the Rev. T. Nutt succeeded the Rev. T. Hill who had followed the Rev. D. Dobrée in 1832. All were curates for the Rev. J. Holmes; Mr. Dobrée lived in Withington, Mr. Hill in Notgrove, "there being no glebehouse" in Compton. Considering the distance and the state of the roads, it cannot have been easy to attend the cure of the souls of Compton from Withington or Notgrove, and as resident Mr. Nutt apparently was no improvement on his absent predecessors, the Dissenters found the field ripe for

harvest and Chapel gave the people what they missed in Church.

The Dissenters were Primitive Methodists and their chapel was the end cottage of "Homestead", now owned by Mr. L. Cooper. Unfortunately, the documents of the Cheltenham Circuit were lost in 1931, so we have to rely entirely on local tradition for the history of the chapel. Despite Mr. Walker's faith in Mr. Mellersh's redeeming powers, the dissenting sheep did not immediately rejoin the proper flock and there are still people in the village who not only remember the chapel, but went there for Sunday School. It was only in the first years of the First World War that it came to an end, and the railed upper storey gallery was removed when the chapel was converted into a dwelling house, probably by Thomas Harris.

This strong, independent religious life no doubt helped in the crisis of 1922, when the dispute with the minister emptied the church and no services were held for a long time - long enough for the organ to perish. Mr. Pritchard who brought up the mail from Andoversford was so distressed about this situation that he organised services in the Big Barn which Mr. Maddy, who led the resistance against the vicar, readily made available. Sunday School, too, was held during this church-less time, and the spiritual life of the village did not suffer as much as it might have. It weathered an unhappy, arid period and did not wither even though it was untended.

The Methodists were the strongest of several nonconformist communities who gathered in private houses and disappeared again with their originators. One centred on the Pikehouse, but nothing is known of it and it is remembered by few. Mrs. Kibble recalled a meeting with "strangers" in the mill, where she had gone with her mother to have their gleaned corn ground. This was in 1890 when Mrs. Kibble was 10 years old.

The strangers had come to live in what is now known as Hillside Cottage and they invited Mrs. Hooper and Ada (later Mrs. James Kibble) to come to their service and "break bread with them". This expression made the invitation unforgettable for Ada. The strangers did not stay long and were thought to have been Mormons and to have gone to Salt Lake City, but the expression "break bread with us" is characteristic of the strict Christians, the so-called Plymouth Brethren, who have no clergy and hand each other the broken bread at Communion. The Mormons had come to the village much earlier, in 1846, when "Jackson William had been received into the Church of Jesus Christ of Latter Day Saints (organized by the will and command of GOD in the USA on April 6th 1830) and ordained a Priest in a branch of the said Church at Compton Abdale, 21st March 1846." But for this certificate which Mr. Alec Mace found among family papers, we should not know that there ever was a branch of Latter Day Saints in Compton.

Mr. Mellersh appointed a curate for Compton soon after he became its minister in 1837. In 1840 he added Salperton (216 persons, £107 5s) to his cures of Shipton and Compton Abdale (188 persons, £81 7s 6d). He resigned in 1845 and two years later the Rev. E. W. Garrow, who had been his curate, became minister in Compton, residing in Sevenhampton. His was one of the longest ministries, lasting till 1867, and he provided the church with an organ by subscription of his friends. The next two curates stayed only a few years, but the Rev. H. Morgan who came to Compton in 1873, remained until his death in 1893. He is commemorated in the Chancel as a "Faithful Kind And True Pastor And Friend" and we have come to know him as a conscientious principal manager of the school and for his contribution to the new vicarage, the modernisation of the church and his notes on its history.

His successor, the Rev. R. P. Norwood, resigned the living after only two years by exchange with the Rev. N. A. Holttum, "because I found the income altogether inadequate". "He (the Rev. Holttum) came with a wife and one child," Mrs. Kibble remembered, "and when they left, there were four. And he worked hard; he had Parson's Field which went with the vicarage, bought a cow, a pig and chickens, and later on a donkey and a cart, and worked his field and so made ends meet. Yes, he worked hard, but he was generous with what he had. He would say: I don't want an egg this morning, put it on the dresser. And he would take that egg when he went visiting and give it to somebody who needed it. And he would take a small flat whiskey bottle with port to an invalid. I can still see him sitting on the handle of a wheelbarrow at a cricket match up on Hill Barn Field; he shared work and play though he was brought up and educated to be a clergyman."

At the request of the churchwardens he wrote a short report about his incumbency in the Parish Book. He leaves church and parish in satisfactory order to his successor. The number of communicants has increased from 8 to 25 (though the attendance at Service could be better), furniture and appointments in the church have been restored and improved, a new stained glass window has been provided in the east end and the fabric of the church is repaired and in good order.

At present, Compton is once more without a minister of its own, and Withington, Hazelton and Compton Abdale form one cure, an arrangement which in all probability will be permanent. The Compton vicarage is now the Old Vicarage, a private house, and the minister resides in Withington. However, the motor car makes light of the two miles "over the hill" - a great improvement on riding on horseback from Notgrove or Sevenhampton.

The Crocodile and other Springs

Springs are a problem in Compton, as the Rev. Nutt did not fail to point out . Though his "to the best of my knowledge it has frequent floods of water in it" sounds rather like hearsay; he would have made more of it, one feels, if he had had personal experience of them. His fair acknowledgement: ..." but it has, likewise, many beautiful springs" has more conviction.

When Mr. Nutt wrote his letter, the brook still ran in its original course and the Crocodile did not yet exist. The spring rises on the east side of the White Way and the brook used to run diagonally across the Square to the lowest level of the valley, past the three cottages which stood where the garage of Compton House now is and past Lower Farmhouse, it then re-crossed the road to Withington beyond Smallhope. The spring in full spate is an imposing sight and can be heard from far off; it is easy to imagine that at such times it flooded the village before it was tamed and confined to the channel under Church Hill.

We get just a glimpse of the old brook in William Wright's will of 1724: "to my daughter Sara Mustoe £5 and that part of my dwelling house she now dwelleth in, with the garden thereunto belonging, that is, from the house she dwelleth in to the brook and no further, to be holden and enjoyed during her natural life. On the Consideration that my said daughter Sara does keep the House and the Mounds in good Repair at all times and for neglect thereof it shall be lawful for my Executrix to enter upon it". The Mounds obviously refer to the banks of the brook. We may remember, too, the clause in the rent agreement between the Prior of St. Oswald and William Rogers in 1530 when the Prior undertakes to protect Rectory Farm against water, wind and rain. A very appropriate combination, water, wind and rain, for it is not only, the brook which causes flooding, but also the many temporary springs thrown out in prolonged rainy weather by the layer of fullers earth which neatly encircles the village and its valley. Because the clay soil prevents rain water from reaching the porous limestone underneath, sudden rainstorms can cause as much flooding as long periods of rain.

In fact, the most spectacular flood within living memory was caused by one of those very local and isolated thunderstorms which occur not infrequently. Rain fell "like poured out of buckets" on the hills north of the village, but south of the A40 and rushed down into the valleys. Mrs. Purvey heard the roar of the water indoors and thought for a moment that the mill dam had burst. But she realised at once that whatever caused this noise was much nearer than the mill pond. When she went out to investigate, she saw a stream of water pouring from Seven Acres into the allotments and, Severn Bore like, rush towards Fern Cottage. There, Mrs. Powell and her daughter Doris and Mrs. Iles, who had gone to stay with them during the thunderstorm, tried to keep the flood out by pressing against the backdoor, but they had to give way and retreat upstairs, where they were marooned until rescued; meanwhile being fortified by cups of tea hoisted up through the bedroom window. The flood, however, had not spent itself in Fern Cottage, but tore down the road, carrying mud, stones and garden ornaments with it. There was no time for Mr. Cosins, the grocer, to take his new, red, motor van to safety on higher ground, and it remained where it had been, namely, standing in front of the shop, ready for its first round, the water swirling about it up to its number plates. The Post Office, then in Manor Farm House, was flooded feet deep, but even so Mrs. Kibble, who then was the postmistress, dispatched the outgoing letters in time, handing them out through the window.

It all happened so quickly that nobody could take evading action and it was so localised that Mr. Purvey who was on his postman's round in Hazelton, only two miles away, would not believe the tale of storm and disaster until he had seen the evidence. Nothing like it has happened since that day in 1922, though the Square has been under several inches of water a few times.

The seasonal springs are scarcely strong enough to cause such sensational flooding, but they can be troublesome enough and ignorance of the configuration of the land and their whereabouts can be costly when choosing a site for a house. This became obvious when the bungalow was built under a bank notorious for producing a row of springs in wet seasons, as everybody knew, - everybody except, apparently, the buyers of the site. Fortunately, it happened to be a wet winter when building began and the nature of the site revealed itself and could be dealt with at the start. Concrete and drainpipes eventually redeemed a place shunned in the days of simple cottages which did not even have foundations; but the necessary drainage and the hefty base for the house on which the building inspector insisted, meant unforeseen and additional expense for the unfortunate owners.

The change of the course of the river and the creation of the Crocodile was undertaken sometime in the second half of the last century. All the information about this great undertaking was gathered in the village and the informants who so kindly and patiently answered so many questions are, alas, no longer with us.

No doubt the project was instigated by the Walkers, who "governed the village", though not without the consent of the lord of the manor. But the man who is associated with the Crocodile is George Curtis, mason. He came from Hazelton in the 1830s and died in 1887, aged 83. He was remembered and spoken of almost with awe because of his understanding of water and springs - "he could make water flow uphill", it was said with affectionate exaggeration.

The following quotation comes from a column titled *Thought for Food* by Denis Curtis which appeared in a now unidentifiable newspaper.

DURHAM LAMB SQUAB PIE. My paternal great-grandfather, George, carved a crocodile's head out of which the Cotswold village of Compton Abdale's spring sprouts. After the carving he took offence at the local criticism and moved to Durham. "A rum thing to do in them days," said my cousin Polly (of the permanently flushed cheeks). "But serve him right for doing such a foolish thing. A crocodile's head indeed!" Years later I followed the old man's trail and found his granddaughter Betty, who was then 94. She lived on the outskirts of Durham in as pretty a setting as you could ever find. Betty cooked her speciality, Squab Pie. It has nothing to do with pigeons nowadays - and there are many variations throughout the country - but I like to think that Betty's is, at least, better than any made in the West Country. (I like the crocodile's head too; and it is still there, albeit slightly worn at the edges).

George not only created the Crocodile, but is credited with a mighty feat of drainage, the devising and laying of the

The Crocodile. Compton Abdale's main spring, constant since time immemorial.

drains on the hills between the Puesdown and the brook in the village, an undertaking which demands an intimate knowledge of the land, the springs and natural water courses. The clay top soil makes drainage an important matter and the poor quality of pre-Enclosure land was caused by poor or non-existent drainage. George Curtis had, of course, neither machines to dig the trenches nor manufactured drainpipes, but man-power was no problem, as we know, and the drains were fashioned from flat stones. These old drains look precarious, but they are astonishingly efficient and long lasting, though perhaps more prone to silting than modern pipes. One still comes across them, sometimes in working order, at least for stretches. In the fields, these now forgotten drainage courses are often damaged by heavy farm machinery.   Near houses and in gardens they are treated with caution and respect; it is obvious they were laid with the knowledge born of close observation and understanding of the nature of the terrain. Though nobody knows anymore where they began and where they ended, and often later building interfered with them, it is best to leave well alone, as long as they still work and do not cause any trouble.

The "many beautiful springs" have largely disappeared into underground channels and the mill race is now private property and inaccessible; it can be heard but not seen where it goes underground at the east side of the Square. Only the brook beside the Pike road and the Crocodile remain. Threatening murmurs are heard now and then against the brook, because the road could be widened if the water were piped and covered over to suit the lorries which now often mangle the bank and use the brook bed itself if they have to draw aside. It would be a pity to sacrifice the companionable, murmuring, open water to mere progress.

The Crocodile - timeworn and weathered, unpretentious and not a bit prettified, sometimes roaring in spate, often quiet but never still, gives the Square and the village character and distinction. There are many Cotswolds villages, some perhaps more picturesque than Compton, but no other can boast a spring like our Crocodile beside the weeping willow in the village Square.

CAMPÁNULA ROTUNDIFÓLÍA
(*Hare-bell*).

The School

A Swedish friend, taken for a mini-Cotswolds tour a few years ago and duly impressed by the beauty of the sweeping hills and the delights of the valleys, was, however, puzzled by the emptiness of the landscape. She said: "I know there must be people to see to all these tidy fields and to look after the cows and sheep - where are they? So far we have not seen one human being." It was true, though being used to it, I had not noticed it. I could only make mechanisation of farming responsible for the absence of humans. A solitary man on a tractor is the biggest crowd you expect to see in the fields these days. The villages, too, if needless to say, not nearly so devoid of people as the fields, are quieter than perhaps at any time in their long history. It is not unusual to walk the length of Compton without meeting a soul; it is remarkable to meet more than three. Where are they?

The majority of the men leave in the morning for work outside. Our 23 schoolchildren are taken by bus or car to their schools and are not much in evidence after their return in the late afternoon either. They are most noticeable around the Council Houses because eight of them live near each other at this end of the village and they enjoy the advantage of a cul-de-sac without traffic. Anywhere else in the village the constant danger from cars and lorries passing through keeps them from playing in the street or the Square, if and when they play outside - television permitting.

To picture Compton in 1851 - "120 years or 4 generations" away - takes as much effort as it does to reconstruct Domesday Book days. There were more than twice as many people as today, all going about their business in and around the village. Lower Farm, the "Manor" and Manor Farm were working farms, not residences, there were carts and wagons rumbling through the village, the smithy in the Square was busy with shoeing horses, rimming wheels and other blacksmith's work, there was the rhythmic sound of hammer on anvil, the screech of the saw from the carpenter's pit, the women fetching water from the Crocodile, there was summer's dust and winter's "abundant adhesive soil", and crowds of children, between 70 and 80 of them under 14, and so far no school. But plans for the school were in hand and it was built in the following year, 1852.

Before the school started we hear very little about education, but the Churchwardens' Disbursement Book and the Registers show that not everybody was illiterate. Edmund Goodrich's handwriting is outstanding and every Goodrich who appears in the registers signs by name, not only the men, but the women as well. So do the Cooks. It is surprising that of the elder Dyers only Josiah is able to write; his second wife, Hester Townsend, Samuel Dyer and his wife, Elisabeth, and Susan Dyer have to make their mark. Josiah's daughters, Mary and Hannah, however, sign by name when they marry. Of 64 couples married between 1760 and 1812, 32 were entirely illiterate; of 16 couples, the man can sign but not the woman; of 7 couples, the woman only can write and of only 8 couples, both were literate. A few of these perhaps could write no more than their name, like Anthony Panter, but we do not know how many, and we might give them all the benefit of the doubt. This is the evidence of the Marriage Register and we have no other; how people were taught to write we do not know; perhaps the curates gave lessons or had some sort of private school.

The Census of 1841 lists Elisabeth Sadler, aged 20, as a member of William Walker's household. She was, in fact, the governess of his five daughters. Thomas Walker had six daughters and a governess for them, too. There was no school in Compton then, and if the eleven Walker girls were to be educated it had to be done at home. That they stayed at home and were taught by governesses shows the status to which the Walkers aspired. William Cobbett and others complained that the farmers tried to live like gentry. It shows, too, the gulf between the farmers and the labourers. Had the girls, the eldest of whom was 15, been labourers' children, all but the youngest would have been at work. Child labour - and exploitation - was accepted as normal and we are very fortunate that we have not to concern ourselves with the wretched fate of the pauper children who were taken by the cartload to the factories in the north. In the next census we find boys of 14, 11, and even 9, listed as agricultural labourers, and as late as 1882, the school-log book records that several boys are absent and illegally employed, illegally because by that time the law prohibited the employment of children under 10, and none of the working boys was yet 10. No father with a weekly wage of 10s. could afford to keep a family of six at home without the older children contributing their share to the family upkeep.

But it was not only the Walkers who had the education of their children at heart, for in 1851 the blacksmith lists four of his six children as "scholars". The same census mentions Priscilla Wakefield, 75, as schoolmistress. She was a relation of the blacksmith's wife and may have taught his children. According to our notions, Priscilla Wakefield was long past retirement, but in her day she would not have been exceptional if she still had worked. There was no State education and there were very few trained teachers, and anybody unfit for other work could - and many did - open a school. Many of these teachers could neither write nor read themselves and had no suitable rooms for their classes. The reports about these "schools" make horrifying reading. We do not know what qualifications Priscilla Wakefield had; she may have been quite able to teach the three R's which was all that was required.

141   These private establishments, however, were not the only places of education. The Quakers had been the first to turn their attention to schools and the experiments of John Lancaster in monitorial teaching developed into the - mainly Non-conformist - British and Foreign School Society (1808). The Church of England, alarmed by Non-conformist influence on education, formed the National Society for Promoting the Education of the Poor in the Principles of the Established Church in 1811. In 1833 the Government made its first contribution to education with a grant of £20,000.

On June 21st 1852 "Henry Francis Hope Esq. by the aforesaid Deed in consideration of £1 paid to him, conveyed to the Minister and Churchwardens of the Parish of Compton Abdale the triangular piece of land" and the "scite of a school" on 21st June 1852; the aforesaid Deed being duly enrolled in Her Majesty's High Court of Chancery on June 29th, 1852. A "neat building with residence for the master was erected" soon after, paid for by public subscription. Unfortunately, we know nothing of the school's early years. Did the Methodists, who at that time were numerous enough in the village to have their own place of worship, object to a National school with its daily religious instruction by the vicar? Did they boycott it or were they resigned as a powerless minority? Then the school building itself - who built it, and to what plans? Was it just to satisfy the Managers or to comply with Government regulations in order to obtain a building grant? The log-book, which is now in the Gloucester Record Office, only begins in 1874; the early ones are lost - if they ever existed - and so the questions about the beginning of the school must remain unanswered. The school had been planned for 50 children and the dimensions of the school room are noted on the fly-leaf of the log-book: Length - 24ft; Breadth - 18 ft; Height - 12ft. It is doubtful if all of the planned for 50 children ever attended, for schooling was neither free nor compulsory. It was only in 1876 that parents were made liable to a fine not exceeding 5s. for not sending their children to school and employment of children under ten was forbidden by law. Even so, school attendance remained a problem for many years. Parents could apply to the Guardians if they could not afford the school fees, but a man had to be very determined and convinced of the value of education to do that and to send the children to school just when they had grown to a useful age.

142   The log-book (2 vols.) beginning in October 1874 at the start of the school year, continues without a break to the closure of the school in 1937. It gives not only a day by day account of school activities, but a continuous report of the weather and an insight into the childrens' background. The inspectors' reports, which had to be inserted into the log-book, provide the official and objective assessment of the school and complement the teacher's point of view. The minutes of the School Managers' meetings from 1894 till 1903 convey some of the difficulties and problems of a school in a small village.

Reading this daily record one can't help sympathizing with the teachers as well as with the children. There they were, teacher and 45-50 children from 5 to 10 years, divided into Infants and 3 Standards, in a room of 24 ft. long, 18 ft. wide and 12 ft. high. This was thought sufficiently large, for the space

officially required per child was 6 sq.ft. Apart from size, the schoolroom did not entirely meet with the approval of H.M. Inspectors. In 1878, he finds it very dark and he does not like the tiled floor. He repeats these strictures in the following years: "Although the difficulty and expense of maintaining a School in this little Parish are fully realised, yet it is hoped that the Managers will see their way in the course of the year to substituting a wooden floor for the present tiles. It seems doubtful if the proposed introduction of larger panes in the windows will sufficiently supply the deficiency of light which is at present very great. A skylight in the roof would perhaps be more effective." The Managers saw their way to provide the recommended changes and the next report comments on the great improvement through the additional window and the wooden floor. Nevertheless, on January 22 1897, it was too dark for normal lessons and so it had to be Tables and Mental Arithmetic.

In 1881 the inspector discovers another flaw: namely, lack of ventilation. The same complaint is made in 1893 (and still in 1926) when it is suggested that "some windows should be made to open", "without delay", the inspector adds sternly, with the warning that otherwise the Government Grant to the school may be in danger - so a ventilator is put in the window instead. In 1898 there is more urging to improve lighting and ventilation without delay, and the Managers decide to provide one of Boyle's Ventilators or a Tobins Tube, and the corrugated window panes are replaced by clear glass.

Heating was a sore point too. The original fireplace, walled up only in 1903, had been replaced by a stove, for which there can have been little room, for the inspector remarks in 1885 that "the Stove when re-erected should if possible be so placed as not to interfere with access to the desk", and the teacher records that the new stove is a great comfort to the children. However, this stove, or its successor, and its misdemeanour are still remembered by Mrs. Purvey who started school in 1900; it was difficult to light and it smoked, and the children often had extra playtime while Mr. Farley, the teacher, wrestled with the recalcitrant apparatus. The children did not mind, but for the teacher it was one more cross to bear. In 1912 the stove was removed from the middle of the room on the insistence of the inspector. Mr. Farley notes the effect of the move in the log-book without further comment:

Northend - 9.30 a.m.: 56°, 10 a.m.: 60°, 10.30 a.m.: 61°
Southend - 9.30 a.m.: 54°, 10 a.m.: 58°, 10.30 a.m.: 59°

The placing of the desks did not satisfy the inspector irrespective of the stove. The infants apparently had to use the same desks as the ten year olds and the teacher could not get at them individually. The positioning was put right in 1883, and six years later the little ones get a small desk which was a great help. Nevertheless, this was not good enough in more enlightened times and in 1893 the inspector suggests that kindergarten desks should be procured for the infants, as the desks he saw were too high for them.

All these shortcomings only come to light in the inspectors' reports, the teachers themselves did not complain it seems, but struggled on as best they could. The schoolroom, however, was not their only handicap, nor even the main difficulty. It was the irregular attendance of the children, caused by weather, illness and the attitude of parents and children to schooling. The weather was so important to attendance that the log-book provides its daily weather report, for example; Dec. 16th and Dec. 17th 1874 - small attendance

because of deep snow. On the 18th the snow was frozen over, access is rendered easier and attendance improves. May 15th - very stormy which keeps children at home. On a dry and mild day, Feb. 7th 1886, 31 children come to school, in March it is very wet and the street is flooded - there are 12 present.

So it goes on throughout the log-book. The winters seem to have been more severe than of late and deep snow before Christmas as well as after occurs nearly every year. In January 1886, it snowed heavily during the night from the 5th to the 6th of January and nobody appeared at school; the snow and the consequent low attendance lasted to the end of the month and for another week at the end of March. Next January the roads are again deep in snow and "slippery as glass, only a few of the older children were able to get up the hill, creeping up on their hands and knees". The teacher adds: "quite unable to work according to Time Table." In January 1895 is "inclement weather attendance low, real steady work impossible", In Feb. 1889 and Dec. 1900 school is closed from Tuesday to Friday because of heavy snow and impassable roads.

These are a few examples of severe weather, but wet and rough conditions were enough to deplete the numbers at the school, and understandably, it was mostly the infants and the children with a long walk to school, as from Cassey Compton, who stayed away.

Allied to the bad weather were colds and sore throats which occurred every winter. Whooping cough, usually in October, and measles in the spring quickly spread throughout the school and twice led to a week's closure. In October 1893, a newly admitted boy died of diptheria and, as he had attended school the week before, the Medical Officer of Health recommended that the school be closed for a week. There was

143

much sickness in the village all through that winter, though no more diptheria, and many children missed school. On February 18th 1881, Mary Smith had been absent for more than a week; on the 21st, the teacher records: "Mary Smith's name to be removed from the Class Register, her illness having ended fatally." In 1907 an epidemic of scarlet fever keeps the school closed for 10 weeks.

Up till the early 1920s the log-book gives the impression that the children have little resistance to illness and that the general state of health is low.

There are some accidents: in 1875 Edwin Luker is killed by the head of a gate on which he was about to swing, he was 7 years old. Rosie Hunt, "one of the cleverest children in Standard I has been so unfortunate as to get her hand very badly cut, sustaining the loss of half a finger" (1885), and severe injury to his hand kept Fred Newman at home in 1898.

The weather and the illnesses, disruptive as they were, did not play havoc with attendance so much as the attitude to school which was prevalent among children and parents. School definitely did not take first place in their lives. During the first two years of the log-book, attendance was not compulsory, but compulsion by law made no difference. Not even the fact that they had to pay school fees made parents send their children to school regularly. "Kate Holyoke returns after several weeks. No particular cause for absence" is a characteristic entry. Their sense of priorities, established from time immemorial, could not be changed in a decade or two. Work came first and, I suspect, school was regarded as a waste of time when there were more urgent calls on the children. On April 21st 1882, attendance is irregular: some boys are working, several children are kept at home to carry dinner to their fathers and brothers. The teacher had refused to let the children go home early at midday to take dinner to the fields, so they do not appear at school at all. The School Attendance Officer calls one Friday morning in October 1881 and finds 17 out of 44 present - though there was no illness. It took the teachers and the Attendance Officers nearly 25 years to achieve full time attendance, and constant vigilance was needed to keep absences low. An entry in Feb. 1890 says: "No attendance Officer for 4 months - parents get careless as to attendance". November 13th 1885 was a historic day because out of 40 on the register 40 were actually present. As late as 1905 Mr. Farley records that everybody is present with the remark that this has not happened for 10 years, and complaints about low attendance are not uncommon much later.

The seasonal work takes precedence over school. It starts in April with potato planting: in May 1875 a boy leaves school to go to plough. Then it is haymaking - "few present". In July it is fruit picking, and before and after the Harvest Holidays school suffers according to the state of the harvest; if it is early, as in 1885 when Rev. Morgan remarks in the log-book: "Harvest seems to have come upon us unexpectedly soon, owing to the long run of hot weather (3.8.)" - then nobody has time to wait for the holidays; if it is late, as in 1878, then school has to wait and the boys do not return before October when potato picking thins the ranks anyway. Charlie Eden returns to school after eight weeks' absence in Dec. 1881; he had been working. He was eight years old and illegally employed, as were several other boys under ten. By August 1882, things had become so bad that Rev. Morgan called in the Attendance Officer who had visited periodically without much effect and presented a list of the twelve worst offenders in the log-book. But improvement was slow and in 1886 even Mr. Tayler, churchwarden and School Manager, is mentioned in the log-book as employing boys on his land in schooltime. An entry in May 1888 laments: "...when the boys attend, the girls are absent, and when the girls are here, the boys are away, and thus the interest in the class is lost." The girls were kept at home to look after the younger children so that the mothers could go to work in the fields.

There were additional distractions: a fire in the village (1878); sales which most of the children attend; a picnic and, most of all mops and fairs in Northleach and other villages. The fairs, especially the mop fairs, were important affairs; they were not just places of amusement, but a kind of labour exchange. Men who wanted to change their place of work or who were seeking employment would go to the mop fair, wearing a token of their trade, so that the farmers who were looking for men could see at a glance if they were dealing with a shepherd, a carter or a stockman.

In the last three decades of the 19th century there was much restlessness in the country, people were moving out of the villages, and from one village to another. Compton's population for instance, which had increased to 258 in 1861, shrank again to 159 in 1901. The log-book refers repeatedly to this moving. In October 1884 "many of the children are leaving the village, owing to their parents' change of residence", in September 1885 the average attendance is 12.9, partly because of gleaning, partly because "several families are leaving the village almost immediately". But other families move in, some return, and the number of children at school stays at about 40. In 1887 the vicar remarks: "It seems an unsettled time of the year just now (Sept./Oct.) as many families are moving about, several fairs and mops in the neighbourhood". In October 1888: "Many changes will shortly take place in the village, as families are leaving", and the entry for Oct. 2nd says: "Mops and fairs in villages around - attendance shaky."

Considering all these impediments it is surprising that the children learned anything at all and that teachers willing to put up with all these difficulties could be found. If in fact the inspectors' reports show that the efficiency of the school depended entirely on the personality of the teacher; they also convey some of the difficulties the Managers experienced in finding suitable staff.

Kelly's Directory of 1856 names Mrs. Jane Gegg as schoolmistress. She was the wife of the shoemaker, but we know nothing more about her and nothing but the name of her successor, Mrs. Anna Maria Greening.

Miss Agnes Lawton "found the children very backward when she took charge of the school 2 months ago (in October 1874). They are now in good order but still at a low point of attainments. She seems painstaking and anxious, and I hope she will be able to show much higher results at the next inspection", this is the first of the yearly H.M. Inspector's reports. He is pleased with order and discipline at his next visit - but Miss Lawton leaves for unknown reasons and Miss Emily Louise Hillman takes over in the spring of 1876. She is doing well, for "this is a very promising little school. The new Mistress appears to be attentive to her duties and the children passed a creditable examination - order and discipline good." The next spring sees her departure and the arrival of Miss Wright who took and passed her Certification Exam the following year. But her Certificate did not save her from a withering comment by the inspector: "Little has been done at present to make the teaching of this school efficient; order is indifferent, as the children freely copy from, and assist, each other. There is no regular supply of Needlework from the Managers, and the little bit produced by one of the elder girls indicates that its teaching is backward." Fortunately, Mrs. Rodgers who follows in November 1879 stays for 3 years and at the end of her period of teaching the school is again "in very fair order and very fairly taught", though she had her share of difficulties besides the usual erratic attendance; for instance, the Managers failed to provide sewing materials for the girls and primers for the infants.

Troubled times follow Mrs. Rodger's departure. There had been no fewer than three teachers between October 1883 and March 1884 when Miss Stateley arrives on the scene. She has a pretty poor opinion of the school and her pupils. The 35 present on her first day make so much noise that it is almost impossible to proceed with the lesson. They are backward in Arithmetic , their singing is loud and harsh and only two can write from dictation - the others copy, including the mistakes. The disapproval is mutual and Rev. Morgan introduces Miss Bessie Smith, 3rd Class certified teacher. Miss Stateley will have none of that and refuses to leave, but eventually cedes victory to Miss Smith.

If ever there was a new broom, it was Miss Smith. She changes dinner hours, locks the school door against late comers, punishes wrong doers during midday break by setting lines for the big ones and makes the infants stand for half an hour with their hands on their heads. She wages war against Mrs. Puffet whose Ernest "ran away in a crafty way when detained", encroaches on the vicar's territory by intoning prayers, including the Creed, twice daily - "This rule will be kept up" - and giving the older children a moral lecture at the end of the school year - in short, she makes

The Old School House.

herself so unpopular that the village rises up in protest and the Managers give her notice after her 3 months' trial. The inspector remarks in his report for this year: "A very earnest and praiseworthy effort has been made by the principal Manager (the Rev. Morgan) to carry on the School under unusual difficulties arising from the illness and misrepresentations of one or the other of the many teachers in charge during the year. Under the circumstances it is not surprising that the attainments of the children in Elementary subjects, singing and needlework are very moderate."

It was fortunate for the children and the Managers, particularly the Rev. Morgan, that at last a good teacher had been found and that she stayed for nearly four years, from October 1884 till February '88. Mrs. Smith had an uphill task, but she seems to have had the magic touch of the born teacher and soon won the co-operation of the children. She records in March that there is great improvement in needlework and that the girls are doing it with great care and very nicely; in June, that the weather is very fine and bright and that "there is an abundance of flowers supplied by the children for the room". In November, she achieves the miracle of 100% attendance, In December 1886 she "was unable to work altogether, according to Time Table, owing to a severe cold, causing total loss of voice", but instead of taking advantage of the disabled teacher, "the children were remarkably good and did their utmost to assist me". The inspector was, of course, pleased with the great improvement of the school and the "abundant evidences of diligent effort on the part of the teacher".

Mrs. Smith's successors benefit from her efforts and a year later the school is still "well worked", but after another year the inspector comes at last to the conclusion that the work is too much for one teacher: "Without any kind of monitress, the teacher has more on her hands than she can well get through, so probably because of it, the children are too talkative, the younger ones do much of their slate work aloud - needlework, as exhibited is fairly satisfactory, but in examination so poorly worked as almost to forfeit the Needlework grant. My lords will look for better results". It took another reminder, and eighteen months, to get the Managers to appoint a monitress, but all is not well yet. The inspector admits that the school is pleasantly conducted and

the Managers have done their best to provide a monitress, but "the one now at work must improve very considerably before she can be of very great use or help to make the staff efficient within the meaning of Art. 105". Miss Hindley and her monitress do their best, but it is not enough. There is a slight improvement under the new teacher, Mrs. M.L. Pippard, Cert. Teacher 2nd Class, in 1893, and the school qualifies again for grant under Article 105, but even so the report finishes on a sinister note: "I am to warn the Managers that in future a class subject must be taught according to Article 85 of the Code or the School will be declared inefficient."

By the time the inspector calls again in June 1894, the school has sunk to its lowest level and the report has not one good word to say about teacher or school: "A general lack of animation is the prominent feature of this school. Efforts should be made to arouse in the children greater and more intelligent interest in their work. Writing and figures are irregular and in some cases cramped. Arithmetic is not very accurate and only 2 problems are correctly worked. In the Sec. Standard, notation is weak. The Grant for Geography is very barely earned and improvement will be expected next year.

Unless the school does much better in all respects, it will probably be declared inefficient next year. The Directress of Needlework reports with regard to the specimens worked at the examination, that marked improvement will be looked for next year. I am to call the attention of the Managers to Article 86 of the Code and to state that unless a more satisfactory report is received next year, My Lords will feel it necessary to give a formal warning under that Article. No grant is payable under Article 105, as H.M. Inspector is unable to report that the Staff is efficient within the meaning of that Article."

But salvation is near, in the person of Mr. Sharman who

was unanimously (by the Managers) elected Master, with Mrs. Sharman to assist him at the Joint Salary of £55 per annum with house rent and fuel free. The first report already is full of praise though a few weak spots still remain: "There has been a change of teacher, but notwithstanding, the tone is more healthy and the attainments of the children have improved. The Reading is generally satisfactory and Arithmetic of the 1st, 2nd and 3rd Standards is exceedingly well done. Spelling and Composition are the weakest subjects. Needlework receives their careful attention. The Infants are taught in a natural kindly and sensible manner, and do well in their examinations." The school keeps on "doing nicely" and Arithmetic which had always been a weak subject is now "more accurate than is usual in small country schools" The report of 1897 remarks: "A good tone and an air of cheerfulness pervades the work of this school which is on the whole very fairly satisfactory. Handwriting on paper should improve. The Infants, the 1st and 2nd Standards are good. Arithmetic is decidedly well done, in fact, it is much above the average in accuracy and intelligence of work. Needlework done very well indeed. The Infants are happy and are doing very well." Along with H.M. Inspector's report, information was received that "My Lords" had sanctioned the omission of next year's examination.

This was gratifying indeed and Mr. and Mrs. Sharman must have been pleased with this appreciation of their labours. The inspector acknowledges in his next report that the school is "conducted with an earnest desire to benefit the children, and that the work of the infants and the 1st Grade deserves special mention (presumably Mrs. Sharman's responsibility), that the children are attentive and take interest in their work." The next (1899) report is the last one concerning the Sharmans, and is as

satisfied as the three previous ones: "The children are under good influences and are orderly and well behaved. Work shows improvement,. especially Handwriting on paper. The Infants and 1st Grade are doing particularly well."

Mr. Sharman resigned on June 24th 1899. The minutes of the Managers' Meeting record the acceptance of the resignation, but give no reason for it. Perhaps it was connected with the sad entry in the log-book for May 9th: "No school - the Master having been called to his son who lay dangerously ill at Gloucester."

So once more the Managers had to find a teacher. They decided to accept the proposal of Mr. Tayler, the Churchwarden to enquire from Canon Stanton of Hazelton what he had done to secure a teacher for the school at Yanworth and then to advertise in the "Schoolmaster" or other suitable papers for a Master. They had several applications and after careful consideration they offered the post of Head Teacher to Miss Jessie Johnston Muir, because "it was thought that a Mistress would be better satisfied than a Master with the salary offered and more likely to settle down in the Parish." The salary was now £60 per annum with house free and garden and fuel.

They also decided to smarten up the teacher's house with a "good pattern tile grate in the sitting room and to apply colour washing with distemper instead of whitening on the kitchen and staircase walls, for an estimated outlay of £7". During the work, two old broken down wooden bedsteads were removed from the Schoolhouse to the premises attached to Mr. Tayler's house. They were in the way, apparently of no value to the school, and he desired to know what to do with them. "It was decided to leave them in Mr. Tayler's hands and he was authorised to give them away to deserving persons in the Parish."

Miss Jessie Johnston Muir arrived in due course and took over the school in October 1899. The Managers soon found the new teacher was not inclined to settle; she started "reforming" straight away - another Bessie Smith. By March, parents complained to the Managers and the School Attendance Officer "expressed the opinion that it was useless his trying to persuade the parents to send their children to the school, unless a competent Mistress were appointed". So Miss Muir was invited to resign. Negotiations with a Mr. Luxton ended unsatisfactorily, "denying liability for breach of contract and offering him the names of their Solicitors if he desired to proceed with the matter". Time was getting short, and Mr. Farley, Assistant Master at Kinver Boys School, Stourbridge, was definitely offered the post. He came to see the school and the house and complained of the condition of the house, so the Managers decided the house would have to be done up for some one and it might as well be done up for him as for anybody else. From the list of repairs one can deduce what sort of home comfort poor Miss Muir enjoyed: "...amongst other things it was decided to board over the top of the bedroom staircase so as to provide a shelf for light articles in the back bedroom; to whiten the ceilings of the sitting room and the kitchen; to put a delf case and cupboard in the kitchen; a new furnace in the wash house and a shelf for saucepans, and to fix the meatsafe against the wall where the coal now lies, to erect a new lean-to coal house and to remove the coal from the wash house into it. The wash house to be provided with a new door. The waterbutt to be made watertight and tarred outside. The fence in the garden made good. The three closets were also to be limed out. The locks and bolts of all doors were to be made good, the school scraper repaired and the chimneys

swept." On inspection, it was found that the waterbutt was leaky and beyond repair and the roof and walls of the washhouse defective, so that both wind and rain were admitted". The need of a slopstone was also apparent.

Messrs. Hartwell & Sons' estimate for the repairs came to £19, the slopstone cost another 10s., and funds were then so low that a galvanised iron watertank was out of the question, so a "cask to hold 180 gallons in good order and condition and properly burned out" which cost 25s. was ordered from Mr. H. Tovey of Cirencester. These expenses came hard on the heel of the £7 which had been spent the year before, in another two years the range in the teacher's house would have to be replaced. These are some of "the difficulty and expense of maintaining a School in this little Parish" to which the Inspector refers already in 1879. It must have been a relief to the Managers when the Board of Education took over the responsibility in 1902 and the financing of the school was transferred to the Committee of the County Council. The grant which is due to the Managers for the part of the school year anterior to the day of take-over enables them to carry out necessary repairs to the school buildings costing £40.

The builders, as is their wont, had not finished their work at the beginning of the school year when Mr. and Mrs. Farley took over the school. Engaged almost in desperation, they proved to be a great success and stayed in Compton until Mr. Farley's retirement in 1926.

We have talked at length about the school, the teacher, the weather and the children without mentioning in particular what it was all about - what did the teachers teach and the children learn? Up to 1881, the log-book is not at all forthcoming with information. There are no lists of subjects, as there are later, and we have to glean what we can from the inspectors' remarks and the occasional complaints about attainment or the lack of it by the teacher. There are, of course, the three R's or rather four: Reading, Writing, Arithmetic and Religious Knowledge. This being a National, that is, Church of England School, the minister is the principal Manager and visits daily to give religious instruction, and the school is subject to inspection by the Diocese as well as by the State. The Rev. H. Morgan was a very conscientious Manager and took great interest in the school. He gave not only religious instruction, but other lessons as well, at least in the first years, he "drilled the boys in Arithmetic", took Spelling and Reading, and during the troubled year of 1883 his "very earnest and praiseworthy effort to carry on the school" was acknowledged by the inspector.

Besides the four main subjects, General Knowledge, Singing and Geography were taught, and - for the girls - Needlework, which was regarded as very important. Timetable and subject matter were determined by the Agricultural Children's Education Act which came into force in January 1875.

The infants started their scholastic career with slates and primers, and counted on their fingers, a habit which tended to persist and was frowned upon in higher Grades. They worked their way up through the Standards to writing on paper, to Dictation and Spelling, and in Arithmetic to Compound Subtraction, and Multiplication and Division of Weights and Measures. Books, slates and other writing material, and material for Needlework were supplied by the school.

"Object lessons" were illustrated by pictures and "objects" ranged from the homely cow, sheep and pig to exotics like the lion, tiger and elephant, the tea plant and the orange. Gradually the scope of Objects expanded; in 1900 the Infants dealt additionally with Wool, Flax, A Light House, The Post Office and A Blacksmith' Shop; Standard II and III with Slate, Furs, Eggs and Chickens, What is a Plaice? Horns and Combs, A Railway Train, Air is a Thing, Silkworm, Beetles, Cricket, The great Worker (Iron), How Knives are made, About Buttons, How Pins are made, What is Water? How Needles are made, Air Currents, Strike a Light and Why a Balloon ascends.

Mr. Farley introduced over-all themes for the Objects so that the Infants and Standard 1 learn about Farm Animals, Dairy Produce and Vegetables while the Upper School concern themselves with Forest and Orchard Trees and Methods and General Cultivation of Crops. The lessons are reinforced by practical demonstrations: the boys work in the garden, and visits to the mill (Corn and Flour) and to neighbouring fields to observe farm operations are organised.   In July 1901, permission by the Managers to close the school is obtained because of the Agricultural Show in Cheltenham. At the suggestion of the inspector, a shelf for plants is provided, and no doubt Mr. Farley made good use of it to demonstrate How A Plant Grows From Seed.

Singing made progress too. Miss Hindley (1889) had complained that the children were quite unable to sing any tune by themselves no matter how well-known. Considering the annual lists of songs -eight for the big ones and four for the Infants - this seems hard to believe. Mrs. Smith introduced action songs which later blossomed into Musical Drill: The Fly, Roll your hands, Song in Motion, Now we little children assembled in school and Would you like to know how bread is made? These are some for the Infants. The Whistling Farmer's Boy, with chorus whistled by the boys, must certainly have appealed to the performers.

The songs they learned are mostly forgotten to-day. God bless the Prince of Wales, Home Sweet Home, Buttercups and Daisies and I love Little Pussy are still known, but who has heard of Gaily the Labourer, The Indian Warrior's Grave, Down at that Cottage, When the Rose of Morn, The Father's Return, or Hail Beauteous Stranger? There are many more like these.

In 1891 Poetry for Recitation is added to the Curriculum. A very few samples of the extensive repertoire must suffice: The Arab's Farewell to his Steed, The first Grief, A Psalm of Life, We are Seven, The Emigrant's Departure and the Deserted Village, by Goldsmith. The most ambitious project is The Trial Scene and The Argument from The Merchant of Venice and 100 lines from The Lady of the Lake and from Scott's Lay of the Last Minstrel, or Marmion.

Geography was not left behind either. Map drawing had always been of importance, but we hear nothing of the lessons until Mr. Farley draws up his list for the year 1900. England with special knowledge of the District, presumably Gloucestershire, for the Upper school, and The Neighbourhood, and Explanations of Geographical Terms as applied to England and Wales for the younger ones. For the next year he proposes Object lessons on Plans and Maps, the chief points of the compass and Fresh and Salt Water. British Possessions in Europe, Asia and Africa are dealt with later. Quite rightly, the inspector remarks that the school should have a map of the world.

History takes care of The Chief Events from the Tudors to Victoria, and The Reign of Victoria.

Mr. Farley could not have dealt with this greatly increased amount of subject matter without the help of Mrs. Farley. She had always taught Needlework and, by the request of the inspector, was made Monitress, responsible for the Infants on three mornings a week. "£5 a year to be paid for her services by way of addition to Mr. Farley's salary." Their joint effort won deserved recognition from the inspectors who expressed their satisfaction with the school year after year in almost identical words: "A creditable state of efficiency", "Great progress, great pains taken with exercises", "Satisfactory progress continued", "Order and discipline good", "Teaching painstaking and intelligent", "Good order, energetically taught." And the Diocesan inspector sums it up: "This is always a most pleasant school to visit."

This is the inspectors' opinion - what about the children? There are six pupils of Mr. and Mrs. Farley still living in the village and when asked for their memories and their opinion of their teacher and their school, none had anything but words of praise and affection. "Mr. Farley was a good man and a good teacher", said Mr. Chris Boulton. "Oh yes, he was strict - but always fair." Mrs. Purvey recalls that he offered to teach her to play the organ, so that she would be able to stand in for him occasionally, for he was organist as well. She started, but to her everlasting regret did not keep it up. Mrs. Farley's kindness to any child feeling poorly came vividly to her mind. Little cakes - "and good cakes they were, made with butter" - and a hot drink by the kitchen stove made a cold almost worthwhile. Mr. Farley's concern for the children who had a long walk home is remembered. He let them go early when a storm threatened - "go straight home and don't loiter". But for all her kindness, Mrs. Farley was a strict teacher and would not tolerate slipshod needlework. "No barleycorns" (coarse stitching) she demanded, and when it comes to patchwork, her pupils' fine and even stitches put us younger ones to shame.

Mr. Farley retired in 1926, after 26 years in Compton, the longest stay of any of the many teachers in the school's life of 84 years. His time included the first World War which, as far as the log-book is concerned, might not have taken place at all. There is a halfday-holiday when the Armistice is signed; the preceding war is not even mentioned. School life is normal during those four years; there is absence due to hay making, and attendance, as usual, suffers from illness and bad weather in winter, particularly in 1916, when 29 school days were lost owing to snowstorms.

New developments occur. Medical Inspections had started in 1913 and from 1921 the School dentist visits and gives treatment there and then - if accepted. In 1924, only one out of twelve examined does so. In 1919 a leaflet about scholarship examinations appears, but it is only in 1932 that two children from Compton are admitted to Westwood's Grammar School in Northleach. This school, originally founded in 1599 by the woolman Hugh Westwood of Chedworth, was revived in 1927 - though it has never been quite dead - and moved from its old quarters (now the R.D.C. Offices) to the new schoolbuildings at the east end of the town. Over the years, more children followed those first two, and in 1971 there are eight who go to Westwoods from the village.

On February 8th 1927, the modern age definitely arrives when the "Time Table is disarranged from 11.20 to 11.45 to allow of the children listening to the broadcast of the procession to the Opening of Parliament."

School Outings take the children to Bristol Zoo in 1931 and to Stratford in the following year.

"I, Annie Gertrude Ducker (nee Thompson) take up duties as Headmistress of this school" on April 12th 1926. There are 22 on the register, present:21. 22 children in school, a monitress and a caretaker - Mrs. Smith who dealt with 45 singlehanded and very well too, would probably have considered Mrs. Ducker's working conditions luxurious. However, the first thing Mrs. Ducker did, was to send an emergency requisition to Shire Hall, a long "list of stock chiefly permanent, urgently required for efficient and up to date working of the school". The log-book does not indicate - naturally - that the working of the school was anything but efficient, and trouble with the inspector flares up quite unexpectedly. After having seen some, but not all, writing books, he tells her bluntly that "there has been no work done in this school since you came". And "He intimated he would make a report to the Council Education Committee that the Headteacher would receive a warning prior to being served with 3 months notice." And all this only because the marking of some books was not up to date. Of course, Mrs. Ducker does not take such strictures lying down, she informs not only the Official Correspondent (as the principal Manager is now known) but the National Union of Teachers. The inspector calls again in July, and "will wipe out the previous report." Another commotion follows immediately: a parent complains that the teacher had punched his son in the kidneys. A Managers' Meeting is called to investigate the complaint. The teacher who maintains that the boy had not been touched, but only spoken to for lying, is exonerated. Another boy who was mentioned by the complaining father, did have a bruise from the teacher's correction, though he had not been given enough punishment to warrant a record being entered in the log-book. "By an accident of nature, tender flesh, this boy did bear a mark for a few days, but the Headteacher had a conversation with his mother at the time who was quite satisfied about the circumstances and the lack of intention to hurt." A year later there is another investigation - altogether three in ten years - Mrs. Turner had complained to the Education Committee about "nailcutting" and spiteful behaviour of the teacher to her daughter Ruth. However, Mrs. Ducker survives these unpleasantnesses. Mr. Farley, too, had to deal with a parental complaint, namely, that he had punished a boy on hearsay. "This is not the case", he records and this is the only time somebody did complain.

145

Mrs. Ducker has her grievance, too. She feels she is not appreciated and records the remarks of the inspector made in conversation with her: "...it was obvious that there had been a lot of hard, in fact, heartbreaking work done as it would take years to set the children in habits of sustained effort after the laxity prior to the present Head Teachers appointment...it was high time the Head Teacher had some encouragement. Furthermore, he offered to do his best when opportunity arose towards securing her a better post.- Summary of his remarks given to the Official Correspondent" (1932). Somehow the opportunity did not occur, Mrs. Ducker and Compton settled down together and she stayed for about 10 years up to the closure of the school. Her efforts met with success, and though the inspectors' reports did not mention any outstanding achievements, they were satisfactory and one points out that "the general friendliness of the children, their natural behaviour and general attitude during lessons make a good impression."

"Order and Discipline good" means praise from the inspectors, and it cannot have been easy in the early years for one woman teacher to create and maintain order in a school of 45 children in a cramped room. Corporal punishment was, of course, the accepted method of dealing with offenders, but detention seems to have been more often used. Disobedience,

rude behaviour, coming late, striking another in school, scribbling and drawing on the walls of the "offices" - these sins have been committed as long as there have been schoolboys, for it is exclusively the boys who have a "criminal" record in the log-book. Difficulties in maintaining order and discipline increased with the raising of the school leaving age from 10 to 12 and then to 14. In 1906, Harry Pitman had to be punished for bad language and kicking in the playground, these offences having lately become a frequent occurrence. A little later Mr. Farley remarks regretfully that the boys are more quarrelsome than of late: and he has to punish Fred Miles for insubordination on the playing field.

Misbehaviour was getting more and more serious. In 1925 stone throwing had to be dealt with severely, this was more than naughty, it was dangerous, and Sylvia Purvey for instance, missed school for a day, having been hit by a stone thrown by Sidney Turner. In 1937, P.C. Ralph from Andoversford came to the school to talk to the boys. They had been annoying the villagers, particularly the shop. "Permission for him to speak was granted in the interest of discipline and good manners."

Two severe cases of temper happened in Mrs. Ducker's time, one boy kicked her and tried to stab her with his pencil; he had to be held down by several other boys until he was "disarmed". Strangely enough, there was no sequel to this attack. Another boy gave much trouble by disobedience and creating disturbance. Teacher, or Head Teacher as she calls herself consistently, remarks in the log-book: "It is a pity that a generally intelligent boy should be ruled by an ungovernable temper so frequently roused without cause." Hardly without cause, for he was a fosterchild, and his aunt and guardian pro temp 'made some rather vague statements about calling in a doctor to see the boy". It would have been better for all concerned if she had, for a year or two later, the boy shot her and her husband dead. This tragedy is still remembered, and if mentioned, which is not often, then not with outrage but with sympathy.

So the school was closed in 1937. Since then the children go to school outside the village, the Infants to Andoversford Primary School, the over-elevens either to the Secondary Modern School in Charlton Kings or to Westwood Grammar School in Northleach. A few children are taken privately to the Convent School in Charlton Kings. The closure of the school is a great loss to a village, but it has to be admitted that in such a small village as Compton, there are too few children to fill a class, let alone a school. But it is hard on the five year olds to be taken away from home for a whole day among strangers, and there is many a tear and heartache until they settle down.

DAUCUS CARÓTA
(*Wild Carrot*)

Fun and Games

Fun and games, or leisure activities to give them their new name, leave little trace; we are, therefore, lucky that the lads who played Nine Men's Morris in the churchyard had no respect for graves and carved the holes for the marbles into the surface of the table-tomb. Thus, at least we know that they gathered in the churchyard in their free time to amuse themselves, even if we know nothing about any other games and pastimes and have to assume that the people enjoyed the same pleasures in Compton as elsewhere, and as King James listed them in his Book of Sports declaration: Dancing, archery, leaping and vaulting, May games, Whitsun ales, Morris dances and setting up of May poles. We do not know how much of this social and sporting life survived the Puritan blight. The churchwardens of St. Oswald's were repeatedly presented for not exhibiting their certificate showing that the Book of Sports had been read at service, and this could mean that they themselves were strongly Puritan and objected to Sunday sport and, moreover, supported their minister who perhaps did not read it, but it could also be that they just resented the royal command to have a good time. Work was hard and working hours were unlimited, and Sunday afternoon was the only free time for sport and recreation, as King James pointed out, but there was no arguing with a Puritan conscience. Before the Puritan era, and particularly before the Reformation, however, there were the feasts of the Christian Calendar, saints' and Holy days, and we can be sure that they were enjoyed and celebrated, though we know nothing of, for instance, mummers or other seasonal customs in our village.

So it is only when we reach the recent past, the last eighty years or so, that we learn a little about the lighter side of life, not only about work but play as well. It is the time of living memory, the old peoples' memory of their youth and the stories they heard from their elders. "Of course we had to amuse ourselves in those days, and we stayed at home more. Getting about was difficult." It was, indeed, for very few people had a pony and cart, and walking was the order of the day. The distances people walked seem incredible to the spoiled slaves of the automobile. Mr. Stanley Mace as a boy often accompanied his grandfather, or uncle, walking from Cold Aston to Compton to work and home again in the evening. It was nothing out of the ordinary to walk to Northleach for a Flower Show or the Mop Fair, or once to Rendcomb to see a plane take off, though this walk ended in disappointment, as the plane did not fly because of strong winds. The walk that is remembered with pleasure is the annual stroll by the women to Chedworth Woods to gather primroses for the Easter decoration of the church. Nowadays, it would be thought a feat of endurance and the primroses are getting scarce. Mrs. Iles, who was very attached to Hazelton and her family there, walked to see them several times a week, even when she was 70, and on summer Sunday afternoons she stayed for tea, afterwards walking together across the fields to Evening Service in Northleach, a roundtrip of 7 to 8 miles which she thoroughly enjoyed.

The doctor came on horseback and only when called, and he was called only if somebody really needed him. A shopping expedition to Cheltenham was truly an expedition and undertaken no more than perhaps three times a year, usually with the carter who had room for three passengers in his pony cart. When old Mr. Perret modernised his transport and replaced his horse and cart by a bus, it started from Shipton and to catch it one walked or cycled over there. Cirencester was reached by train from Withington and a three miles' walk from Compton to the station, but the Mop Fair there made the effort worthwhile.

These outside diversions were rare and entertainment was mostly centred on the village and home made. There is now nobody left who took part in the dancing in the Square, dancing to drums and a penny whistle and later to Mrs. Kibble's melodeon by the light of candles stuck on the Manor Farm garden wall. Mrs. Kibble and Mr. E. Jones, who both died in the sixties, were the last to remember the sociable evenings there with a barrel of beer and cheese, and a singsong.

The school log book, too, records holidays and special occasions, in fact, it starts with a treat never to be repeated: a lecture at night with Magic Lantern, on Astronomy with Music and Ventriloquism on December 3rd 1874. The treat for the schoolchildren at the Vicarage was an annual event, tea on the lawn and races in the vicarage field with prizes of sweets and nuts. Whit Monday should have been an ordinary school day, but was regularly declared a holiday probably because nobody would have come to school anyway, for this was the annual Club meeting. No further explanation is given for everybody knew that it was the Conservative (Savings) Club and the eagerly awaited first social event of the year. Mrs. Purvey remembers the thrills, the Dinner at the Puesdown Inn, the Roundabout (powered by a pony), the Swingboats, the Aero-like brown rock made the evening before, and the dancing on the lawn to the Chedworth Band.

Summer, of course, is the season for games and gatherings and the most summery thing is cricket, and cricket was played in a field at Hill Barn - the nearest and possibly the only field without a slope and flat enough to play on. The men played and the women came to watch and brought food for a picnic at the end of play.

Coronations and other national events were celebrated in great style. The children had a holiday, the bells were rung and there were dinners and teas in the Barn, everybody contributing 2/6 to the expenses. At Queen Victoria's Jubilee, the men climbed to the top of the churchtower and sang God Save The Queen.

But there were no village fetes until 1922 when the first one was organised to raise funds to equip the village hall which had been given by Mr. Maddy. Mr. Maddy's name crops up again and again when the talk turns to the past. He was the last squire; he took part in village life, he led the revolt against the autocratic parson, he organised the fetes; in short, he was the leader of the village. The fetes always took place in the Manor garden and in the Barn. There were dress parades, and decorated bicycles, a march down the village street to the Square where the judging took place, tea in the Barn and dancing on the Manor lawn - Compton fetes were famous in the neighbourhood. The good old days. "There was more fun and games in my early days", Mr. Jones remarked in 1958, and another voice later enlarged on that: "The village was different then (before the 1939 war). There was only one big house, the Manor, and many more cottages and more people. The war finished it all. Compton has never been the same. Now there are so many big houses, and the people in them take no part in the village. Keep themselves to themselves..."

Nevertheless, the fete has been revived, and whatever happens or does not happen during the rest of the year, this is the one day when everybody, big houses and cottages, natives and newcomers, lends a hand and does whatever he or she has been asked to do by the fete committee, from rummage to skittles, from produce stall to children's sports, and the village is united, particularly in praying for good weather.

The emphasis has shifted, however, the fetes are held not so much for the amusement of the village but of the visitors and for the raising of funds for the Church and the Village Hall. For the village they are nothing so much as hard work, yet there are fetes in other villages, where we can take our turn as visitors and enjoy ourselves without worrying if the ice cream will go round or if the donkeys will arrive on time.

There is no more cricket because there are not enough men in the village to make a team, and no football either, for the same reason. Whoever wants to play has to go to Withington.

No school, no cricket, no football - what is left? The *148* fete, Guy Fawkes, the Social Club and the Women's Institute - or is it irreverent to mention the W.I. in a chapter headed Fun And Games? It - the chapter - could easily be re-named: Social Activities, but it would sound so much duller and come to the same thing. So it shall stand without being allowed to detract from the serious purpose of the Women's Institute which is: "to give countrywomen the opportunity of working together to improve and develop the conditions of country life and of putting into practice the ideals for which it stands" - the ideals of "fellowship, truth, tolerance and justice".

I am afraid we are not always conscious of this high purpose when our small band assembles in the Village Hall for our monthly Meetings. We should perhaps remember more often that we are members of the Association of the Country Women of the World, but we firmly believe that the fellowship in the Institute is of great value to the women of the village and we do try "to improve and develop the conditions" in the

village and we do not forget the needs outside our valley. However, we do not let the serious side of life overwhelm us and have, after all, no objection to being included in a chapter which has the word Fun in its heading.

RÚBUS FRUTICÓSUS
(*Blackberry*)

Journey's End

We have tried to follow the fortunes of Compton through nearly 45 centuries, and in concentrating our attention on the village, we may have fallen into the error of seeing it in isolation, tucked away in its "hole", out of this world. It would be an error indeed, for right from the beginning of the story, in about 2500 BC until comparatively recently, this Cotswold village was never remote from "the great world" outside. In the very early period, the New Stone Age, the hills and wolds were the most important part of Britain, in fact, the only inhabited part, and we may remember the Long Barrows which by their great number indicate how well populated the Cotswolds were in that Age. The limestone ridge carried the highways and trade routes between south and north - in contrast to present times when the hills are a hindrance to roads and traffic and the area is regarded as inaccessible and a backwater which can be disregarded in plans for the development of the County.

The trackway which ran closest to Compton was the White Way, and it was still an important route in the times of the Romans who adapted it to link their villa estates with Cirencester. Compton villa was one of these estates and was thus brought within the orbit of this important town, the capital of Britannia Prima. Cirencester kept its importance till the end of the Roman occupation and even after their withdrawal, for it is named among the three cities which the Saxons took from the three defeated British kings after the battle of Dyrham in 577. After the Saxon conquest, however, the centre of gravity shifted to Gloucester, and this city held its prominent place for many centuries and a good deal of English history was made in it.

We know how close were the ties between Compton and the Priory of St. Oswald "besyde Gloucester" since 909, and how lively the traffic between the two. When down in the city, the men from Compton no doubt did not restrict themselves to business with the canons, particularly when some exciting event took place, and it may well have been that there were some onlookers from Compton among the crowd who watched William the Conqueror ride into the city to wear his crown and hold his court, when Domesday Book was discussed and decided upon in 1085.

Many kings, after the Conqueror, came to Gloucester or fought over it, for the possession of the city was a deciding factor in the struggle for power from Stephen and Maud to Cromwell. The tides of war and civil war swept over the Cotswolds often, but we have no direct evidence that Compton was ever engulfed by them, and while the village - despite its seeming isolation - was sometimes near enough to events which affected the whole nation, its involvement with the ordinary everyday life of the neighbourhood was more permanent and more important. As long as it was a member of the Barony of Churchdown, Compton was in touch, not only with Churchdown, but also with the other manors. The Manor Court was not always held in Compton, as the Bailiff of the Barony met the reeves of the hill manors together in one place, sometimes in Oddington, at others in North Cerney or in Compton. The reeves no doubt brought back from their journeys to the Courts news - and gossip perhaps?

In 1260, Northleach was granted the right to hold a market and this market was a meeting place for the villagers of the surrounding country. But Northleach was more than the place where the local fair took place, it was a woolmarket of national importance. The Staplers came here from London to view and buy wool and they brought the atmosphere of the wide world beyond the Cotswolds with them, of big cities, ports and trade overseas. True, they dealt with the woolmerchants and not with the farmers, but there were ways and means of meeting them, as the delightful tale of match-making in the Cely Papers shows, or if you were a friend of a woolmerchant, as John Rogers was. The Lombards were travellers from overseas, too; they were riding over the Cotswolds trying to buy wool from the farmers, which was illegal, as the Staplers had the monopoly of the wool trade, but which was done nevertheless.

149

By the end of the sixteenth century, the Priory had disappeared, Compton had been separated from the manors which once formed the Barony of Churchdown, the wool trade had lost its importance, and Compton was no longer a part of a larger unit; it became parochial, a "village in the valley". The greatest degree of isolation was perhaps reached in the 19th century, in the age of the railway. The previous era of the stage coach had not exactly benefited Compton, but it must at least have provided entertainment and interest for the people working in the fields, for they could watch the coaches on what is now the A40 bound for fashionable Cheltenham. No fewer than 10 coaches in 24 hrs. passed up and down between Cheltenham and London or Oxford. Absolutely everybody who was anybody had to take the waters there, and whoever came from London had to pass the Compton fields. Could one hope to see the Royal family or perhaps the Duke of Wellington? Even if one was not so lucky, there was still The Regulator (Improved Safety Coach) or, The Defiance or The Roebuck (Coach for Invalids to Oxford), or if nothing else, Dawes, Fly-Waggons. These were freight waggons "with

guards" and made the journey from Cheltenham to London in four days, while the coaches took only one day. The Regulator left the Royal Hotel in Cheltenham at 6.30 in the morning and arrived at the New White Horse Cellar in Piccadilly at 7 pm, provided there were no overturns and no hold-ups.

All this bustling life on the roads, which was thought to go on for ever, was extinguished by the railways in a very few years. Thousands of Turnpike Trust shareholders were ruined, and life and prosperity declined all along the now empty coach routes - grass is said to have grown in Northleach Market Place. Railways were built everywhere, except over land of objecting landowners. Lord Eldon objected strongly to the railway from Andoversford through Withington to Chedworth and Cirencester, but his objections were overcome and the line was built. Lord Sherborne was more successful and the proposed connection between Oxford and Cheltenham via Burford did not go beyond the drawing board. The plan for the line from Andoversford to Northleach is deposited in the Gloucestershire Record Office and shows what we have been spared. The trains would have come up from Shipton, run just below the A40 and recrossed the road at Rooks Hill Lane. It is easy to picture the redbrick bridge over the Pike Road which would have disfigured the landscape as the redbrick walls disfigure Chedworth and Withington even now, years after the branchlines were closed.

The railways ousted traffic on the roads, but after a century's supreme rule were overcome in their turn by the internal combustion engine and the roads came into their own again. The network of lines contracted, the branchlines were closed, the rails taken up, the stations abandoned or converted into houses, the tracks are deserted and are reclaimed by the farmers holding adjacent land or become bridlepaths and nature reserves. The A40 is busy again, if not so entertaining to watch, life and, we hope , prosperity has returned to Northleach, though it pays a high price for it by being shaken and assaulted by the thunder of the heavy traffic along its narrow High Street.

Not only the High Streets and main roads, but the lanes, the villages and the fields have been taken over by the motor and life in the country has been radically altered by it. In 1851, 53 men were employed on a farm of 700 acres, in 1971, in the whole parish of more than 2,000 acres, 7 men work on the land - 7 men on tractors. The working horses of course, are gone, but the few who remember them, do so with affection and nostalgia; the sight of them all trotting up the hill to Horse Common in the evening and the days in the fields with them are not forgotten. One man, speaking for many, said, "that's what I should like doing again: ploughing a field, walking behind a pair of horses. Of course, you come home tired, but you had a lot of healthy exercise, you heard the birds sing, you smelt the earth and you had the horses to talk to. Now you have a tractor. True, you can do a bigger field in half the time. But you sit on that noisy, rattling, draughty thing and drive. It hardly matters whether you plough or drill or harrow. You are alone, can't hear nor smell a thing. It is a lonely, monotonous, unhealthy life. When you have finished you are shaken up, cold, half deaf and you have sat in one seat all day long, if you are unlucky." The price of progress.

There are horses, but they are not the plodding, ploughing kind, they are race horses and they were trained by Mrs. Brutton under National Hunt Rules. Mrs. Brutton also farmed 1,300 acres at Spring Hill.

The mechanisation of farming is, of course, only one aspect of the rule of the motor. There are still about 100 people in the village, and only 11 men work in farming; the mobility which cars and buses bring enables many to work outside in a variety of occupations: in 1971 we had four Highway Department employees, one of the Waterboard, 2 business men, 1 Estate Agent, 1 Headmaster, 1 Foreign Office Official, 1 Secretary, 2 Motor Mechanics, 1 Hairdresser, and 2 Sales Women. Of these, 8 worked in Cheltenham, one in Stow-on-the-Wold and one in Birmingham which, by motorway, can now be reached in little more than one hour.

Shopping in Cheltenham is no longer an event but an everyday occurrence, ten miles are no distance worth mentioning. The butcher, the baker, the milkman, the fishmonger who bring their wares fresh to our frontdoors, the travelling shop (which sells anything from paraffin to dustbins) and the Library Van, we take them all for granted, but perhaps we should sometimes remember the blessings of the motor age, about its curses we grumble often enough.

All this shows how great is the change from the purely agricultural, self-contained village which Compton once was - to what? Nobody knows yet. At least Compton still is a residential village, people live here, there are no week-end cottages as in many other villages. The future of all villages, not only Compton, is problematical. Only 7% of the entire population of Britain work on the land, and thousands still leave every year. Who then is going to live in villages? Change is inevitable, and change is nothing new; the 19th century Compton of 49 farm labourers and 2 farmers was very different from the 18th century village of yeomen, but Compton still remained Compton. In the end, it is people who make a place what it is - a challenge to us and whoever comes after us.

Notes

1 - A Village in the Cotswolds

1   William Camden, *Brittania, or a chorographical description of Great Britain and Ireland with the Adjacent Islands*, translated by Philemon Holland, 2nd Edition 1636. p. 364.

2   A.H.Smith, *The Place-Names of Gloucestershire*, Cambridge University Press, 1964 Part I, p. 2.

2 - "Compton Abdale"

3   H.P.R.Finberg, *Roman and Saxon Withington*, Leicester, The University Press, 1959, p. 22.

4   *Gazetteer of the British Isles*, ed. by J.G.Bartholomew, London, 1904.

5   Ralph Bigland, *Historical Monumental and Genealogical Collections, Relative to the County of Gloucester,* 1791.

6   A. Hamilton Thompson, *The Jurisdiction of the Archbishops of York in Gloucestershire.* Bristol and Gloucestershire Archaeological Society (Hereafter BCAS) Vol 43, 1921 p. 85ff. I owe nearly all the information about the Priory of St. Oswald and the Barony of Churchdown to this exhaustive survey of the Jurisdiction from 972 till the Reformation.

7   Notebook No. 56, p. 191. Dr. W. St.Cl. Baddeley's Notebooks are kept in Gloucester Public Library, where I was allowed to see them.

8   Place-Names IV, pp. 76 and 134

3 - Prehistory

9   Nicholas Thomas, *A Guide to Prehistoric England*, B.T.Batsford Ltd. London 1960.

4 - 2500BC - AD43

10   O.G.S.Crawford, *The Long Barrows of the Cotswolds.*

11   H.E. O'Neil, *Sale's Lot Long Barrow, Withington, Gloucestershire*, 1962-65, BGAS, Trans. Vol.85, 1966.

12   The floor of a Round Barrow has since been uncovered by deep ploughing in the field next to Sale's Lot.

5 - A.D.43 - 410

13   B.H.St. and H.E. O'Neil, *The Roman Conquest of the Cotswolds*, The Archaelogical Journal Volume CIX, July 1953.

14   Dr. W.St.Cl. Baddeley, *Notes on Portions of a Late and Secondary Road System (c AD 220-390) in Gloucestershire*, BGAS Vol LVII 1930 p. 152.
H.P.R. Finberg, *Roman and Saxon Withington* p. 11

15   A.L.F. Rivet, *Town and Country in Roman Britain*, Hutchinson University Library, London 1958.

16 Information supplied by Mr. Irving, Curator of the Chedworth Villa Museum.

17 Mr. W.G. Hewer mentions Chalkhill in Turkdean, Chattles in Hazelton, and sites in Farmington and Sherborne in a letter, written in 1891.

18 Dr. W. St.Cl. Baddeley *Ancient Roads to and from Corinium,* BGAS Trans. Vol. 47 1925.

19 The finds of the 1931 excavation were deposited at the Cheltenham Museum and are still there.

20 Spring Hill BGAS Vol. 61

21 Mrs. O'Neil wrote (in pencil) on her map of Compton Abdale on Homeground next to the Manor: Ruins?
Capt. John Green, when asked for confirmation of Dr. Baddeley's story, replied that he had not heard of these finds. His father had never mentioned them.
An exploratory trench across one of the linear humps, did not reveal anything, not even what might have been the foundation of a field wall. The marks are, however, still "visible" in conditions of hoar frost or light snow.

6 - The Saxon Settlement

22 *Anglo-Saxon Chronicle AD 449.* Translated and edited by G.N.Garmonsway New ed. London - Dent 1972 (Everyman's Library No 624)

23 *Anglo-Saxon Chronicle AD 577*

7 - Mercia

24 Northumbrian Princes connected with Mercia (Gloucestershire)

Oswald, Saint, King and Martyr. Died 642.
Oswy, King Oswald's younger brother.
Alfrid, son of Oswy.
Cyneberge, his wife, first abbess of the minster of St. Peter in Gloucester.
Osric, Viceroy of the Hwicce and later King of Northumbria.
Oshere, founder in 692 of a minster in Withington. (grandson of Penda and nephew of Cyneberge).
Ostritha, Queen, daughter of Oswy.
    Rescues St. Oswald's bones from the battlefield, takes them to Bardney. Niece of St. Oswald.

25 *The Venerable Bede's Ecclesiastical History of England.* Edited by J.A. Giles, Geo. Bell and Sons, London 1875, Book III, Chapter 21, 5th Edition

8 - St. Oswald, King and Martyr

26 Bede, Book III, Chapter 3

27 Bede, Book III, Chapter 6

28 Bede, Book III, Chapter 2

29   William of Malmesbury, *Chronicle of the Kings of England*, Translated by J.A. Giles, Henry Bohn, London 1847. Book I, Chapter 43, p. 47.

30   Bede, Book III, Chapter 9

31   Francis Bond, *Dedications and Patron Saints of English Churches*. Ecclesiastical Symbolism, Saints and their Emblems. Oxford University Press 1914.

9 - Queen Aethelfleda

32   Bede

33   William of Malmesbury's *Chronicle*, Book I Chap. 4

34   William of Malmesbury's *Chronicle*, Book II Chapter 5

35   F.T.Wainwright, *Aethelfleda Lady of the Mercians*, in: The Anglo-Saxons, Studies in some Aspects of their History and Culture presented to Bruce Dickins, ed. by Peter Clemoes, Bowes and Bowes, London 1959.

10 - The Priory of St. Oswald in Gloucester and the Archbishops of York

36   *The Itinerary of John Leland, the Antiquary*, Published from the Original MS in the Bodleian Library by Thomas Hearne, Oxford 1710-1712, Fol. 173.2, Vol IV, p. 63.
"...whereupon he (the Archbishop of York) practized with the Prebendaries of a new Foundation, and that they should be Chanons Regular. Some were content, some would not; but the B. brought his purpose to pass by Power; and there instituted a House of Chanons Regular; impropriating Benefices unto them and giving them Coyletts of Land; reserving the goodly land to the Church of Yorke that at this tyme (ca 1534) be yet possessed of it".

37   Archbishop Giffard's Register.

38   Kirby's Inquest.

39   Sir Robert Atkyns, *the Ancient and Present State of Gloucestershire*, London 1712 p. 717
F.B. Welsh, *Gloucestershire in the Pipe Rolls* BGAS Trans. Vol. LIX, 1937.

40   BGAS Trans. Vol.36, 1913 .

41   See: H.S. Bennett, *Life on the English Manor*, Cambridge, University Press, 1960

11 - Domesday Book

42   *Anglo-Saxon Chronicle.*

43   *Domesday Survey of Gloucestershire* edited by J.S.Moore. Publisher, Phillimore & Co. 1982.
The photocopy from which this facsimile was taken came from the Cheltenham Reference Library.

44   Charles S. Taylor, *An Analysis of the Domesday Survey of Gloucestershire*, BGAS Bristol, C.T. Jefferies & Sons, 1889.

45   However, in an interview on the occasion of her diamond wedding Mrs. M. Iles of 5 Upper Park Street, Cheltenham recalled her father ploughing with a team of eight oxen. Mrs. Iles is 77 years old. (Gloucestershire Echo March 8 1977). Oxen were used on the Stowell Park Estate until the First World War. There were 22 oxen at Hill Barn and Mrs. Kibble could remember the names of the team: Spot, Merriman, Traveller, Beauty, Stout, Short, Captain and Colonel.

46   Samuel Rudder, 1791 *A New History of Gloucestershire*, p. 332 under Chedworth.

47   During his term of office the reeve incurred considerable expenses which were refunded out of the income of the Manor. In addition he had a privileged holding of land. One virgate is mentioned in the compotus of 1441, and as late as 1804, when the ancient demesne (Compton Farm) is sold, it is mentioned that the owner's Title of Claim to the farm excludes "a certain parcel of meadow called Reeves Close, reserved thereout by Indenture of Lease and Release 30th November / 1st December ,1686 to one John Rogers".

48   *The Domesday Geography of Midland England.* Edited by H.C. Darby and T.B. Terret, Cambridge, At the University Press 1954.

49   Domesday Geography p. 22.

50   The finds were examined and dated by Mrs. H.E. O'Neil.

51   I regret that I cannot find the source of this quotation.

12 - The Manor and its Lord

52   Helen E. Cam, *The Hundreds and the Hundreds Rolls*, London, Merlin Press 1963, p. 186.

53   Cal. Pat. 1266-72, 59. Quoted from Victoria County History 1965, p. 94 for Oddington.

54   William Marshall, *The Rural Economy of Gloucestershire*, 1789, Volume II

13 - The Lord visits his Manor

55   By that time Compton had slipped from the second place in the Barony with it held in the Domesday Book. Archbishop Zouche's Register of 1347/8 gives the value of Churchdown as 40 Mark, Norton 30 Mark, Sandhirst 20 Mark and Compton 15 Mark.

56   L.F. Salzman, *Edward I*, Constable, London 1968 p. 34

57   Doris May Stenton, *English Society in the Middle Ages (1066-1307)*, The Pelican History of England, 3rd Edition 1962, Re-print 1964, p. 221.

58   Pat. 19 Edward I, 066/110

59   W. Stubbs, *The Constitutional History of England* in its origin and development, 1893 Volume III, Chapter XXI p. 555.

15 -Stone

60   L. Richardson, *The Country Around Cirencester*, Geological Survey of Great Britain, H.M. Stat. Off. 1933.

61   In the words of the compotus: iiii. s. de firma i quarrere petri sic diss custod fabrice ecclesie de Surcestr hoc Anno.

62   *A History of Cirencester* by Welbore St. Claire Baddeley 1924, Cirencester Newspaper Compay Ltd. p. 278 passim.

63   W. Marshall, *Rural Economy* p. 16 passim

64   L. Richardson, p.p. 41 and 106.

65   W. Marshall p. 24 passim.

66   W. Marshall, p. 17. Mr. Muller of Naunton, who is a builder, told me that scrapings were still used when he was young and confirmed the excellent quality of the mortar.

16 - 15th Century

67   Translation of the beginning of the compotus for Compton Abdale, 1399/1400: "Compton: Account of/by Thomas Hawkyns, the reeve there (in Compton) for: the day after the feast of St. Michael, the Archangel of the first year of the reign of Henry the Fourth since the conquest of England until the same day of the second year of the reign of the afore said Henry the Fourth - that is for one entire year."

68   When Edmund Chamberlayne sold the manor to Sir Richard Grubham in 1608, the Indenture stipulates that he sell it "Together also with all manner of deeds . . Charters, exemplifications, terrars, scripts, minimi, court rolls. rentals, copies of court rolls and other writings whatsoever", and the manorial records should be at Stowell Park or at the County Record Office. But they seem to have disappeared in the course of time. However, a few court rolls and compoti of the whole Barony of Churchdown, including Compton Abdale, remained in the possession of the Chamberlayne family and were handed over to the County Record Office by Miss Ingles-Chamberlayne in 1952. (BGAS Trans. Vol. 1952, Irvine E. Gray, *Some recent discoveries in Local Records*).

69   A.R. Myers, *England in the Late Middle Ages* (1307-1536). The Pelican History of England 1952 p. 16.

70   The compotus of 1413 defines Mondayland as belonging to men "of which each one is

accustomed to work each Monday of the year". In the Manor of Painswick Mondayland carried the obligation to watch and keep prisoners taken within the manor one day and one night apiece and to bring all such prisoners to the next Justice or to the king's goal at their own cost or charge (*A Cotteswold Manor being the History of Painswick* by W. St. Cl. Baddeley, Longman Green & Co. London 1929). We do not know if Mondayland in Compton carried the same or any other obligation.

71   The eight yardlands (or virgates) of Compton Farm are in 1804 defined as 320 acres in the Common Fields (and 61 acres in Closes and small fields).

72   Translation of the end of the compotus for Compton Abdale for the year 1467. Reeve, William Aylsworth:
"The whole sum, including allowances and payments in money as said above is £16 4s 11d. And so the accountant withdraws quit."

Quietus = quit, means his account is free of discrepancies or deficit. The auditors found every item correct, a satisfaction and a relief for the reeve who was personally liable for any sum missing. This annual reckoning of every small item for the whole of the manor was a considerable achievement for a nativus who could neither read nor write.

17 - Sheep

73   William Midwinter leaves 20d to each of the churches of these villages. The church of Naunton, however receives 6s 0d and Chedworth and Broad Rissington 3s. The Will is preserved in Gloucester.

74   William Camden, *Brittania* p. 364

75   Gloucestershire Echo June 24 1968.

76   Information supplied by Mr. C. Summers for Compton Farm and Mr. C. Curtis for Manor Farm.

77   VCH II, p. 256.

78   Gloucester Consistory Court 1551, Gloucester Diocesan Register (Hereafter GDR). (Hockaday Abstracts).

18 - The Reformation

79   Hockaday Abstracts

80   GDR Will No. 93.

81   *Foxe's Book of Martyrs*, ed. Dr.A. Clarke, Ward Lock & Co. London p. 421.

82   *Gloucester Diocese under Bishop Hooper*, BGAS Trans. Volume 60, 1938.

83   GDR Volume 6, p. 124.

84   Bishop Hooper's Act Books

85   "... I entreat you to recommend master Hooper to be more moderate in his labour: for he preaches four, or at least three times every day; and I am afraid lest these over abundant exertions should occasion a premature decay by which very many souls now hungering after the word of God, and whose hunger is well known from the frequent anxiety to hear him, will be deprived of both their teacher and his doctrine..." Ann Hooper to Henry Bullinger, April 3 1551.
Original Letters Relative to the English Reformation Etc. Edited for the Parker Society by the Reverend Hastings Robinson, Cambridge, The University Press MDCCCXLVI (1846).

19 - Rectory Farm since the Reformation

86   Indentures, rent agreements, valuation and correspondence referring to Rectory Farm and the three cottages from 1530 to 1857, are kept at Bristol City Archive.

87   Parish Book, Notes by the Reverend H. Morgan.

88   Lam. Lib. Ms989 fol 112 (Hockaday Abstracts).

20 - The Priest House

89   The Indenture and the Leases of the Priest House are kept at Bristol City Archive.

90   Parish Book.

21 - Trees and Woods

91   William Cobbett, *Rural Rides*, abridged and edited by S.E. Buckley. Geo. Harrap & Co., London 1948. pp. 25, 34, and 256.

92   W. Marshall, *Rural Economy.*

93   Gary Hogg, *Country Crafts and Craftsmen*, Hutchinson of London, 1959 p. 56.

94   Frederic Burgess, *English Churchyard Memorials*, Lutterworth Press, London 1963. p. 25.

22 - The Manor after the departure of the Archbishop of York

95   Reverend A.L. Brown, *Richard Pates, MP for Gloucester*, BGAS Trans. Vol. 5 1934.

96   Rudder, p. 705.

97   Hockaday Abstracts for Prestbury.

98   (Cassey Compton) This description is fortunately out of date. The house has been repaired and modernised and is lived in once more.

23 - Reformation to Restoration

99   Neville Williams, *Elizabeth Queen of England*, Weidenfeld and Nicolson, London 1957. p. 57.

100   Neville Williams, *op. cit,*. p. 84.

101   Robert Vaughn, *The History of England under the House of Stuart*, 1840. p. 25.

102   Vaughn, p. 32. Printed from the MS in Hallams's Constitutional History of England 1,331 and 1,332.

103   State Papers. 16/387/64

104   Vaughn. p. 122

105   GDR, Volume 175

106   GDR, Volume 191

107   Vaughn, p. 535

108   A.G.Mathews, *Walker Revised*, Clarendon Press 1948. p. 171 Quoted from Gloucestershire Records Office (Hereafter GRO) D2052

109   GDR Volume 97 p. 165 (GRO D2052)

110   Lambeth Library MS 968 fol.135, 999 fol. 125, 995 539, 987 fol. 109, 989 fol. 112. Hockaday Abstracts, GDR.

111   Vaughn. p. 535

112   *The Nonconformists Memorial*: Being an Account of the Ministers, who were ejected or silenced after the Restoration etc. etc. Originally written by the Reverend and Learned Edmund Calamy DD. Now abridged and corrected by Samuel Palmer, London 1778.

113   John Stanley, *"In days of Old"*: Memories of the Ejected Ministers of 1662. Hereford 1913. p. 81 Cong. Hist. Soc. Trans XIII, 164. Both quoted from GRO D2052.

24 - "Whole in minde and sycke in body..."

114   All the wills quoted here are in the Gloucester Diocesan Records in Gloucester Public Library.

115   William Harrison, *An historical description of the Island of Britayne* (Holinshed's Chronicle of 1577). Quoted from G.M.Trevelyan, *English Social History*, Penguin Books 1967. See also *Life on the English Manor* p. 233, H.D.Bennet Cambridge University Press 1960.

116   *Men and Armour of Gloucestershire 1608*, John Smith.

25 - Parish Registers

117   Bishop's Transcripts exist for the years: 1616-17, 1620-23, 1625-26, 1629, 1637-38, 1640, 1662-65, 1670-72, 1675-76, 1679-82, 1684-87, 1689, 1692, 1695, 1700-03, 1705-16, 1718 (2), 1719-24, 1726-29, ?1730, 1731, 1734-37, 1758 (2), ?1759, 1760-1803, 1805-12.

118   The Cottage between the mill and Cornbow was called Freeman's before it was renamed Manor Cottage.

119   On the 1843 Tithes Commutation Map, Ridgeway is the field which is now called Horse Common. Perhaps it is no coincidence that Compton's only

footpath runs along the upper edge of the former Ridgeway.

26 - The Church

120 Ulric Daubeny, *Ancient Cotswold Churches*, E.J.Burrow, Cheltenham and London, also G.L.Copley, *English Place Names and their Origins*, David and Charles, Newton Abbot, 1968. p. 15L. Pope Gregory's much quoted letter to Abbot Melitus (Bede, *Eccles. Hist.* Book I Chapter 29, AD 601) recommends "that the temples of the idols ought not to be destroyed" and "it is requisite that they be converted from the worship of devils to the service of the true God", "that the nation ... may the more familiarly resort to the places to which they have been accustomed".

121 Daubeny

122 The Parish Book is kept in the Parish chest in the church.

123 The lamp brackets are now (in 1990) back in the church, some were given back by people who had bought them, some were retrieved from sheds and even a coal bunker. All were lovingly and expertly restored by Mr. Ron Owens, a Compton resident. They - all eight of them - now bear candles at Christmas and flowers at weddings and add much to the beauty of the church.

124 Kelly's Directory, 1910.

125 Dr. Baddeley records in his Note Books(No. 52) in 1925 that he found the church shut when he came to the village on one of his tours through his territory and learned locally that, owing to the vicar's strange behaviour the parishioners boycotted the Services. The last straw had been that he had bought a piano and had put it into the school without consulting anybody about spending money which had been collected in the parish. The bells were rung by his garden boy or his daughter, but nobody came to church. This had been going on for four months, when Dr. Baddeley found the church locked, the churchyard untidy, uncut and most woebegone. This story explains a few cryptic remarks in the school log-book about a piano which appears and is soon taken away again, and is confirmed, though very reluctantly, by people in the village. See also Curates, Methodists and Others.

126 Reverend F.E. Broom Witts, *Old Bells in Gloucestershire Belfries*, BGAS Trans. VII, 1882.

127 Mr. George Lane of A.T. Wheeler, Lower Slaughter.

27 - The Churchwardens' Disbursement Book.

128 It is kept in the Parish Chest in the church.

129 Kelly's Directory for 1870, however, still lists "Clock and 4 bells".

28 - Enclosure

130   The Compton Abdale and Chedworth Enclosure Act is to be found in the Bristol City Archive; the Map in Gloucester Record office.

131   W. Marshall, *Rural Economy* p. 24.

132   The Compotus of 1413 gives the statistics of the Manor and accounts for 399 acres, one and a half rod of arable in 30 fields and furlongs.

29 - Farmers and Labourers

133   Reverend Nutt's letter and the correspondence with Mr. Capel Cure are to be found in Bristol City Archive.

134   Thomas Rudge, *General View of the Agriculture of the County of Gloucester*. Drawn up for the consideration of the Board of Agriculture and Internal Improvement, 1807.

135   Census 1851.

136   Rudge, *op cit*, p. 13.

137   Rudge, *op. cit*, p. 49.

138   The allotment is also the place where the breast plough was last used. Originally its purpose was to pare off the turf when downs were converted to arable. After drying it, the turf was burnt to gain fertilizer from the ash (Rudge). On the allotment, however, the breastplough was used to mound potatoes. No breastplough nor any other pre-tractor agricultural implement has survived in the village.

139   W.E.Tate, *The Parish Chest*, A study of the Records of Parochial Administration in England, Cambridge University Press, 1946, reprinted 1960.

30 - Curates, Methodists and Others.

140   BGAS Trans. XX, 197, XIV, 338.

32 - The School

141   S.J. Hibbert, *History of Education in Great Britain*, University Tutorial Press, London, 4th Edition 1957. p. 208.

142   The log-book is deposited in the Gloucestershire Record Office. The log book in the Compton Abdale Parish Chest belongs to Haselton School.

143   Mr. C. Boulton who went to school at the beginning of the century and who then lived at Compton Cassey has since told me that a cart and three horses had to be sent to the school to fetch the children home.

144   The problem does not seem to be solved yet. "One in four children 'play truant'" is the heading of an article in the Daily Telegraph of June 29, 1971. Though this figure was challenged, the attendance in London had dropped from 89.18% to 87.81% between May 1970 and May 1971. On a national scale absenteeism ranged from 10 to 12%.

145   "Nail cutting" does not mean shortening the finger nails with scissors, but cutting across with them with the sharp edge of a ruler.

33 - Fun and Games

146   There is a narrow straight strip of rough ground beside the road to Rookshill, between the wall and the field, which strangely enough has retained its name, it is called the Butts. Well defined and easily recognised even now. This strip may indicate that archery was practised and that this was the exercise ground.

147   Mr. C. Boulton has since told me that he remembers Mummers and mentioned that Mr. Charles Paish of Yanworth probably knows more about them, because they came from Yanworth. Mr. N. Irvine (of the Roman Villa) came to my help once again and introduced me to Mr. Paish. Mr. Paish remembers not only the Mummers but the words they used, and which he heard last 70 years ago. (He is 80). He took the trouble to write them down for me. I am grateful to all three gentlemen for this help. (May 1972).

The Mummers used to go from house to house and performed for whoever asked them in, not only in Yanworth but in the neighbouring villages, Compton included. There were six characters and Father Christmas began.

In comes I, old Father Christmas,
Welcome in or welcome not
I hope old Father Christmas
Will never be forgot.
I brought my bisum to sweep up the house
I brought my bissum to kick up a doust
Mince pies hot, mince pies cold
Mince pies in the pot, nine days old.

Royal Prucey King:

I am the Royal Prucey King
Many long battles I've been in
Fighting for St. George our king.

Valiant Soldier:

I am the valiant soldier bold
Bold Flasher is my name
Sword and buckle by my side
I long to win this game

Doctor:

In come old Doctor Lero
Very well known at home and abroad
I've been all over the country
And never far from home.
I have some pills, they are the best
Very well known from East to West
I have some pills they are but few
But they search the body and the stomach through.

Old Woman:

.... Mr. Paish regrets, he cannot remember a word she said.

Jack Vinney:

> In come I that ain't been it
> With my great yud (head) and little wit
> My yud so big and wit so small
> We'll play a tune to please you all.

148   The Foundation Meeting of the Womens' Institute was held on February 27th 1945.

34 - Journey's End

149   Richard Serche signs John Rogers' will as witness in 1498. He was probably related to Robert Serche, "Mercer" of Northleach, who died in 1501.

A portion of the unusually complete Brass of Robert and Anne Serche. The brass measures 5ft 2ins x 2ft and is to be found in Northleach Church.

Compton People

The year or years refer to a date associated with the person, or is the year of birth or death as indicated

A

Adams, Edmund		1551	110
Archers, Mrs & 4 Misses		1742-64	76
Ardwey, Katherin		1545	99
Ardwey, Richard		1545	99
Ardwey, William		1545	99
Aylworth, Joshua		1715	136

B

Baker, Eve (restorer, mural)		1965	117
Beckett, Rev. W.		1662	96
Beckford, Col & Mrs		1963	116, 122
Brawn, tenants of Rectory Farm		1659-1742	76
Brown, Rev. John		1642	97
Brown, Rev Will		1599	97
Brushe, John		1530ca	110
Brutton, Mrs. Jackie		1965	117, 163
Bustede, William		1552/3	107

C

Capel Cure, tenant of Rectory Farm		1811-57	77, 82, 130
Cappar, Elena		1545	99
Casswell, James		17**	110

Cassey, John		1498	72, 99
Cassould, Ann	d	1685	100
Cassould, Edmund			101
Chamberlayne, Edmund		1580	90, 91, 128
Chamberlayne, Thomas		1544	90, 44
	d	1580	85, 127
Colston, Alexander, Esq		1760	136
Cook, Betty		1742	106
Cook, John		17**	108
Cook, William		1742	106
Cooper, J.H. (Grove House)			10, 122
Cooper, Leslie	d	1989	138
his wife, Sylvia daughter of Harry & Gladys Purvey			157
Corbett, Mary	d	1685	102
Cosins, Josiah		1857	131
Cosins, Mr (grocer)		1922	140
Crosse, Dorothy			17, 122
Crosse, Elsie			17, 122
Curtais, Thomas (Henry VIII)			65
Curtais, William		1400	64
Curtais, William		1441	65
Curtis George		1856	131, 140f
Curtis, Thomas		1854/74	131

D

Davies-Evans, Lt.Col.Delmer		1939	116
Dean, Sarah		1742	106
Dean, William		1844	131
Despenser, Adam Le		1284	33
Despenser, Thurstin Le		1266	33
Dobrée, Rev. D.		1832	138

The Compotus is the reeve's account of the finances of the manor for one year. Rent paying tenants and officers would be mentioned by name, but by no means would every villager be mentioned. Following are the decipherable names listed in the compoti for the years shown.

Compotus of 1390

Adam, Robert
Aylworth, William
Basse, Gilbert (?)
Cartor (?), Richard
Curtais, William
Colyne, Johannis
Godman, R
Gibbs, Roger
Grokke, John
Hancock, Galfrid
Hancock, Walter
Hawkyns, Thomas
Hawkyns, William
Jarman, Johannes
Lyelebroke, R
Milneward, Will
Packe, Richard
Pekke, Richard
Poole, Johannes
Roger, Robert
Roger, Thomas
Roger, William
Shepherd, Henry

Smyth, Galfrid
Verne, Johannes
Verne, Richard
Verne, William
Whyte, William
Taylor, Richard
(see Cartor)

Compotus of 1432/3

Adam, Robert
Aylworth
Cartor, Richard (?)
Curtois, Thomas
Curtois, William
Colles(?), Johannes
Godman, Roger
Hancock, Galfrid
Hawkyns, Galfrid
Hawkyns, Johannes
Hawkyns, William
Lillbroke, R.
Milward, William
Poole, Thomas
Rogers, Johannes
Rogers, Robert
Rogers, Walter
Shepherd, Henry
Verne, Johannes

Compotus of 1437/8

Adam, Robert
Cartor, Johannes
Curtoys, William
Hancock, Galfrid
Hawkyns, Galfrid
Hawkyns, Johannes
Hawkyns, William
Lillebroke, Richard
Pole, Johannes
Roger, Johannes
Rogers, Roger

Field Names

Compotus for 1413

Brokhole
Croxfurlong
Dedfurlong
Dephefurlong
Foxhole
Garston
Garstonhoverd
Gronhull (Greenhill)
Halkewell
Hexfurlong
Hoggefurlong
Lamburcroft
Litellhaye
Lytillfurlong
Midilcroys
Morwell
Pesefurlong
Pittes
Ryefurlong
Schortgrove
Smaldengrove
Soursfurlong
Southmore
Tadcombe
Totestonfurlong
Tulverhanfurlong
Wodefurlong
Wodestyght
Wyndumhill
Yneshay

1545   Joan Rogers' Will

Court Field

1597   Robert Rocke's Will

Berry Mead

1685   Lawrence Wright's Will

Brassington's Yardland

1695   Priest House Lease

Hawkwell Furlong
Lingsbury Hedge
Squire Hedge Way

1696

Ditch Acre Close
Grass Furlong
Moor Slade"
Squire Hedge Close
Thistle Goare
Westwales

1795   Josiah Dyer's Will

Hill Hay
Rudgeway
Small Hope

1804   Compton Farm (now Lower Farm) Miss Heart

Calfs Close
Grove Chure
Land Dew or Land Dew Bottom
Mead Bottom
Mead Hill
Puesdown Close
Pidgeon House Close
Reeve's Close
Slatters Mead
Stancombe

1811   Lord Chedworth's Sale

Compton Cassey

Bury Mead
Compton Great Park Pasture
Compton Little Park Pasture
Hopyard Meadow
Long Mead
Round Close
The Orchard
Upper Court Field

Parsonage Farm

Brook Close
Compton Downs
Dyer's ground
Eastfield
Home Close

East Farm

Bransdons Meadow
Chalkwell
Dry Close
Fatcombe

Home Close
Slatter's Mead
Square Hedge Close
The Croft

West Farm

Home Ground
Home Meadow
The Hitching

Mr. William's Farm

Breaches and Brook Close
Dyer's Close
Grove
Grove Chure
Home Field
Lower Close
Westfield

1821   Thomas Hope Estate

Brooks Meadow
Bull Bank
Coulbrington Hill
Downs Close
Farm Combe
Foxalls
Grove Chure
Harps Hill
Holly Bush Piece
Hunter's Horn
Landew
Little and Great Stankham
Long Close
Mead Hill
Measdown Hill
Moss Hill

Rough Bank
Small Hope
The Moors
The Piece
Westfield

1826   Valuation of the Rectory

Brook Close
Compton Downs
Eastfield
Grove
Home Close
Parsonage Meadow

1843   Tithes Commutation Map

Arkel
Arnot Bank
Assmore Ditch
Barn Ground
Beech Ground
Boar Acre
Brandon
Brooks Meadow
Bull Bank
Butts
Church Hill
Compton Park
Coultangton Hill
Downs
Eleven Acres
Fair Acre Furlong
Farmcomb Piece
Fleetgo
Forty Acres
Foxalls

Grafton
Great Park
Great Puesdown
Green Hill
Grove Chure
Grove Field
Harps Hill
Holly Bush Piece
Hopyard
Hunter Horn
Ladder Ground
Landen
Langet
Little Park
Little Puesdown
Long Breach
Long Close
Long Meadow
Lower Close
Lower Compton Hill
Lower Court Field
Lower Hutnach
Lower Larkall
Lower Meadow
Mead Hill
Measdown Hill
Moor Hill
Oat Hill
Pigeon House Close
Pigeon House Ground
Pike Ground
Ridgeway
Rooks Hill
Rough Bank
Seven Acres
Shippy Bank
Shippy's Close
Small Hope Bank

Stoney Bank
Tatley
The Moors
The Piece
Thirty Acres
Twenty Acres
Under the Downs
Upper Court Field
Upper Close
Upper Compton Hill
Upper Hutnach
Upper Larkall
West Field
Windmill Field
Woman's Go

1962

Arkell
Assmoor Ditch
Barn Ground
Beech Patch
Boar Acre
Brandin
Brimsdon
Bull Bank
Church Hill
Church Piece
Coldrington Hill
Crow Patch
Eleven Acres
Far, Middle, Near, Downs
Flitgo
Forty Acres
Grafting
Green Hill
Grove Chure
Harps Hill

Holly Bush Piece
Home Ground
Horse Common
Hunters Horn
Islands Ash
Ladders Patch
Landew
Langet
Larkhill
Long Bratch
Lower Compton Hill
Lower Ground
Lower Meadow
Mead Hill
Measdown Hill
Moors Hill
Pidgeon House Ground
Pike Ground
Pound Ground
Puesdown Ground
Rookshill
Rough Bank
Seven Acres
Sheppey
Slatters Mead
Stable Ground
Stancombe Wood
Tadcombe
Tately
The Butts
The Clays
The Close
The Hopyard
The Moors
The Park
The Patches
Thirty Acres
Twenty Acres

Under Downs
Upper Compton Hill
West Field
Windmill Ground
Woman's Go

     The ancient Court Field is now called Lower Ground.
     Horse Common was formerly Ridgeway.

     Arnot's Bank is now part of Horse Common, but the dip is still known as Arnold's Pitch or Arnold's Hollow.

     The Court Field (1545) surfaces again in 1811. It was situated beside the White Way the field nearest to Compton Cassey

     The Hopyard belongs to the same neighbourhood, the White Way slope of the brook valley, as remembered and confirmed by old Mrs. Ada Kibble.

Wild Plants

This list was compiled by Mrs. B. Rideout after a year's search and research in field and books. She does not claim that it is fully comprehensive, but it would have to be a very elusive plant if it escaped her patient and thorough hunt in the fields, the pastures and the Grove. I am most grateful for this contribution to the history of Compton Abdale.

The classification is according to W. Keble-Martin, *The Concise British Flora in Colour*, 1965.

Ranunculaceae

Old Man's Beard	Clematis Vitalba
Wood Anemone	Anemone nemorosa
Goldilocks	Ranunculus auricomas
Common Meadow Buttercup	Ranunculus acris
Creeping Buttercup	Ranunculus repens
Bulbous Buttercup	Ranunculus bulbosus
Lesser Celandine	Ranunculus ficaria
Marsh Marigold	Caltha palustris

Papaveraceae

Common Red Poppy	Papaver rhoeas
Long Smooth-headed Poppy	Papaver dubium
Long Rough-headed Poppy	Papaver argemone
Round Rough-headed Poppy	Papaver hybridum
Welsh Poppy	Meconopsis cambrica
Greater Celandine	Chelidonium majus

Fumariaceae

Yellow Corydalis	Corydalis lutea
Fumitory	Fumaria offiicinalis

Crucifarea

Water Cress	Rorippa nasturtium aquaticum
Comon Yellow Rocket (Winter Cress)	Barbarea vulgaris
Cuckoo Flower (Lady's Smock)	Cardamine pratensis
Hairy Bitter Cress	Cardamine hirsuta
Hedge Mustard	Sisymbrium officinale
Garlic mustard (Jack-by-the-Hedge)	Alliaria petiolata
Black Mustard	Brassica nigra
Charlock	Sinapis arvensis
White Mustard	Sinapis alba
Sheperd's Purse	Capsella bursa-pastoris
Field Pepperwort	Lepidium campestre
Field Pennycress	Thlapsi arvense

Resedaceae

Wild Mignonette	Reseda lutea

Cistaceae

Common Rockrose	Helianthemum chamaecistus

Polygaceae

Common Milkwort	Polygala vulgaris

Violaceae

Sweet Violet (Blue)	Viola odorata
Sweet Violet (White)	Viola odorata Var. dumetorum
Hairy Violet	Viola hirta
Common Violet	Viola riviniana
Dog Violet	Viola canina

Field Pansy   Viola arvensis
Field Pansy   Viola arvensis Var.
obtusifolia
Tricolour Pansy   Viola tricolor
    (Heart's Base)

Caryophyllaceae

Bladder Campion   Silene vulgaris
White Campion   Silene alba
Red Campion (scarce)   Silene dioica
Ragged Robin   Lychnis flos-cuculi
Clustered Mouse-ear   Cerastium glomeratum
Common Mouse-ear   Cerastium holosteoides
Chickweed   Stellaria media
Greater Chickweed   Stellaria neglecta
Greater Stitchwort   Stellaria holostea
Slender Sandwort   Arenaria leptoclados

Hypercaceae

Square-stalked St. John's Wort Hypericum tetrapterum
Hairy St. John's Wort   Hypericum hirsutum

Malvaceae

Musk Mallow   Malva moschata
Common Mallow   Malva sylvestris

Tiliaceae

Common Lime   Tilia vulgaris

Linaceae

White Flax   Linum catharticum

Geraniaceae

Meadow Cranesbill   Geranium pratense
Soft Cranesbill   Geranium molle

GERÁNIUM PRATÉNSÉ
(*Meadow Crane's-bill*)

Cut-leaved Cranesbill	Geranium dissectum
Dove's-foot Cranesbill	Geranium columbium
Shining Cranesbill	Geranium lucidum
Herb Robert	Geranium robertianum

Oxalidaceae

Wood Sorrel	Oxalis acetosella

Aquifoliaceae

Holly	Ilex aquifolium

Celastraceae

Spindle	Euonymus europaeus

Aceraceae

Sycamore	Acer pseudoplatanus
Common Maple	Acer campestre

Papilionaceae

Restharrow	Ononis repens
Black Medick	Medicago lupulina
Red Clover	Trifolium pratense
Zigzag Clover	Trifolium medium
White or Dutch Clover	Trifolium repens
Hop Trefoil	Trifolium campestre
Lesser Yellow Trefoil	Trifolium dubium
Bird's Foot Trefoil	Lotus corniculatus
Kidney Vetch	Anthyllis vulneraria
Horseshoe Vetch	Hippocrepis comosa
Sainfoin	Onobrychis viciifolia
Tufted Vetch	Vicia cracca
Bush Vetch	Vicia sepium
Common Vetch	Vicia sativa
Yellow Meadow Vetchling	Lathyrus pratensis

Rosaceae

Blackthorn (Sloe)	Prunus spinosa
Wild Plum	Prunus domestica
Bullace	Prunus insititia
Meadow Sweet	Filipendula ulmaria
Salad Burnet	Poterisum Sanguisorba
Lady's Mantle	Alchemilla vestitia
Barren Strawberry	Potentilla sterilis
Silverweed	Potentilla anserina
Creeping Cinquefoil	Potentilla reptans
Wild Strawberry	Fragaria vesca
Blackberry	Rubus silvaticus
Blackberry	Rubus ulmifolius
Dewberry	Rubus ceasius
Wood Avens	Geum urbanum
Dog Rose	Rosa canina
Trailing Rose	Rosa arvensis
Lesser Sweet Briar	Rosa micrantha
Crab Apple	Malus sylvestris
Common Hawthorn	Crataegus monogyna

Saxifragaceae

Rue Leaved Saxifrage	Saxifraga tridactylites

Crassulaceae

Orpine, Livelong	Sedum fabria
Wall Pepper, Yellow Stonecrop	Sedum acre

Onagraceae

Rose Bay	Chamaenerion angustifolium
Great Willow Herb	Epilobium hirsutum
Hairy Willow Herb	Epilobium parviflorum
Broad Leaved Willow Herb	Epilobium montanum
Enchanter's Nightshade	Circaea lutetiana

Cucurbitaceae

White Bryony   Bryonia dioica

Umbellifereae

Hemlock   Conium maculatum
Goutweed, Ground Elder   Aegopodium podagraria
Burnet Saxifrage   Pimpinella saxifraga
Cow Parsley   Anthriscus sylvestris
Fool's Parsley   Aethusa cynapium
Wild Parsnip   Pastinaca sativa
Hogweed, Cow Parsnip   Heracleum sphondylium
Hedge Parsley   Torilis japonica
Wild Carrot   Daucus carota

Araliaceae

Ivy   Hedera helix

Cornaceae

Dogwood, Cornel   Thelycrania sanguina

Caprifoliaceae

Elder   Sambucus nigra
Wayfaring Tree   Viburnum lantana
Guelder Rose   Viburnum opulus
Honeysuckle   Lonicera periclymenum
Snowberry   Symphoricarpos rivularis

Rubiaceae

Crosswort   Cruciata laevipes
Lady's Bedstraw   Galium verum
Upright Bedstraw   Galium erectum
Goosegrass, Cleavers   Galium aparine
Sweet Woodruff   Galium odoratum
Field Madder   Sheradia arvensis

SENÉCIO JACOBÆA
(*Common Ragwort*)

Valerianaceae

Lesser Valerian	Valeriana dioica
Valerian	Valeriana officinalis

Dipsaceae

Common Teasel	Dipsacus fullonum
Field Scabious	Knautia arvensis

Compositae

Daisy	Bellis perennis
Yarrow, Milfoil	Achillea millefolium
Corn Marigold	Chrysanthemum segetum
Ox-eye Daisy	Chrysanthemum leucanthemum
Wild Chamomile	Matricaria recutita
Wild Chamomile	Matricaria matricarioides
Mugwort	Artemisia vulgaris
Coltsfoot	Tussilago farfara
Groundsel	Senecio vulgaris
Ragwort	Senecio jacobaea
Carline Thistle	Carlina vulgaris
Common Burdock	Arctium pubens
Spear Thistle	Cirsium vulgare
Wooly Thistle	Cirsium eriophorum
Ground Thistle	Cirsium acaulon
Creeping Thistle	Cirsium arvense
Brown Knapweed	Centaurea nemoralis
Great Knapweed	Centaurea scabiosa
Chicory	Cichorium intybus
Nipplewort	Lapsana communis
Common Cat's Ear	Hypochoeris radicata
Hieracium	Hieracium pilosella
Beaked Hawks Beard	Crepis vesicaria (taraxafolia)
Smooth Hawks Beard	Crepis capillaris
Rough Hawkbit	Leontodon hispidus
Dandelion	Taraxacum officianale
Common Sow Thistle	Sonchus oleraceus
Corn Sow Thistle	Sonchus arvensis
Prickly Sow Thistle	Sonchus asper
Lesser Goat's Beard	Tarapogon minor

Campanulaceae

Clustered Bell-flower	Campanula glomerata
Harebell	Campanula rotundifolia
Venus' Looking-glass	Legouisa hybrida

Primulaceae

Primrose (scarce)	Primula vulgaris
Cowslip	Primula veris
False Oxlip	Primula veris vulgaris
Scarlet Pimpernel	Anagallis arvensis
Blue Pimpernal	Anagallis arvensis

Oleaceae

Ash	Fraxinus excelsior
Privet	Ligustun vulgare

Gentianaceae

Common Centaury	Centarium erythraea
Yellow-wort	Blackstonia perfoliata

Boraginaceae

Hound's Tongue	Cynoglossum officinale
Water Forget-me-not	Myosotis scorpioides
Common Forget-me-not	Myosotis arvensis
Early Forget-me-not	Myosotis ramosissima

Convolvulaceae

Bindweed	Calystegia sepium
Lesser Bindweed	Convolvulus arvensis

Solanaceae

Woody Nightshade	Solanum dulcamara
Duke of Argyle's Tea Tree	Lycium chinense

Scrophulariaceae

Common Mullein	Verbascum thapsis
Dark Mullein	Verbascum nigrum
Ivy-leafed Toadflax	Cymbalaria muralis
Round Leaved Fluellen	Kickxia spuria
Small Toadflax	Chaenorhinum minus
Common Toadflax	Linaria vulgaris
Scarce Water Figwort	Scrophularia umbrosa
Figwort	Scrophularia nodosa
Ivy-leaved Speedwell	Veronica hederifolia
Persian Speedwell	Veronica persica
Wall Speedwell	Veronica arvensis
Common Speedwell	Veronica officinalis
Germander Speedwell	Veronica chamaedrys
Wood Speedwell	Veronica montana
Brooklime Speedwell	Veronica beccabunga
Common Eyebright	Euphrasia nemerosa
Red Bartsia	Odontites verna
Hayrattle	Rhinanthus minor

Labiateae

Marjoram	Origanum vulgare
Wild Thyme	Thymus serpyllum
Larger Wild Thyme	Thymus pulegioides
Cushion Calamint	Clinopodium vulgare
Ground Ivy	Glechoma hederacea
Self Heal	Prunella vulgaris
Wood WoundWort	Stachys silvatica
Common Hemp-Nettle	Galeopsis tetrahit
Henbit	Lamium amplexicaule
Purple Dead-Nettle	Lamium purpereum

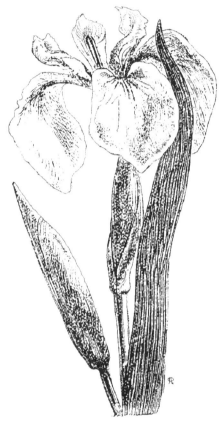

ÍRIS PSEUDÁCORUS
(*Yellow Iris, Flag, Corn Flag*)

White Dead-Nettle	Lamium album	*Thymlaceae*	
Yellow Archangel	Galeobdolon luteum		
Horehound	Ballota nigra	Spurge Laurel	Daphne laureola
Bugle	Ajuga reptans		
		Ulmaceae	
Plantaginaceae		Wych Elm	Ulmus glabra
Great Plantain	Plantago major		
Hoary Plantain (Lamb's Tongue)	Plantago media	*Urticaceae*	
Ribwort Plantain	Plantago lanceolata	Stinging Nettle	Urtica dioica
Chenopodiaceae		*Betulacaea*	
Fat Hen	Chenopodium album	Silver Birch	Betula pendula
Good King Henry	Chenopodium bonus henricus		
Common Orache	Artiplex patula	*Corylaceae*	
Polygonaceae		Hazel	Corylus avellana
Black Bindweed	Polygonum convolvulus		
Common Knotgrass	Polygonum aviculare	*Fagaceae*	
Common Knotgrass	Polygonum arenastum	Pedunculate Oak	Quercus robur
Common Persicaria	Polygonum persicaria	Beech	Fagus sylvatica
Sharp Dock	Rumex conglomeratus		
Broad Leaved Dock	Rumex obtusifolius	*Hippocastanaceae*	
Common Sorrel	Rumex acetosa	Horse Chestnut	Aesculus hippocastanum
Loranthaceae		*Salicaceae*	
Mistletoe	Viscum album	Common Osier	Salix viminalis
		Great Sallow	Salix caprea
Euphorbiaceae		Black Poplar	Populus nigra
		Aspen	Populus tremula
Sun Spurge	Euphorbia helioscopia	Weeping Willow	Salix babylonica
Petty Spurge	Euphorbia peplus		
Dwarf Spurge	Euphorbia exigua	*Orchidaceae*	
Caper Spurge	Euphorbia lathyrus		
Dog's Mercury	Mercurialis perennis	Twayblade	Listera ovata
		Pyramidal Orchid	Anacamptis pyramidalis

Early Purple Orchid	Orchis mascula
Common Spotted Orchid	Dactylorhiza fuchsii

Iridaceae

Yellow flag	Iris pseudacorus
Stinking Iris	Iris foetidissima]

Dioscoreaceae

Black Bryony	Tamus communis

Liliaceae

Crow Garlic	Allium vineale
Bluebell	Endymion non-scriptus

Juncaceae

Field Woodrush	Luzula campestris

Araceae

Lords-and-Ladies, Cuckoo Pint	Arum maculatum

Cyperaceae

Common Sedge	Carex nigra
Wood Sedge	Carex sylvatica

Pinaceae

Scots Pine, Scots Fir	Pinus sylvestris
European Larch	Larix decidua
Norwegian Spruce	Picea abies
Austrian Pine	Pinus nigra

Taxaceae

Yew	Taxus baccata

FRAGÁRIA VÉSCA
(*Wood Strawberry*)

Birds of Compton Abdale

Compiled and contributed by Wendy and Peter Sparks of The Old Vicarage. Sightings of birds between November 1968 and February 1992.

REGULAR (71 Species): birds which can be seen in the Parish without too much difficulty, at least at some time during the year.

LESS COMMON (33 Species): birds which have been seen in the Parish, but which are not regular.

Barn Owl - formerly regular: now occasional
Black-headed Gull - regular: winter
Blackbird - regular: common: breeds
Blackcap - regular: breeds
Blue Tit - regular: common: breeds
Brambling - irregular: winter
Bullfinch - regular: breeds
Buzzard/Common Buzzard - regular: breeds nearby
Canada Goose - irregular
Carrion Crow - regular: breeds
Chaffinch - regular: common: breeds
Chiffchaff - regular: breeds
Coal Tit - regular: breeds
Collared Dove - regular since 1970's: common: breeds
Common Crossbill - one bird seen 16.1.1977; pair at pond 1991
Common Gull - regular: winter
Common Sandpiper - one bird seen 22.9.69
Coot - regular: breeds
Corn Bunting - probably still regular in small numbers
Corncrake - probably regular before 1940's *
Cuckoo - irregular
Dipper - regular?: thought to breed, at Cassey Compton

Fieldfare - regular: winter
Garden Warbler - ? regular
Goldcrest - regular: breeds
Golden Plover - irregular: winter
Goldfinch - regular: breeds
Great Spotted Woodpecker - regular: breeds
Great Tit - regular: common: breeds
Green Woodpecker - regular: breeds
Greenfinch - regular: common: breeds
Grey Partridge - regular: now less common
Grey Wagtail - regular: breeds
Hawfinch - irregular, seen 20.12.69, 9&11.12.76
Hedge Sparrow/Dunnock - regular: common: breeds
Hen Harrier - occasional, winter
Heron/Grey Heron - regular
Herring Gull - regular: winter
Hobby - two birds seen once
Hoopoe - one bird seen in May 1990
House Martin - regular: common: breeds
House Sparrow - regular: breeds
Jackdaw - regular: common: breeds
Jay - regular: breeds
Kestrel - regular
Kingfisher - occasional: one bird, male, watched fishing autumn 1971 and one bird autumn 1976
Lapwing - regular: breeds in small numbers
Lesser Black-backed Gull - regular: winter
Lesser Whitethroat - three birds seen/heard in July 1972 and one heard singing later the same year
Levant Sparrowhawk - one seen on one occasion
Linnet - regular: number reduced
Little Grebe/Dabchick - regular: breeds
Little Owl - regular: breeds
Long-eared Owl - seen once, winter 1983-4
Long-tailed Tit - regular: breeds
Magpie - regular: breeds: (formerly common)
Mallard/Wild Duck - regular: common: breeds

Marsh Tit - regular: breeds
Meadow Pipit - regular: breeds
Mistle Thrush - regular: breeds
Moorhen - regular: breeds
Mute Swan - irregular
Nutcracker - one bird seen once in 1968 by Mrs. Sadlier
Nuthatch - regular: breeds
Pheasant - regular, common, breeds
Pied Flycatcher - one bird seen on one occasion in 1991
Pied Wagtail - fairly regular
Quail - heard once, 27.6.77
Red-legged Partridge - regular: probably breeds annually
Redshank - one bird seen on two occasions
Redstart - fairly regular: breeds occasionally
Redwing - seems to be less regular than formerly
Reeve's Pheasant - one bird fed below bird table, winter late 1970's
Robin - regular: common: breeds
Rook - regular: common: breeds
Ruddy Shelduck - seen once 1970's - escapee?
Short-eared Owl - seen once, 8.12.76
Shoveler - three birds, seen once, winter 1970's
Siskin - irregular: winter
Skylark - regular: common: breeds
Snipe - irregular: one bird autumn 1971
Snow Bunting - occasional
Song Thrush - regular: breeds
Sparrowhawk - regular
Spotted Flycatcher - less regularly than formerly: breeds
Starling - regular: breeds: numbers reduced latterly
Stock Dove - regular: breeds
Stonechat - ocasional on migration
Swallow - regular: common: breeds
Swift - regular in small numbers: breeds
Teal - probably regular
Tree Sparrow - regular: common: breeds
Treecreeper - regular: breeds
Turtle Dove - formerly regular: not seen since 1970's

Water Rail - possibly regular
Wheatear - occasional on migration
Whitethroat - not seen since April 1976
Wigeon - some (number unknown) seen winter 1970
Willow Tit - seen once
Willow Warbler - regular: breeds
Woodcock - probably regular: winter; possibly breeds
Woodpigeon - regular: common: breeds
Wren - regular: common: breeds
Yellow Hammer - regular: breeds

* Corncrake. Mr S.G.Mace described to P.H.Sparks some years ago, a bird which used to occur regularly, and which was called locally "Wet-me-'ook" (Sharpen my hook; i.e. scythe, sickle, billhook)

Mammals of Compton Abdale

Seen by P.H. and G. Sparks between November 1968 and February 1992. This list is not conclusive.

Badger	Hedgehog
Bank Vole	House Mouse
Brown Hare	Mole
Brown Rat	Polecat
Common Long-eared Bat	Pygmy Shrew
(One Larger Bat,	Rabbit
not positively identified)	Stoat
Common Shrew	Water Shrew
Fallow Deer	Water Vole
feral Ferret	Weasel
Fox	WoodMouse/Longtailed Field
Grey Squirrel	Mouse

Index

PAPAVER RHÆAS
(Common Red Poppy)